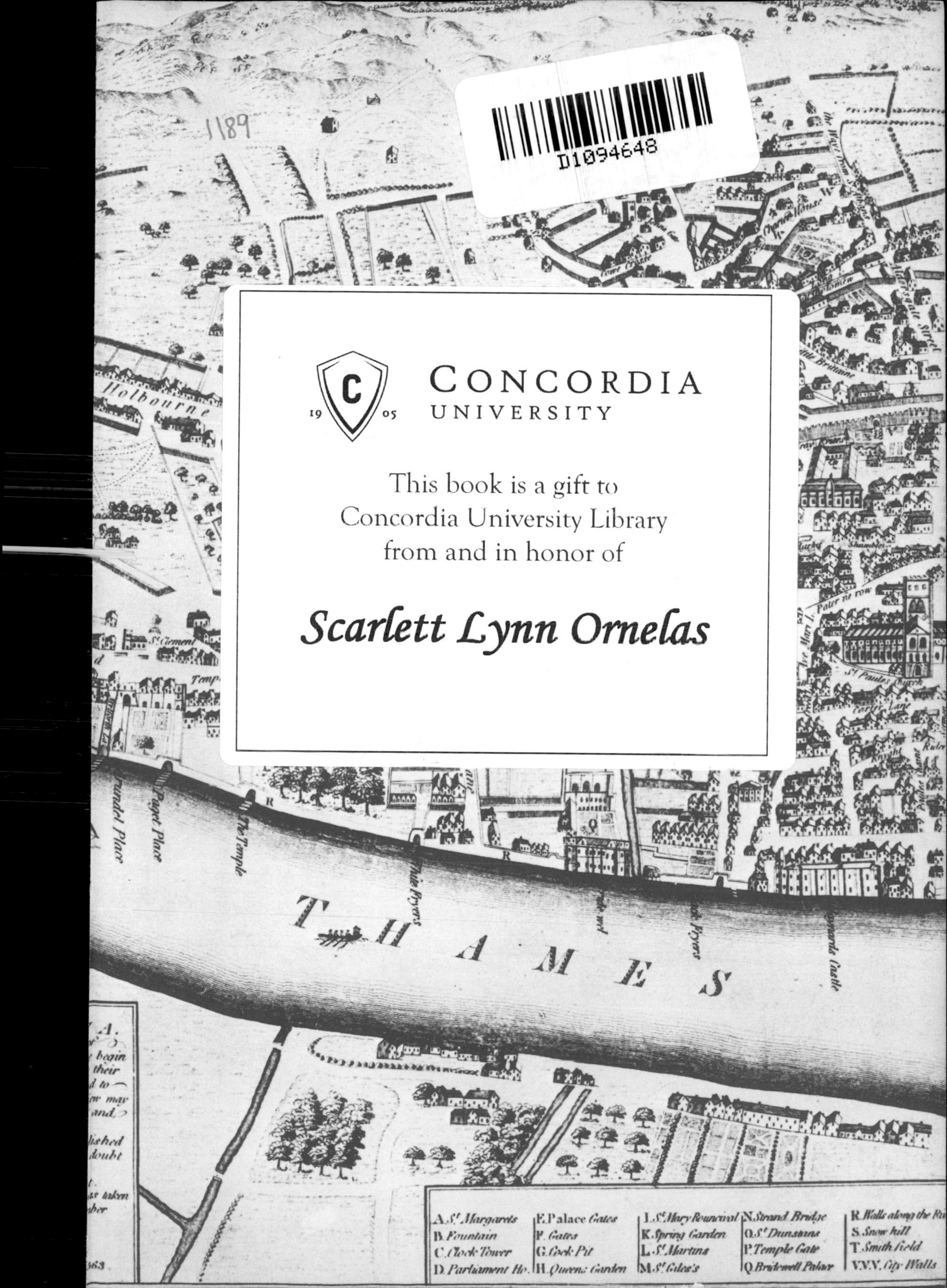
Holbourne
St. Clement
Temple
Arundel Place
Paget Place
The Temple
White Fryers
THAMES
Castle
Charter House
Aldersgate Street
Little Britaine
Pater no row
St. Paules Church
A. St. Margarets
B. Fountain
C. Clock Tower
D. Parliament Ho.
E. Palace Gates
F. Gates
G. Cock Pit
H. Queens Garden
I. St. Mary Rouncival
K. Spring Garden
L. St. Martins
M. St. Giles's
N. Strand Bridge
O. St. Dunstans
P. Temple Gate
Q. Bridewell Palace
R. Walls along the Ri
S. Snow hill
T. Smith field
V.V.V. City Walls

Shakespeare Oxford Society

Victor Crichton Collection

THE BLACK BOOK OF KNAVES AND UNTHRIFTS

In Shakespeare And Other Renaissance Authors

PLATE 1. Jacques Callot, Beggar with Dog. Meaume Collection, British Museum.

THE BLACK BOOK OF KNAVES AND UNTHRIFTS

In Shakespeare And Other Renaissance Authors

BY JAMES A. S. McPEEK

THE UNIVERSITY OF CONNECTICUT
PUBLICATIONS SERIES

Library of Congress Catalog Card No.: 68–59484

TO

KATHLEEN GIBSON MCPEEK

To dyspyse poore folke is not my appetite
Nor suche as lyve of very almsdede
But myn intent is onely for to wryte
The mysery of suche as lyve in nede
And all theyr lyfe in ydlenesse dooth lede
Whereby dooth sue suche inconvenience
That they must ende in meschaunt indygence.

ROBERT COPLAND, C. 1535

PREFACE

> Gentlemen, I knowe you have long expected the comming foorth of my *Blacke Booke,* which I long have promised, and which I had many dayes since finished, had not sickenes hindered my intent: Neverthelesse be assured it is the first thing I meane to publish after I am recovered.—*The Black Bookes Messenger.*

THIS PRESENT BOOK is not the *Blacke Booke* which Robert Greene had planned, with its revelation of all the names of the rogues and knaves in and around London in 1592. It is not a roster of the "rowsey, ragged rabblement of rakehelles" and unthrifts in Renaissance England; but it does consider the scope and variety of the social phenomenon represented by these beings and their impact on the life and literature of the time.

This study had its inception in an essay entitled "Shakspere and the Fraternity of Unthrifts," published in *Harvard Studies and Notes in Philology and Literature* in 1932. This essay, along with other studies on aspects of the subject, especially "The 'Arts Inhibited' and the Meaning of *Othello*" and "The Thief 'Deformed' and Much Ado About 'Noting' " (*Boston University Studies in English,* 1955, 1960), led ultimately to the project of the present book, first begun in 1958 with the help of a grant from the American Council of Learned Societies and further sustained by an award from the University of Connecticut Research Foundation in 1962. My study was aided by the generous policy of sabbatic leave practiced by the University, which made it possible for me to spend nine months in London in 1958.

In a work of this sort one is always indebted to many

predecessors, and I have benefited particularly from the excellent studies in the socio-literary history of rogue and knave life and tradition by Frank Aydelotte and Professor A. V. Judges. My obligations to these and many other scholars are recorded in the progress of the work.

I am grateful to various persons who have assisted me in diverse ways in the development of this book. First, I wish to thank those who served with the late Professor Hyder Edward Rollins as sponsors for the project, namely Professor Douglas Bush and Professor Bartlett Jere Whiting of Harvard University and Professor Austin Wright of Carnegie Institute of Technology. I am indebted for valuable suggestions to Professor William Rosen of the University of Connecticut and to Professor Brents Stirling of the University of Washington, who have read the complete manuscript. Where I could do so, I have profited from their advice.

I wish to thank the officers and attendants of the British Museum Library, the Bodleian Library, and the Harvard University Library for extensive unfailing courtesies. Likewise I am grateful to Mr. J. P. Harthan, Keeper of the Library of the Victoria and Albert Museum, for permission to read works in the Dyce Collection. Not least I would thank Mr. John P. McDonald, Librarian of the University of Connecticut, and his staff, especially Miss Gail Hitchcock and Mrs. Ruth Raines, for their many services.

And I must express gratitude to several others: to Mrs. Barbara Nelson-Smith of the British Museum Typing Service, who first reduced my difficult manuscript to type; to the University of Connecticut Research Foundation, whose typist, Mrs. Marjorie M. Bentley, prepared the final manuscript for the printer; to Miss Harriet Babcock of the English Department staff for her patient consideration in unnumbered clerical matters; and to Miss Leba Goldstein of Birkbeck College, London, Assistant Professor Richard W. Bailey of the University of Michigan, Dr. Daniel C. Dawes, and Dr. Lydia G. Dawes of Cambridge, Massachusetts, for various contributions.

Moreover, I wish to thank Associate Professor Alex G. Medlicott of the University of Connecticut, Mr. Robert Neff, Art Director, and Mr. Raymond Buck, Director of the University Publications, who were responsible for the arrangements for publishing this book and seeing it through the press. Finally I acknowledge a debt to my wife, without whose aid this book would not have been written.

The University of Connecticut
Storrs, Connecticut

J. A. S. McP.

ACKNOWLEDGEMENTS

For permission to reproduce various materials the author is grateful to the officers and trustees of the following institutions:

the British Museum for Plates 1, 5, 6, 7, 9, 10, 11, 13, 14, 15, 16, 17, 19, 20, 21, 22, and the end-leaves;

the Pierpont Morgan Library for Plates 2, 3, 8;

the Bodleian Library for Plates 12, 18;

the London *Times* for Plate 23.

Contents

Illustrations

> half a yeare after which by a great chaunce was found by hunteres for conneys, for one chaunced to runne into the same bushe where my caudren was and being perceaved one thrust his staffe into the same bushe and hyt my caudren a great blowe the sound whereof dyd cause the man to thinke and hope that there was some great treasure hidden, wherby he thought to be the better whyle he lyved. And in farther searching he found my caudren, so had I the same agayne unloked for.[2]

'hen Harman discovered that his copper cauldron had :en stolen from his own backyard, he acted, as we see, with ispatch and sent a man to Southwark, to Kent and Bermond-·y streets, to inquire about it among the tinkers.

Some of the tinkers of Bermondsey (today the scene of ıe Friday "rag fair") and Kent streets were doubtless estab-shed craftsmen, but others were itinerant (not easily distin-uished from vagabonds), usually wandering about the coun-·y with their sowskin budgets and returning periodically to outhwark or other centers for supplies and good fellowship. ιny of these might be approached by thieves with stolen oods, and Harman had good reason to expect his cauldron o turn up in Southwark; but his quick action forestalled the robable intention of the thieves. Harman knew also that if he cauldron reached a Thames ferry, the dens for thieves and

. *A Caveat / for Commen Cur / setors vulgarely called / Vagabones, set forth y Thomas Harman, / Esquier. for the utilite and proffyt of hys / naturall Countrey. Newly agmented* [*sic*] */ and Imprinted Anno Domini. / M. D. LXVII.* ¶ *Vewed, examined and allowed, according unto the / Queenes Maiestyes niunctions* [Cut of rogue whipped at cart-tail] */ Imprinted / at London in Fletestret at the signe of the / Faulcon by Wylliam Gryffith and are to be / olde at his shoppe in Saynt Dunstones / Churche Yarde. in the West.* See sig. 3 iv verso of this copy (Harvard, STC 12787). There are only two other copies f this date (O., B.M.). The first edition, of which no copy is known, appeared n 1566 (see Viles and Furnivall, pp. iv–vii). See p. 21 of this study for an ac-count of this important pamphlet. Harman's work is largely reproduced in *The Groundworke of Connycatching* (1592); the unknown editor presumably borrows his title in part from Greene, and the opening pages, narrating the cozening tricks of the "visiter" and the "shifter," promise a collection of cony-catching tales; but he then reproduces Harman, thus confusing conycatching with common vagabondage, a mistake not made by Awdeley, Harman, and Greene.

A Plague of Sturdy Beggar
Men, and Paupers

THE STORY Thomas Harman[1] t
cauldron offers a summary impress
tween rogue and citizen in Tudor Engla

> I latly had standing in my wel house wl
> bȧckeside of my house, a greate cawdron
> full of water, havinge in the same halfe a d
> well marked, and stamped with the conn
> whiche being well noted when they were tak
> the water powred out, and my caudren ta
> suche bygnes that one man unlesse he were
> not able farre to carye the same. Not withst
> one night within this two yeares convayed m
> from my house, into a common or heth. An
> great firbushe. I then immediatly the next da
> to Londõ, and there gave warning in Sothwa
> Barmesey streete to all the Tynckars ther
> any such caudorn came, thether to be sold
> should be stayed, and promised twenty shylli
> gave also intelligence to the water men that k
> such vessell should be eyther convayd to Lo
> promising the lyke reward, to have underst
> my doing was well understand [*sic*] in many
> that the feare of espyinge so troubled ye consc
> that my caudoren laye untouched in the thicke

1. For a good summary of Harman's life and his inf
and F. J. Furnivall, *The Rogues and Vagabonds of Sh*
don, 1907), pp. vii–viii.

In 1569, three years after the publication of Harman's *Caveat,* as many as thirteen thousand wanderers and masterless men were arrested throughout England in one of the many attempts to suppress vagabondage. Though the numbers were gradually to decrease as the measures taken for the relief of the poor and the suppression of vagrancy became more effective, the size of the vagabond class was to remain indefinitely a continuous concern. The beggar and his crew were a familiar part of the landscape:

> Hark, hark, the dogs do bark:
> The beggars are coming to town.

They were familiar, but feared; every man's hand was against them, but they were still a part of the social fabric, a force to be reckoned with. To understand better the scope and nature of the literary response to this social phenomenon, we must briefly review the principal causes for it here.[4]

To begin with, we observe the paradox of great wealth and abject poverty existing side by side throughout the pe-

---

hanged 72,000 "great theeves, pettie theeves and rogues" in his time. Aydelotte, pointing out that Cardan (who cites the Bishop of Lisieux as his authority) says that 72,000 perished in the last two years of the reign, discredits the statement as gossip.

4. The best concise studies of these causes and their underlying economic and social conditions are those of Frank Aydelotte, pp. 3–20, and A. V. Judges, *The Elizabethan Underworld* (London, 1930), pp. xiv–xxvi. For an illuminating study of the change of the English economy to that of a capitalist state, see L. C. Knights, *Drama and Society in the Age of Jonson* (London, 1937), pp. 30–95. D. B. Thomas (*The Book of Vagabonds and Beggars,* p. 4; see ch. 1, note 16 of this text) finds that the general cause of the widespread vagrancy throughout Western Europe in the Middle Ages lay in the nature of the Christian civilization itself: "Vagrancy as opposed to mere migration was almost unknown in an inelastic social structure in which each person, be he noble, serf, or artizan, had his own appointed niche. But as soon as Western Europe became more settled principally as a result of the civilizing penetration of Holy Church, the foundation of the Monastic Orders, their subsequent consolidation as great landed proprietors, and the growth of schools and universities, the thief and outlaw became a vagabond, and vagrancy entered upon its golden age."

knaves in such places as the Barbican, Turnmill street, and Houndsditch would have swallowed his property as if it had been cast into the murky river itself.

Not every citizen could have been so resourceful as Harman in meeting the common menace to every householder of the time, a menace present at all times to some extent, but then greatly augmented by vast economic and social upheavals, which were producing swarms of vagabonds. Everyone was touched by this threat, this constant danger to security, a danger that could not be wished away. To the very poor the danger was so palpable as even to affect their actual livelihood; many lived so near the border of pauperism that over night thieves might steal away all their claims to respectability. To the more substantial citizens the drains on their substance in alms and from losses in theft and robbery and, not less important, the constant apprehension or actual experience of disorder and violence were a serious concern. To all thoughtful citizens the menace represented a great social problem affecting the basic welfare of the nation. It is not surprising that a problem so gravely important to all the people in general, and to the clergy, the magistrates, and the statesmen guiding them, should arrest the attention of literary men and that we should encounter evidence of their interest in it almost everywhere we turn. The story of the multitudes of rogues recorded in pamphlets, ballads, and plays mirrors in curious ways their living presence in the land.

Just how numerous these beggars were in England as a whole cannot be determined with any accuracy, but official estimates indicating that there were as many as one thousand beggars in London in 1517 and twelve thousand in 1594, suggest that the national total must have been alarmingly high.[3]

3. For these figures, see Frank Aydelotte, *Elizabethan Rogues and Vagabonds, Oxford Historical and Literary Studies,* I (Oxford: Clarendon Press, 1913), pp. 4–5. These figures are, however, not so startling as those of William Harrison (*The Description of England,* Book II, Ch. XI, New Shakespeare Soc., London, 1877, p. 231), who says that according to Cardan, Henry VIII

A Plague of Sturdy Beggars, Masterless Men, and Paupers

THE STORY Thomas Harman[1] tells about his copper cauldron offers a summary impression of the conflict between rogue and citizen in Tudor England:

> I latly had standing in my wel house which standeth on the bắckeside of my house, a greate cawdron of copper being then full of water, havinge in the same halfe a doson of pewter dyshes, well marked, and stamped with the connizance of my armes, whiche being well noted when they were taken out were set a side the water powred out, and my caudren taken away, beinge of suche bygnes that one man unlesse he were of greate strength was not able farre to carye the same. Not withstanding, the same was one night within this two yeares convayed more then halfe a myle from my house, into a common or heth. And ther bestowed in a great firbushe. I then immediatly the next day sent one of my men to Londõ, and there gave warning in Sothwarke, kent streete, and Barmesey streete to all the Tynckars there dwelling. That if any such caudorn came, thether to be sold, the bringar therof should be stayed, and promised twenty shyllinges for a reward. I gave also intelligence to the water men that kept the ferres that no such vessell should be eyther convayd to London, or into essex promising the lyke reward, to have understanding therof. This my doing was well understand [*sic*] in many places, about, and that the feare of espyinge so troubled ye conscience of the stealer, that my caudoren laye untouched in the thicke firbushe more then

1. For a good summary of Harman's life and his influence, see Edward Viles and F. J. Furnivall, *The Rogues and Vagabonds of Shakespeare's Youth* (London, 1907), pp. vii–viii.

> half a yeare after which by a great chaunce was found by hunteres for conneys, for one chaunced to runne into the same bushe where my caudren was and being perceaved one thrust his staffe into the same bushe and hyt my caudren a great blowe the sound whereof dyd cause the man to thinke and hope that there was some great treasure hidden, wherby he thought to be the better whyle he lyved. And in farther searching he found my caudren, so had I the same agayne unloked for.[2]

When Harman discovered that his copper cauldron had been stolen from his own backyard, he acted, as we see, with dispatch and sent a man to Southwark, to Kent and Bermondsey streets, to inquire about it among the tinkers.

Some of the tinkers of Bermondsey (today the scene of the Friday "rag fair") and Kent streets were doubtless established craftsmen, but others were itinerant (not easily distinguished from vagabonds), usually wandering about the country with their sowskin budgets and returning periodically to Southwark or other centers for supplies and good fellowship. Any of these might be approached by thieves with stolen goods, and Harman had good reason to expect his cauldron to turn up in Southwark; but his quick action forestalled the probable intention of the thieves. Harman knew also that if the cauldron reached a Thames ferry, the dens for thieves and

2. *A Caveat / for Commen Cur / setors vulgarely called / Vagabones, set forth by Thomas Harman. / Esquier. for the utilite and proffyt of hys / naturall Countrey. Newly agmented* [*sic*] */ and Imprinted Anno Domini. / M. D. LXVII. / ¶ Vewed, examined and allowed, according unto the / Queenes Maiestyes Iniunctions* [Cut of rogue whipped at cart-tail] */ Imprinted / at London in Fletestret at the signe of the / Faulcon by Wylliam Gryffith and are to be / solde at his shoppe in Saynt Dunstones / Churche Yarde. in the West.* See sig. B iv verso of this copy (Harvard, STC 12787). There are only two other copies of this date (O., B.M.). The first edition, of which no copy is known, appeared in 1566 (see Viles and Furnivall, pp. iv–vii). See p. 21 of this study for an account of this important pamphlet. Harman's work is largely reproduced in *The Groundworke of Connycatching* (1592); the unknown editor presumably borrows his title in part from Greene, and the opening pages, narrating the cozening tricks of the "visiter" and the "shifter," promise a collection of conycatching tales; but he then reproduces Harman, thus confusing conycatching with common vagabondage, a mistake not made by Awdeley, Harman, and Greene.

riod of the Renaissance,[5] a difference in social conditions much more pronounced than in medieval times. England was in the process of changing both in its living and thinking from a medieval agrarian state into a modern one of trade and commerce, and the transformation, like all other revolutionary changes, disrupted the lives of many who had had a certain security in the old order. The chief exemplification of this change seems to have been the practice of land-enclosure, or the enclosing by the landlords for sheep pasturage of lands hitherto used for tillage by the people.[6] Among many who protest this practice, Sir Thomas More (in the guise of Hythloday) sympathetically interprets its consequences to the people who were dispossessed of their rights as tenants:

> There is an other [cause for theft], whych, as I suppose, is pper [proper] & peculiar to you Englishmen alone. What is that, quod the Cardinal? forsoth my lorde (quod I) your shepe, that were wont to be so meke and tame, & so smal eaters, now, as I heare saye, be become so great devowerers and so wylde, that they eate up, and swallow downe the very men them selfes. They consume, destroye, & devoure whole fieldes, howses, and cities. For looke in what partes of the realme doth growe the fynest, and therfore dearest woll, there noble men, and gentlemen: yea and certeyn Abbottes, holy men no doubt, not contenting them selfes with the yearely revenues and profytes, that were wont to grow to theyr forefathers and predecessours of their landes, nor beynge content that they live in rest and pleasure nothinge profiting, yea much noyinge the weale publique: leave no grounde for tillage, thei inclose al into pastures: they throw doune houses: they plucke downe townes, and leave nothing standynge, but only the churche to be made a shepehowse . . . Therfore that on covetous and unsatiable cormaraunte and very plage of his natyve countrey maye compasse aboute and inclose many thousād akers of grounde to gether within one pale or hedge, the husbandmen be thruste owte of their owne, or els either by coveyne and fraude, or by

5. As R. H. Tawney says, "The brilliant age which begins with Elizabeth gleams against a background of social misery and squalor" (*The Agrarian Problem in the Sixteenth Century,* London, 1912, p. 193).
6. See Tawney, *The Agrarian Problem,* for a thorough study of this practice; also L. C. Knights' briefer but informative discussion, pp. 96–108.

violent oppression they be put besydes it, or by wronges and iniuries thei be so weried, that they be compelled to sell all: by one meanes therfore or by other, either by hooke or crooke they muste needes departe awaye, poore, selye, wretched soules, men, women, husbandes, wives, fatherlesse children, widowes, wofull mothers, with their yonge babes, and their whole houshold smal in substãce, and muche in numbre, as husbandrye requireth manye handes. Awaye thei trudge, I say, out of their knowen and accustomed houses, fyndynge no place to reste in. All their housholdestuffe, whiche is verye litle woorthe, thoughe it myght well abide the sale: yet beeynge sodainely thruste out, they be constrayned to sell it for a thing of nought. And when they have wandered abrode tyll that be spent, what can they then els doo but steale, and then iustly pardy be hanged, or els go about a beggyng. And yet then also they be caste in prison as vagaboundes, because they go aboute & worke not: whom no mã wyl set a worke, though thei never so willyngly profre themselves therto.[7]

It has been estimated that between thirty to fifty thousand people were displaced in this process.[8] As late as 1597 Francis Bacon still felt that the basis of the increase in vagabondage and national poverty was to be found in this practice of enclosure and, in introducing legislation for poor relief in Parliament, spoke vehemently against it:

Inclosure of grounds brings depopulation, which brings first Idleness, secondly decay of Tillage, thirdly subversion of Houses, and

7. STC 18095 (Huntington 12572): *A frutefull / pleasaunt, & wittie worke, / of the beste state of a publique / weale, and of the newe yle, called Uto / pia: written in Latine, by the right wor / thie and famous Syr Thomas More / knyght, and translated into Englyshe by / Raphe Robynson, sometime fellowe / of Corpus Christi College in Ox- / ford, and nowe by him at this se- / conde edition newlie peru- / sed and corrected, and / also with divers no- / tes in the margent / augmented. / Imprinted at London, by / Abraham Vele, dwellinge in Pauls churchyarde, at the signe of the Lambe* [1556]. See fols. 14^v–15^v. Aydelotte (p. 6) quotes this passage. See also Robert Crowley's *The Way to Wealth* (London, 1550), *The Select Works of Robert Crowley* (London, 1872), pp. 132–133. Crowley, a busy printer and, later, archdeacon of Hereford and Vicar of St. Giles, finds the great farmers, merchants, and lords responsible for sedition: "They take our houses over our headdes, they bye our growndes out of our handes, they reyse our rentes, they leavie great . . . fines, they enclose our commens!" But in this work, as elsewhere, Crowley counsels absolute submission to authority.

8. Judges, p. xx.

> decay of Charity, and charges to the Poor, fourthly impoverishing the state of the Realm. A law for the taking away of such inconveniences is not to be thought ill or hurtful unto the general State. And I would be sorry to see within this Kingdom, that piece of *Ovids* verse prove true, jam seges ubi Troja fuit, so in England, instead of a whole Town full of people, nought but green Fields, but a Shepherd and a Dog.[9]

Yet other important causes contributing to the increase in vagabondage lay in Henry VIII's battle with the church and his dissolution of the monasteries and other religious houses, with its sad complement of displaced persons; the incessant wars, with their jetsam of discharged soldiers; heavy taxation, which forced noblemen to reduce the number of their retainers; and the immigration of the Gypsies into England and Scotland. The displaced religious of the monasteries, numbering around eight thousand according to Cardinal Gasquet,[10] were variously provided for, but some, even if only a small part of their dependents, estimated to number between thirty-five to eighty thousand,[11] must have been forced into beggary. The friars, who, from the time of the establishment of their orders, had been, with the sanction of religion, the most successful beggars of all, and who by their practices had inspired imitation, seem likewise to have been largely able to avoid lives of unemployed beggary.[12] Their

9. Sir Simonds D'Ewes, *The Journals of all the Parliaments during the Reign of Elizabeth* (London, 1682), p. 551. On Bacon's stand in this matter, see Edward D. Cheyney, *A History of England from the Defeat of the Armada to the Death of Elizabeth* (London, 1926), II, 262–265. In his argument for a law abolishing enclosures at the expense of those who created them, Bacon adopts for himself the recommendation of Hythloday in the *Utopia,* fol. 17^{v}.

10. *Henry VIII and the English Monasteries,* by Abbot Gasquet (London, 1906), pp. 359–360 (cited by Judges, p. xxiv). A. N. Savine, excluding the friars, estimates the number of religious at about seven thousand; see his *English Monasteries on the Eve of the Dissolution, Oxford Studies in Social and Legal History,* ed. P. Vinogradoff (Oxford: Clarendon Press, 1909), I, 222.

11. See Savine, p. 265, for the lower figure and Cardinal Gasquet, p. 190, for the higher.

12. G. Baskerville, "The Dispossessed Religious After the Suppression of the Monasteries," *Essays in History Presented to R. L. Poole,* ed. H. W. C. Davis (Oxford, 1927), p. 462 ff. (cited by Judges, xxiii).

disappearance from the roads eliminated one of the most picturesque types of wanderers who for many years had searched all parts of the land "As thikke as motes in the sonne-beem." Their brothers in mendicity, the pardoners, whose profession was cancelled by the Council of Trent in 1562, also faded from the scene, some perhaps entering into various types of vagrancy, and some possibly becoming proctors or collectors of charity for hospitals and other institutions.[13]

A more serious immediate danger to the commonwealth was the increase in the number of discharged soldiers, who, returning from wars on the Continent, too often found themselves with little pay and no employment and consequently swelled the ranks of vagrancy. These were the most formidable of all the beggars and sometimes begged and robbed in groups. On one occasion, after the expedition of Norris and Drake to Portugal in 1589, a band of five hundred of these masterless men threatened to plunder Bartholomew Fair, and later in the same year the Lord Mayor had to call out two thousand of the city militia to disperse another large group.[14] And it was probably a like band that assembled in Somerset in 1595 and boldly took a cartload of cheese, according to the letter of Edward Hext, a justice of the shire:

> And this yere there assembled lxxx in a Companye and tooke a whole Carte loade of Cheese from one dryving yt to a fayre & dispersed yt amongest them, for wch some of them have indured longe imprisonment and fyne by the Iudgmt of the good L Chief Iustice att our last Crismas Sessions, wch may grow dangerous by the ayde of suche numbers as are abroad especyally in this tyme of dearthe, who no dowpt anymate them to all contempte bothe of nobel men and gentlemen contynially Bussynge into there eares that the ritche men have gotten all into ther hands & will starve the poore. And I may Iustlye saye that the Infynyte numbers of the Idle wandrynge people & robbers of the land are the chefest cause of the dearthe . . . for they lye Idely in the ale howses daye &

13. Judges, xxi; see also K. S. Latourette, *A History of Christianity* (New York, 1953), pp. 869–870.
14. Cheyney, I, 182–185.

> nyght eatinge & drynkynge excessively. And within these iij monethes I tooke a thief that was executed this last assizes that confessed unto me that he & too more laye in an Alehouse three weeks in wch tyme they eate xxti fatt sheepe whereof they stole every night on, besydes they breake many a poore mans plowghe by stealing an Oxe or too from him . . . And when these lewde people are comytted to the gayle, the poore Cuntry that ys robbed by them, are inforced to feede them which they greve att . . .[15]

Moreover, the number of discarded serving-men or retainers of noble houses seems to have increased greatly during the first half of the century.[16] These serving-men varied in type from the cashiered honest knaves scorned by Iago (such as Adam in *As You Like It*) to "superserviceable, finical rogues" like Oswald. A large number of these were doubtless of the same temper as Bardolph and Pistol, in their role of discarded retainers of Sir John in *The Merry Wives of Windsor;* and it was perhaps this group that furnished most of the rogues who, like Brainworm, feigned records of military service. Apprentices also, always ready for a riot, appear to have joined with the masterless men and other vagrants in assaulting Lincoln's Inn and plundering several chambers in 1590.[17] Sometimes bold knaves passed themselves off as serving-men of great nobles, and even Elizabeth was not exempt from their

15. B.M. MS. Lansdowne 81, No. 62: John Strype, *Annals of the Reformation . . . during Queen Elizabeth's Happy Reign* (Oxford, 1824), IV, 405–412. Aydelotte (pp. 167–173) called my attention to this letter. In 1591 by proclamation the Queen decreed that any wandering soldier not able to produce a valid passport should be committed to prison as a felon and suffer the same penalty as that for soldiers deserting the army (B.M., G.6463.300).

16. Aydelotte (p. 14) says: "From 1485 to 1550 we hear more and more of this class of thieves." For an admirably clear statement of the conditions behind this particular charge, see L. C. Knights, pp. 108–117, "The Dislocation of Social Classes and the Decay of Housekeeping."

17. B.M., G.6463: *A Book containing All Such Proclamations as were Published During the Raigne of the Late Queene Elizabeth,* collected by Henry Dyson (London, 1618), No. 283B. Elizabeth issued special proclamations against rogues and vagrants in London, requiring them to leave the city, in 1576, 1578, 1580, 1593 (February 21, June 18), 1596, 1598, 1599, 1600.

deceptions, as is evident from her proclamation in 1596 against abuses by "divers lewd and audacious persons falsely naming themselves Messengers of her Maiesties chamber." By means of clever ruses, such as pretended warrants from one lord to another, these knaves extorted various sums of money, and though many were set in the pillory and deprived of their ears, this abuse of the law seems to have continued.[18]

Much less dangerous than these wandering ex-soldiers and dismissed retainers, as Hext remarks, was "that wycked secte of Roages the Egipsions," but nevertheless these add a new set of vagabonds whose recorded history in England begins in the first years of the sixteenth century, and who, though at times confused with the purely English vagabonds, in general form a distinct group with their own special fascination for the people as well as the writers observing them.[19] And in addition to the Gypsies there were others who in any circumstances would be wanderers, creatures who, as Dr. Otto Fenichel observes,[20] have a strong liking for various peculiar actions, to whom wandering is like a private perversion, almost a mania, as exemplified in the obsession of Richard Brome's Springlove.[21]

Still another cause for the thriving of beggary at this time may be found in the charitable disposition of the people. Many rogues appear to have been utterly conscienceless, like Barnardine in *Measure for Measure,* without guiding principles or any shade of religion, preying upon a populace religious to the point of superstition. The people, swayed by mixed motives of fear, pious charity, and human compassion for the apparent sufferers with huge cleyms (sores) and for a feeble Autolycus with his piteous tales, were good picking, and hence the vulnerability of the people themselves resulted

18. B.M., G.6463, No. 334.
19. See Chapter IX.
20. Otto Fenichel, *Perversionen, Psychosen, Charackterstörungen* (Vienna, 1931), p. 59. I am indebted to Dr. Daniel C. Dawes for this reference.
21. See page 168.

in a thriving beggar population. This attitude is well illustrated in Robert Crowley's crude verse homily "Of Beggers."[22] After urging that counterfeit beggars should be forced to work for their food, Crowley tells of overhearing two beggars talking of their loathsome sore legs which they kept raw and red to elicit pity. If they did not have these self-inflicted wounds, they would be forced to go to work or be beaten as sturdy beggars. Yet another beggar complains that he will never thrive: he has only taken in sixteen pence that day but has spent eighteen. But a man must have drink:

> Go fyll me thys quarte pot
> full to the brynke.
> The tonge muste have bastynge,
> it wyll the better wagge,
> To pull a Goddes penye
> out of a churles bagge.

Yet this astonishing vicar-to-be of St. Giles would give alms even to these wretches, presumably because of the difficulty in distinguishing between the truly indigent and the knave:

> Yet cesse not to gyve to all,
> Wythout anye regarde;
> Thoughe the beggers be wicked,
> thou shalte have thy rewarde.

Sir John Cheke well sums up the enormity of the menace at the middle of the sixteenth century and points to the need for more stringent measures to deal with it:

> Is it not then dailye hearde, howe men be not onlye pursued, but utterly spoiled, and few may ryde safe by the kinges waie, excepte they ryde stronge, not so muche for fear of their goodes, whiche menne esteme lesse, but also for daunger of their lyfe, which everye man loveth. Worke is undone at home, and loiterers linger in stretes, lurk in ale houses, range in highewaies, valiaunte beg-

22. Crowley, *Select Works,* pp. 14–15; see also "The Beggars Lesson," pp. 57–59. The influence of Copland's *Hye way to the Spyttell hous* (see p. 59 of this study) is felt in the first of these verse-homilies.

> gers play in tounes, and yet complaine of neede, whose staffe if it be once hoat in their hande, or sluggishness bred in their bosome, they will never be allured to labour againe, contenting them selves better with idle beggary, then with honest and profitable labour. And what more noisom beastes be in a comune wealth? Drones in hives sucke oute the honie, a smal matter, but yet to be loked on by good husbãdes, caterpillers destroye the fruyte, an hurtefull thinge and well shifted for, by a diligente overseer. Diverse vermine destroye corne, kill pulleyne, enginnes and snares be made for thẽ. But what is a loyterer, a sucker of honeye, a spoyler of vytaile, a sucker of bloud, a breaker of orders, a seker of breakes, a queller of lyfe, a basiliske of the comune wealth, whiche by companie and syght doeth poyson the whole contreye, and staineth honeste myndes with the infection of his venime, and so draweth the commune wealthe to deathe and destruction.[23]

There was no evading the problems posed by this ever-multiplying horde of wanderers. Out of the many proposals for dealing with them issued much legislation, some at first so harsh and brutal as to be self-defeating, but gradually modified to win a fair degree of success. For a long time offenders guilty of even petty theft were condemned to death,[24] with the result that many citizens, motivated either by sympathy or fear of reprisal, evaded the law by failing to press charges against culprits or even taking their punishment into their own hands. Quite early, attempts were made to harmonize the law and the pragmatic response to it, as may be witnessed by the efforts of Edward VI to arrive at a solution of the problem in 1552–1553. Moved by a plea by Ridley, then Bishop of

23. B.M., C.40.a.9 (STC 5109): *The / hurt of sedici- / on howe greve- / ous it is to a / commune welth. / M.cccc.xlix,* sig. E4^v.

24. This penalty held for burglary, robbery, horse-stealing, and theft of every sort above the value of a shilling, save for its remission through benefit of clergy when the guilty party might be branded, imprisoned, and whipped, or subjected to any of these penalties. James F. Stephens (*A History of the Criminal Law of England,* London, 1884, I, 467) notes that towards the end of the seventeenth century the crimes listed, along with high treason, petty treason, murder, arson, rape, and abduction with intent to marry, were all excluded from benefit of clergy. Hythloday in *Utopia* argues against the folly of this law.

London, Edward, as Holinshed tells us,[25] sat down with the Bishop in Westminster and at the latter's suggestion, initiated plans for using the indigent of London as an experimental group in improving the lot of the poor in the realm. With the aid of the Mayor of London, Sir Richard Dobbs, a committee of twenty-four aldermen and commoners was appointed, who logically analyzed the situation confronting them and then proposed sound measures which ultimately were to prove as good basic solutions as were to be arrived at in the age. First they categorized the indigent into nine kinds of three degrees; then with admirable thoroughness, they devised provisions for all:

The poore by impotencie. Poore by casualtie. Thriftless poore.	Three degrees of poore.

1. The poore by impotencie are also devided into three kyndes, that is to say:	1. The fatherless or poore mans chylde. 2. The aged, blinde and lame. 3. The diseased person, by Leprie, Dropsie, &c.

25. B.M., 598.h.4 (STC 13568): *1577. The / Laste volume of the / Chronicles of England, Scot- / lande and Irelande, with / their descriptions. / Conteyning, / The Chronicles of Englande from William Con- / queror untill this present tyme. Faithfully gathered and compiled / by Raphaell Holinshed. / At London, / Imprinted for Iohn / Harison. / God save the Queene.* See p. 1713. E.M. Leonard (*The Early History of English Poor Relief,* Cambridge, 1900, pp. 34–35) says that Bridewell was not finally established before 1557; see her discussion of this action of Edward and Ridley and the functions of the hospitals, pp. 30–39.

Ridley's famous plea, as recorded in Glocester Ridley, *The / Life / of Dr. Nicholas Ridley, / sometime / Bishop of London / shewing the / Plan and Progress / of the / Reformation in which he was a principal Instrument and suffered Martyrdom / for it in the Reign of Queen Mary* (London, 1763), V, 377, reads: "Good Mr. Cecil. I must be a suitor unto you in our good Master Christ's cause; I beseech you be good to him. The matter is, Sir, alass! he hath lain too long abroad (as you do know) without lodging, in the streets of London, both hungry, naked and cold. Now, thanks be to Almighty God! the citizens are willing to refresh him, and to give him both meat, drink, cloathing and firing: but alass! Sir, they lack lodging for him. For in some one house I dare say they are fain to lodge three families under one roof. Sire, there is a

2. The poore by casualtie are also three kyndes, that is to saye:
   4. The wounded souldior.
   5. The decayed housholder.
   6. The visited with grevous disease.

3. The thriftlesse poore are three kyndes, that is to saye:
   7. The riotour that consumeth all.
   8. The vagabond that will abide in no place.
   9. The ydle person, as the strumpet and other.

For these sortes of poore were provided these severall houses: first for the innocent and fatherlesse, whiche is the beggers childe, and is in dede ye seede & breeder of beggerie, they provided ye house that was late Gray friers in London, & nowe is called Christs hospital, where the poore children are trayned in the knowledge of God and some vertuous exercise to the overthrowe of beggerie.

For the second degree is provided the hospitall of S. Thomas in Southwarke, and Saint Bartholomewe in West Smithfielde, where are continuallie at least two hundred diseased persons, which are not onely there lodged and cured, but also fed and nourished.

For the third degree, they provided Brydewell, where the vagabonde and ydle strumpet is chastised & compelled to labour, to the overthrowe of the vicious lyfe of ydleness.

They provided also for the honest decayed housholder, that he shoulde be relieved at home at his house, and in the parishe where he dwelled, by a weekelie reliefe and pencion. And in lyke maner they provided for the Lazer to keepe him oute of the Citie from clapping of dyshes, and ringing of Belles, to the great trouble of the Citizens, and also to the dangerous infection of manye, that they shoulde bee relieved at home at their houses with severall pensions.

---

wide, large, empty house of the King's Majesty's called Bridewell, that would wonderfully well serve to lodge Christ in, if he might find such good friends in the court to procure in his cause. Surely, I have such a good opinion of the King's Majesty, that if Christ had such faithful and hearty friends who would hartily speak for him, he should undoubtedly speed at the King's Majesty's hands. Sir, I have promised my brethren, the citizens to move you, because I do take you for one that feareth God, and would that Christ lie no more abroad in the streets." I am indebted to Dr. Richard W. Bailey for copying this text.

Some of these hospitals had been serving in these roles already, but the new proposals defined their functions more specifically and placed them under the authority of the City of London with the king himself as founder and patron of the establishment.

Sound as these provisions were, the vagabonds were so numerous and the problems they presented so complex that conditions did not improve for several decades. In some respects, these measures worked to better the lot of the helpless poor; but perhaps because the Bridewell experiment was not extended as widely as it should have been or ineptly administered, many of the sturdy rogues still remained unregenerate, resisting all attempts to change their behavior. Throughout the century various punishments for these offenders were tried with little success towards their reformation and the solution of the social problem, punishments such as stocking, whipping (often at the tail of a cart), the cutting off of one or both ears, branding with a V, and hanging (see Plate 2).[26]

As Aydelotte points out, more effective than all the other measures was the prescription of work in Bridewell and other corrective houses: ". . . the one effective punishment for sturdy vagabonds and beggars was to set them to work."[27] And it was the extension of this penalty in the important law of 1597 for the punishment of rogues, vagabonds, and sturdy beggars (39° Eliz. c.4) that put teeth into the statute and made it, together with the accompanying statutes for the relief of the poor (39° Eliz. c.3) and the building of local hospitals or workhouses (39° Eliz. c.5), as Cheyney describes it, "the foundation of the English system of dealing with the problem of pauperism . . ."[28] In this new law, superseding all

26. See Aydelotte's summarizing chapter, "Laws against Vagabonds," pp. 56–57.

27. Aydelotte, p. 57.

28. *The Statutes of the Realm, Printed by Command of his Majesty King George the Third . . . From Original Records and Authentic Manuscripts,* IV, Pt. II (1819), pp. 892–902, 39° Eliz. c.3, "An Acte for the Releife [*sic*] of the Poore"; 39° Eliz. c.4, "An Acte for the Punishment of Rogues, Vagabonds and

A whyp is a whyskar, that wyll wrast out blood,
Of backe and of body, beaten right well.
Of all the other it doth the most good.
Experience techeth, and they can well tell.

¶ O dolefull daye, nowe death draweth nere,
Hys bytter styng doth pearce me to the harte,
I take my leaue of all that be here,
Nowe piteously playing this tragicall parte,
Neither stripes nor teachinges in tyme could conuert,
wherefore an ensample let me to you be,
And all that be present, nowe praye you for me.

PLATE 2. Rogue at the Gallows. *A Caveat for Commen Cursetors*, H1v. The Pierpont Morgan Library.

previous statutes, justices of the peace were empowered to build Bridewells in their various jurisdictions. As in the statute of 1572 (14° Eliz. c.5) and successive laws on the subject, this new law listed as rogues, vagabonds, and sturdy beggars, roughly ten categories of begging wanderers, namely, all such persons calling themselves scholars; sea-faring men pretending losses of their ships; all using subtle crafts, such as unlawful games, physiognomy, palmistry, and other devices of fortune-telling; proctors or collectors for jails and hospitals; entertainers such as fencers, bearwards, players of interludes (except those under the patronage of a noble), and minstrels; jugglers, tinkers, pedlars, and other petty chapmen; loiterers and common laborers refusing to work for legal wages; persons freed from jail, begging for their fees; persons pretending loss by fire; and those pretending to be "Egyptians." Any such person was to be arrested and, with the advice of the parish minister and another citizen, was to "be stripped naked from the middle upwards, and . . . openly whipped untill his or her bodie be bloody." Then the offender was to be given a letter signed and sealed by any two of the officers, testifying to the punishment and its date and requiring the bearer to go directly within a specified time to the place where he had been born or had last lived for a year or the place where he had last passed through without punishment. Having returned to any of these places, he must be taken to the local Bridewell or the county jail until placed in service. If found unfit for work, he was to be put in an almshouse.

Provisions were made in the statute for the relief of the poor for the aid of "the lame, ympotente, olde, blynde . . . poore and not able to worke." The churchwardens and two to

---

Sturdy Beggars"; 39° Eliz. c.5, "An Acte for erecting of Hospitalls or abiding and working houses for the Poore." See also Cheyney's discussion (II, 262) of the provisions and effects of these statutes, and Leonard, pp. 68–70. The latter (p. 133) remarks that the statute on poor relief was given its final form in 1601.

four substantial householders were appointed yearly in each parish as overseers of the poor. They were to meet after divine service on Sunday once a month to consider courses of action, and they were enabled to assess taxes to buy materials to provide work for their charges, to build needed housing, and to take care of the helpless. Licenses to beg for food, but not for money, were granted to various poor persons unfit for work.

The provisions of these statutes were so complete, effective, and sensible that they were to remain essentially unchanged, Cheyney tells us, for two and a half centuries. Of course these statutes did not eliminate vagabondage or pauperism; these problems were to continue and remain important down even into the days of the modern welfare state, but the height of the tide of vagabondage was reached in the days of Elizabeth and began ebbing in the first quarter of the seventeenth century.

So remarkable a social and economic phenomenon as this increase in vagabondage with all its associated concerns for all citizens would inevitably have its impact on the literature of the time, and the effects are felt early and late. They are seen in tracts and petitions such as those of Simon Fish[29] and Robert Crowley;[30] in crude but vivid works of narrative verse by writers such as the author of *Cocke Lorelles Bote*

29. Simon Fish's well-known pamphlet, *A Supplicacyon for the Beggers*, c.1529 (B.M., C.21.b.45: STC 10883), represents a curious early rhetorical use of a beggar metaphor as a satire to further the Reformation. The beggars complain to Henry VIII because of inadequate alms: their number has been so "sore encreased" by the influx of "strong, puissant and counterfeit holy, and ydell beggers," whose numbers have grown to a kingdom, that the real beggars are dying of hunger. On this polemic see Percy Dearmer, *Religious Pamphlets* (London, 1898), pp. 12–13, 55–56. It is interesting, in view of More's concern in answering this "petition" (see his *The Supplicacyon of soulys*), to note that Fish probably derived his inspiration for his metaphor from the jest of the scoffer in *Utopia* regarding the distribution of beggars into houses of religion.

30. For the several pamphlets by Crowley, see *The Select Works*. Especially pertinent are *The Way to Wealth* and *An information and Peticion agaynst the oppressors of the pore Commons of this Realme* (1550).

and Robert Copland; in pamphlets shading from fact to fiction, such as those of Harman, Greene, and Dekker; in ballads like "The Blind Beggar's Daughter of Bethnall Green" and "The Gaberlunzie Man"; and in drama of all sorts, most strikingly in the works of Dekker, Shakespeare, Jonson, Fletcher, and Brome. At times in these works we appear to be in the presence of actual living rogues and knaves, especially in the eye-witness narratives of Harman and portions of Dekker. More commonly we observe the rogue of tradition, sometimes idealized, with his very vices dusted over with the gilt of romance. And times without number, rogue, unthrift, knave, madman, and thief became metaphor, symbols describing patterns of behavior.

The response of the authors to this knave and beggar world exhibits myriad shades of sensitivity and emotion. It varies from tolerant, robust laughter at knavish tricks and intrigues to harsh reprobation of evil; from unsparing condemnation of rogues in high station to tender sympathy and mercy for wretches who have lost their way, homeless wanderers in the night of error and folly. Shakespeare and Ben Jonson stand first among these authors recreating this world of knaves, rogues, and unthrifts because they perceive them as an integral part of the human condition. They knew that the passions of kings lay fettered like wretches in prison and might break out, that "uncleanly apprehensions / Keep leets and law days" in the purest minds. And it was this knowledge that led them, while they condemned vileness and corruption for itself, to be humanely considerate of the malefactor. No short book can adequately encompass all the manifestations of this subject. Here we shall look at only the most notable examples, many of which will be familiar, but all of which illumine the subject as the subject illumines them.

I

The Fraternity of Vagabonds and the Quartern of Knaves and Their Origins

THE MASTERLESS MEN who took the cart of cheese in Somerset and those who menaced London were creatures of flesh and blood. Side by side with them stride the rogues and knaves of tradition, almost always coloring the reality and imparting to it at times a curious glamor. This mingling of reality and tradition is well illustrated in Thomas Harman's *Caveat for Commen Cursetors* (1566),[1] the most widely known pamphlet on vagabondage in the Elizabethan period and one of the basic sources for later rogue literature (Plate 3).

At one time a justice of the peace, Harman got much of his information at first hand: we can believe him when he tells us that he had talked daily with many of the "ragged rabblement of rakehelles" at his home in Crayford in Kent, where, he says, "povertye daylye hath and doth repayre, not without some releife . . ." (Aii). After exacting his promise not to reveal their identity, some of these rogues have uncovered to him the nature of their strange order of vagabondage and their secret language known as "peddelars Frenche." But, as he tells us also, he derives at least "a glymsinge lyghte" from "a small breefe set forthe of some zelous man to his countrey . . . well worthy of prayse," manifestly an allusion to John

1. See Introduction, Note 2, p. 2.

A Caueat
FOR COMMEN CVR
SETORS VVLGARELY CALLED
Vagabones, set forth by Thomas Harman.
Esquier. for the vtilite and proffyt of hys
naturall Countrey. Newly agmented
and Imprinted Anno Domini.
M. D. LXVII.
¶ Vewed, examined and allowed, according vnto the
Queenes Maiestyes Iniunctions

IMPRINTED
at London in Fletestret at the signe of the
Fauleon by Wylliam Gryffith and are to be
solde at his shoppe in Saynt Dunstones
Churche yarde. in the West,

PLATE 3. *A Caveat for Commen Cursetors*. Title page. The Pierpont Morgan Library.

Awdeley's *Fraternitye of Vacabondes* (1561)[2] which had appeared five years earlier. And, as we shall see, he doubtless knew other works on the subject as well.

Awdeley had catalogued as many as nineteen kinds of vagabonds[3] as constituting an actual brotherhood,[4] most of

2. See Viles and Furnivall, p. ii. There appear to have been three early editions of this work, 1561, 1565, 1575. No copy of the first (1561) has been preserved and only the title of the second (1565) still exists. The title page of the 1575 edition (STC 12790: Bodl. 4° R.21. Art. Seld. [8]) reads *The Fraternitye of / Vacabondes. / As wel of ruflyng Vacabondes, as of beg- / gerly, of women as of men, of Gyrles as / of Boyes, with their proper names and qualities. / With a description of the crafty com- / pany of Cousoners and Shifters. / Wherunto also is adioyned the. xxv Or- / ders of Knaves, otherwyse called / a Quartern of Knaves / Confirmed for ever by Cocke Lorell.*

The Uprightman speaketh. /

Our Brotherhood of Vacabondes,
If you would know where dwell:
In graves end Barge which syldome standes,
The talke wyll shew ryght well.

Cocke Lorell aunswereth.

Some orders of my knaves also
In that Barge shall ye finde:
For no where shall ye walke I trow
But ye shall see their kynde. /

Imprinted at London by Iohn Aw- / deley, dwellyng in little Britayne / streete without Aldersgate. / 1575.

3. The first recorded use (1404: *OED*) of *vacabond* (OF *vacabond*) appears to be in a passage from a letter by Reynold of Bayldon, a keeper of Conway, to William Venables, Constable of Chester, and Roger Brescy, reading as follows: "Also I have herd my selfe mony of the gentilmen & of the commyns of M'yonnyth shire & of Caern'shire swere that al men of the forsaede shirs exepte fowre or five gentilmen & afewe vacaboundis, woldin faene cum to pees so that Englishemen were lafte in the cuntre for to helpe to kepe hom from mysdoers, and namely for to cum into the cuntre whil the weddir were colde." See Henry Ellis, *Original Letters, Illustrative of English History; Including Numerous Royal Letters: From Autographs in the British Museum and One or Two Other Collections, Second Series* (London, 1827), I, 36–37.

4. This fanciful idea, based obviously on the craftsmen's guilds, may have been suggested to Awdeley by Copland's casual allusion to the twenty-four orders of knaves or Lydgate's Order of Fools or Nigel Wireker's *Speculum Stultorum*. Whatever its source, the tradition persisted. Though Harman avoids the term *fraternity* and speaks of their "fleeting fellowship," he accepts the idea of an order and even provides for leaders (upright men) and a ritual of initiation

whom are faithfully accounted for by Harman in his much expanded treatise. A comparison of the categories listed by the two illustrates how closely Harman follows Awdeley even though he varies his approach. Essentially he adopts Awdeley's outline, rearranging its parts, and then, with additional details and anecdotes from experience or hearsay, endows the outline with entertaining substance.

(Lists correspond to the order of details in each text. Numbers in parentheses show Harman's correspondences to Awdeley. Brief definitions follow Awdeley's terms and Harman's added terms.)

Awdeley's "Vacabondes"	Harman's "Cursetors"
1. Abraham man (Bedlam beggar)	1. Ruffler (2)
2. Ruffler (sturdy vagabond)	2. Upright man (7)
3. Prigman (common thief)	3. Hooker (an angler)
4. Whipjack (fresh-water mariner)	4. Rogue (8)
5. Frater (licensed proctor)	5. Wild rogue (15)
6. Quire bird (horse thief)	6. Prigger of prancers (6)
7. Upright man (chief vagabond)	7. Palliard (9)
8. Curtal (rogue with short cloak)	8. Frater (5)
9. Palliard (beggar in patched cloak with artificial sore)	9. Abraham man (1)
10. Irish toyle (beggar selling points and laces)	10. Whipjack (4)
11. Jackman (counterfeit license-maker)	11. Counterfeit crank (beggar feigning falling sickness)
12. Swigman (peddler with pack)	12. Dommerer (one feigning dumbness)
13. Washman (palliard of lower rank)	13. Tinker (14)
14. Tinker	14. Swadder (12)
15. Wild rogue (born vagabond)	15. Iarke man and patrico (11, 19)

(the "stalling" of the rogue). This picture of a brotherhood is elaborated by Dekker, who makes much of one of their quarter-dinners (see p. 144) and the author of *Martin Mark-All,* who credits them with a guildhall (Maunders' Hall) and formal statutes regulating their behavior.

16. Kitchin co (*Kindchen;* boy beggar)
17. Kitchin mort (young girl beggar)
18. Doxy (female lace-seller)
19. Patriarke co (*patring cove,* hedge-priest)

16. Demander for glimmer (woman feigning losses by fire)
17. Bawdy basket (a female Autolycus)
18. Autem mort (married woman beggar)
19. Walking mort (unmarried female vagabond)
20. Doxe (harlot beggar) (18)
21. Dell (a "ripe" kynchin morte)
22. Kynchin morte (17)
23. Kynchin co (16)

Awdeley adds as a separate group (not vagabonds) under the heading "The company of Cousoners and Shifters" three special cozeners, namely, a courtesy man (confidence man), a cheater or fingerer (card sharp or false-dice player), and a ring-faller (one who gulls with gilded rings), knave types probably derived from *A manifest detection* (1552), a pamphlet devoted to the arts of cozening.[5]

Of the nineteen types of vagabonds listed by Awdeley, Harman has retained all but three, the curtal, Irish toyle,[6] and washman, though he has new names for some of Awde-

5. Bodl., 8° K.3. Art. BS.: *A manifest de- / tection of the most vyle and detestable / use of Diceplay, and other practises lyke / the same, a Myrrour very necessary for / all yonge Gentilmen & others soden- / ly enabled by worldly abũdãce,* to loke in. *Newly set forth for their behoufe* (Richard Tottyl, 1552). This work was printed also by Abraham Veale (n.d.). It was reprinted by Halliwell in 1850 for the Percy Society, and by Judges, pp. 26–50. For a review of the book and the plagiarism of it by various writers, see Aydelotte, pp. 121, 125–127, 175–177. See also p. 101 of this study.

6. Though Harman does not include the Irish toyle as one of the orders, at the end of his list of rogue names he speaks of over a hundred wandering Irish beggars who claim to have been despoiled by the Earl of Desmond and have come to England in the past two years. These "toyles" were possibly the same creatures as the "towlers" of *Cocke Lorelles Bote.* Wright (*Dialect Dict.*) defines *toweller* as "a wild or disreputable character" and associates the word with *towel.* To "rub down" with a blackthorn or oak towel was to beat or cudgel.

ley's beggars (*prigger of prancers* for *quire bird, swadder* for *swigman*). He saw at once that the washman was a palliard.[7] Though he lists the *patrico* and *jackman* (*iarke man*), he rejects them as nonexistent types. Since he is interested only in professional beggars, he naturally omits cozeners. To Awdeley's list of vagabonds proper, he adds seven new types, namely, *counterfeit crank* (see Plate 4), *dommerer, demander for glimmer, bawdy basket, autem mort, walking mort,* and *dell.* Besides adding types, Harman always improves on the parsimony of Awdeley's descriptions with more complete accounts of the behavior of each sort. Awdeley's document is a brief catalogue; Harman's work is a vivid and curious piece of literature.

How many of these "orders" had actual or merely fictive being is a nice question. Harman was probably right in rejecting the jackman (*iarke man*)[8] as a special type; and the patrico was possibly derived from Gypsy lore.[9] One may surmise that just as on occasion rufflers turned highwaymen and

7. L. Sainéan (*Les Sourçes de L'Argot Ancien,* Paris, 1912, I, 351) speaks of a band of "Paillards" as early as 1183 in France: "en 1183 on recontre une autre bande, celle des Paillards. Ils'attaquaient en particulier aux eglises." *OED* defines *palliard* as literally a vagabond who sleeps on straw in barns (Fr. *paillart* 13th c., *paille,* straw); its first recorded use is in 1484 (Caxton, *Fables of Æsop,* II, xviii, "The foxe was but a theef and a payllart and a knave of poure folke").

8. *OED* notes that *Jackman* is a misprint of the 1575 edition of Awdeley for *iarkeman,* probably thus spelled in the first edition of 1561. *OED* defines *Jark* (*iarke*) as "Old Cant, a seal," and a jarkman was a maker of counterfeit seals and licenses. *OED* notes further that the misprint (*Jackman*) was "sometimes taken as the right form." In actuality it seems to have replaced *iarke man* in later rogue lore.

9. In discrediting the existence of the patrico, Harman appears to have been right in regarding the type as non-English. The patrico (more properly, as in Copland, *patring cove*) seems of Gypsy origin, the one possibly specific Gypsy contribution to the supposed "order" (see Aydelotte, pp. 19–20). The curious rogue ceremony performed by the patrico in which he married vagrants till death should part them (that is, until they wearied of each other and shook hands in farewell over a dead animal) is traced by Walter Simson in his *History of the Gypsies* (1865), pp. 270–275, to related Gypsy customs. Later writers, including Dekker, Jonson, and Brome, find the patrico too useful to discard.

This is the fygure of the counterfet Cranke, that is spoken of in this boke of Roges, called Nycholas Blunt other wyse Nycholas Gennyngs. His tale is in the xvii. lefe of this booke, which doth showe vnto all that reades it, woundrous suttell and crafty desett donne of & by him.

PLATE 4. Nicholas Blunt in the Pillory. *A Caveat for Commen Cursetors,* H2. The Pierpont Morgan Library.

upright men turned peddlers, most of the other orders merged into one another as opportunity invited. Though some beggars would find certain practices of trickery more suitable than others, most, like Autolycus, would play the field, using whatever shifts advantaged them. The "orders" consequently should be visualized not so much as representing well-defined divisions as the functions of the supposed fraternity in general. That Harman himself basically accepted this view is attested by his giving us the presumed names of the members of only three orders, the upright men, the rogues, and the palliards, about whom he says, "And although I set and place her[e] but iii. orders, yet good Reader understand that all the others named are derived and come oute from the upright men and Roges. Concerninge y[e] number of Morets [Morts] and Doxes, it is superfluous to write of them."[10]

That Harman was led to assume (perhaps for the literary effect) the reality of his twenty-two orders (excluding the patrico and jackman) by the example of Awdeley's "fraternitye" can hardly be doubted; and Awdeley himself was so taken with the passion for establishing order in this society of disorder that he not only provides us with a fraternity of vagabonds (and a company of cozeners) but goes yet further and adds a second part, "the / xxv. Orders of Knaves, / otherwyse called / a Quarterne of Knaves, / confirmed for ever by Cocke Lorell." The title itself Awdeley owes in part to Robert Copland, who speaks of the "orders. viii tyme thre /

10. Sig. Gi; Viles and Furnivall, p. 78. *Roge* (*rogue*), according to *OED,* was introduced mid-sixteenth cy. to designate beggars and vagabonds. It is possibly related to *Roger,* probably with hard *g,* based on *rogacyon* and indicated originally a begging scholar, or vagabond pretending to be one (see Copland, *Hye Way,* l. 391: "Cometh not this way / Of these rogers that dayly sing and pray, / With Ave Regina or de profundis?"

Mort: origin unknown (*OED*); used commonly with qualifying word, as *autem mort, strolling mort*; first recorded use in Awdeley, 1561. *Doxy:* origin unknown; possibly continental; first recorded use, *Hickescorner,* c.1530 (Hazlitt, Dodsley, I, 188: "Of the stews I am made controller . . . There shall no mon play doccy . . . Without they have leave of me."

Of knaves onely" (Eiii^{v}) as being inmates of the hospital for unthrifts. Presumably Awdeley adds a twenty-fifth order for the sake of a catchy title: "a Quarterne of Knaves." The odd work itself is more interesting for its implications about sources than for information about rogues. It is made up of twenty-five brief definitions of various types of shiftless and more or less tricky rascals, all cousins of Lydgate's "froward Maymond" (*A Ballad of Jak Hare*), who can shake his master's doublet with one hand and cut his purse with the other, and reads almost like a book of manners for servants, designed to warn them by bad examples against misconduct. Awdeley is using the term *knave* in its common basic meaning, namely *servant* or *serving-man,* though with pejorative force.[11] The names of these knaves suggest their natures, as, for example, *Jeffrey Gods Fo, Nichol Hartles, Simon Soone Agon, Chop-logyke, Unthrifte, Ingratus.* Clearly these are not vagabonds but ne'er-do-well serving-men, a group, however, that by virtue of the practices set down by Awdeley, as well as other causes, continually swelled, as has been observed, the ranks of vagrancy. As well as most other Elizabethans, Awdeley would subscribe to Thomas Nashe's aphorism: "An ill husband is the first step to a knave."

Harman varies the procedure by adding to his first part a general section on the lodging and behavior of his rogues and "doxes" at night. His second part is a new feature, a catalogue of the names of the rogues whose nature he has been describing. Presumably the roster of 214 names (215 are listed, but John Gray is named twice) is composed of actual vagrants. Aydelotte furnishes a list of eighteen rogues bearing names cited by Harman who were punished as vagabonds between 1571 and 1589 in the middle and southern counties, and who, allowing for possible duplications, may have been

11. *Knave* (*OE cnafa,* originally, *boy, male child*) quite early (c.1000) was used to designate a boy servant, and hence a male servant in general (*OED*). The debased sense (of low character, rogue) is noted as early as 1205. The distinction between the two meanings doubtless depended on the tone of expression.

known to Harman.[12] This is strong evidence, as Aydelotte asserts, for supposing that most of the names may have been those of real vagabonds, though a few may seem fictive, such as "Core the Cuckolde," "Sothegard," and "Dowzabell skylfull in fence." Perhaps, however, they are no more unreal than those of some recent unthrifts in New Orleans named "Charlie the Mole," "Atomic Bum," "Gondola George," "Knapsack Jack," and "Horrible Example."[13] Most of the names in Harman's list are familiar English ones, such as Jackson, Cook, Brown, Gray, and Wilson, occasionally identified with a brief comment or tag. Thus John Howard is described as a well-digger who takes half his payment in advance and, after working two or three days, runs away. He has a possible relative in Richard Howard, a bawdy drunkard of nearly eighty years, who can bite a six-penny nail in two. White-bearded William Gynkes (Jenks) roams the country seeking work as a plasterer, but very little work suffices him. Harry Smith drivels when he talks. John Donne has one leg, and Robert Brownsword wears his hair long. Slight as such details are, they help to suggest the rogues behind the names as contrasted with the patent fabrication of the list in *Cocke Lorelles Bote*[14] with its morality names such as Adam Avarice, Cicely Clatterer, and Fabian Flatterer.

Harman improves further on Awdeley by adding a third part to his *Caveat* describing the private language or cant of the vagabonds, the nature of which will be considered later.[15]

I
Early Vagabond Documents: the *Warnung* of Basel and the *Liber Vagatorum*

As has been intimated, both Awdeley and Harman appear to have gleaned much of their information about rogues

12. Aydelotte, pp. 150–151.
13. Assoc. Press Report, *Hartford Courant,* July 14, 1961, "Charlie the Mole Buried; Lived Subterranean Life."
14. See p. 48.
15. See p. 39.

and knaves from earlier works on the subject. Both probably knew Alexander Barclay's version of Brant's *Narrenschiff* and *Cocke Lorelles Bote;* and both may have known some version of the *Liber Vagatorum,* though it is unlikely that either was acquainted with the immediate ancestor of the *Liber,* a manuscript in the archives of the City of Basel of an advisory issued by the Senate, which was copied in the *Chronicle* (c. 1479) of Johannes Knebel, a chaplain of the Cathedral of Basel.[16] The basic source for Knebel's copy (hereafter named the *Warnung* for convenience) is thought to date possibly as early as the first quarter of the fifteenth century, and it has been suggested that its publication may have coincided, oddly enough, with the first coming of the Gypsies to Basel in 1422. Knebel's copy shows the *Warnung* as having three divisions: first, a listing and description of twenty-three types of beggars and rogues; secondly, a brief discussion of several unclassified vagabonds; thirdly, a short account of their argot, named *Rotwelsch,* and a handful of Rotwelsch terms. This short document appears to have been first used in a literary way by Brant in his discussion of the beggars in his *Narrenschiff,*[17] which was written and published (1494) while Brant

16. D. B. Thomas (*The Book of Vagabonds and Beggars. With a Vocabulary of their Language. Edited by Martin Luther in the year 1528. First Translated into English by J. C. Hotten and now edited anew by D. B. Thomas,* London, 1932, p. 10) finds that three MSS. inventories, all based on a common source, are preserved in the Basel Archives and that the second of these was used by Knebel in his *Chronicle.* Thomas dates the first MS. between 1426–37 on the ground that it is written in a hand like that used in the Town Council Minutes of the same period. P. Ristelhuber (*Liber Vagatorum. Le Livre de Gueux,* Strasbourg, 1862, p. vi) lists three later printings of the *Warnung:* Johann Heumann's, in *Exercitationes iuris universi praecipue germanici* (Altdorff, 1749), "De lingua occulta," No. 13, pp. 174–180; Daniel Brückner's, in *Versuch einer Beschreibung historischer und näturlicher Merkwürdingkeiten der Landschaft Basel,* 1752 [1753], pp. 855–865; and Heinrich Schreiber's, in *Taschenbuch für Geschichte und Alterthum in Suddeutschland* (Freiburg in Breisgau, 1839), pp. 333–343. Ristelhuber says that Schreiber's text is the first exact copy of Knebel's and notes that Brückner and Heumann agree in dating the basic *Warnung* from the entry of the Bohemians (Gypsies) into Basel in 1422.

17. See *Sebastian Brants Narrenschiff,* ed. Friedrich Zarncke (Leipzig, 1854), p. 62, ch. 63, "von betlern."

was living in Basel; and it was accepted as a model by the anonymous author of the remarkable little quarto of twelve leaves known as the *Liber vagatorum / Der betler orden,* printed by Johann Weissenberger at Nuremberg perhaps as early as 1510 (see Plate 5).[18] The *Liber Vagatorum* was reprinted several times in the fifteenth century, and had the distinction of being edited in 1528 by Martin Luther, with a characteristic preface, under the title *Von der falsschen Betler büeberey.*[19] Since this edition faithfully reproduces the subject matter of the original work and has the added interest of containing some of Luther's views, it may be profitably examined here.

Despite Luther's preoccupation with many affairs at this time, like other churchmen and statesmen of the decades to come, he was much concerned about the dangers that the increasing numbers of the vagabonds represented to law and the spiritual welfare of society. These vagabonds (at least the greater part of them) he considers agents of the devil and a symbol of the devil's power in the world (and this view has some currency through the Renaissance and later):

> Ich habs aber fur güt angesehen / das solch büchlin nicht allain am tage blibe / sonder auch fast überal gemain würde / do mit man doch sehe ungriffe / wie der tewfel so gewaltig in [der] welt regiere / obs helffen wolt / das man klüg würde / und sich fur im ein mal fursehen wolte (sig. Ai^{v}).

Luther observes that the essential purpose of the booklet is to warn princes and other officials to be on guard in dealing

18. *Liber vagatorum. Der betler orden.* / [woodcut]; n.p., n.d.; listed in B.M., C.53.bb.g(4) as follows: Johann Weissenberger: Nuremberg, 1510? Avé-Lallement (as cited by Ristelhuber, p. xvi) believes that the lost first edition was printed between 1494 and 1499 at Basel and that the author was either Bergmann de Olpe or Brant. Ristelhuber argues for either Brant or Thomas Murner.

19. B.M., 12330.f.30: *Von der falsschen Bet / ler büeberey / Mit einer Vorrede / Martini Luther. / Und hinden an ein Rotwelsch / Vocabularius / darauss man die wört / ter so in dysem büchlein ge / braucht / verstehen kan. / Wittemberg. / M.M[D].XXVIII.*

Liber vagatorum.
Der betler orden.

PLATE 5. *Liber vagatorum*. Title page. British Museum, C.53.bb.9(4).

with beggars and to quit distributing them alms, under the persuasion of the devil, which really should go to honest poor folk. He goes on to prescribe sound methods of dealing with the problem which foreshadow summarily those adopted in the English poor laws of 1597 and 1601. All towns and villages should, he says, register their own paupers and take care of them, and strange or alien beggars should not be tolerated unless they can show letters or other testimony justifying their wandering. If every city kept track of its vagabonds, knavish tricks would soon be ended. He himself, he confesses, like Harman later, has frequently been a victim of these rogues and knaves: "Ich bin selbs dise iar her also beschyssen und versucht von solchen landstreichern und zungenddreschern / mer den ich bekennen wil."

The purpose, plan, and scope of the work are clearly stated in the introduction. The three-fold design (corresponding to that recorded by Knebel for the *Warnung*) establishes the pattern employed loosely or more exactly by authors of succeeding pamphlets, narrative verse, and even books on rogue life and manners from Robert Copland's *Hye way to the Spyttell hous* down to the long picaresque story of Meriton Latroon in the *English Rogue* (1665). The scheme is followed partially by Awdeley, more closely by Harman, but, as we have seen, both authors naturally vary the contents of their pamphlets, apparently adapting them to the conditions of English vagabondage. Yet Harman appears aware of the artificial nature of the scheme which he is imposing on English rogue life;[20] and the source, whether direct or indirect, of this excessive categorizing seems to lie in the pattern established by the *Liber Vagatorum* and its progenitor, the *Warnung* of the Senate of Basel.

The first part of the *Liber* describes twenty-eight different types of beggars and knaves, devoting a brief paragraph to each. Most of these are more fully delineated than those of

20. See p. 28.

Brant and could have served as models for the sketches in Awdeley and Harman, though there seems to be no direct relationship. Among those of special interest are the *stabeylers, lossners, klenckners, dobissers, grantners, voppers, dützbetterins,* and *biltregerins.* The *stabeylers* wander from shrine to shrine, wearing their patched cloaks, and they are beggars by inclination: once the beggar's staff grows warm in their hands, they never work again. The *lossners* are knaves with forged letters who claim to have been freed by miracles from imprisonment in pagan lands (a characteristic Gypsy claim). The *klenckners* sit at church doors, some with legs tied up as if maimed, others with arms smeared with salve. One of these, named Peter von Kreutzenach, tied up one of his legs under his cloak and sat with a dead thief's leg extended from his knee. Seeing a sergeant coming, he ran off faster than a horse ("ein pferd möcht in kaum erlauffen haben"). The *dobissers* are false clerics, pretended friars, who beg for linen thread for their altar cloths (that is, a dress for a harlot), or money to restore a ruined chapel (the drunkard's chapel beneath their noses). The *grantners* counterfeit the falling sickness, collapsing with soap-foam in their mouths (like Harman's counterfeit cranks). Some of these thrust straws up their noses to make them bleed (Falstaff knew of this trick too). The *voppers* (cousins of the English Bedlam beggars) pretend to be possessed of demons, they behave like madmen and beg for offerings in saints' names to remedy their affliction. Among the most picturesque in the group are the *dützbetterins,* women who lie covered with sheets in front of the churches, pretending to have lost children at birth or to have borne monsters, and the *biltregerins* who, like Doll Tearsheet, feign pregnancy by putting pillows under their clothes.

If the close resemblances between some of these knaves are taken into account, the list could be reduced to twenty-four or five, and one can see how, in fitting the types to conditions of English beggary, Awdeley and Harman possibly modified the numbers in their fraternities to 19 and 22 orders respectively. The descriptions of the various types themselves would appear to have helped the English pamphleteers in their classifications. Several of the German vagabonds have no clear parallel in the English pamphlets, but both Awdeley and Harman recognize several types, such as the klenckners, dobissers, kammesierers (wandering students), grantners, voppers, lossners, kandierers (fraudulent merchants, with false certificates, pretending to have losses from overseas or robbery, somewhat like the whipjacks), Christianers (fraters), and seffers (palliards). Even so, the debt is not one of free translation, but one of general outline and suggestion, not unlike, but not so conclusive as the debt of Harman to Awdeley. Harman's more extensive development of his material does not show the resemblances of translation in any part, and there is nothing to show positively that either English author knew the German work.

In the second part the *Liber Vagatorum* gives a general account (not classified) of other wanderers hardly less interesting, such as those who pretend to find hidden treasure, those who cripple their children to gain alms through pity, those who trick people into buying a counterfeit silver finger (like the ring-fallers of Awdeley), peddlers selling inferior wares, quack doctors, gamblers at cards and dice (Awdeley's cozeners), and tinkers whose women go ahead of them (suggestive of Harman's tinkers and their "doxes").

The third part of the *Liber Vagatorum,* the vocabulary of rogue words (*Rotwelsch*), lists and defines 227 terms used as a secret language by these vagabonds in their activities. As will be seen, the origins and development of this jargon and its currency are somewhat obscure. Some of the words are derived from Hebrew, such as *betzam* (*betzah*), egg; *beth* (*beth*), house; *joner* (*janah*), gambler; *lehem* (*lekhem*), bread. A few come from Latin, such as *caval* (*caballus*), horse; *kabas* (*caput*), head; *terich* (*terra*), country; *cass* (*casa*), house. Yet others represent compounds or corruptions of familiar German words (*gackenscherer,* chicken, from *gacken,* to cackle, and *scheren,* to vex or plague; *lissmarckt,* the head, louse-market).

D. B. Thomas has shown that this Rotwelsch vocabulary appears to be derived from Konrad Ammenhausen's *MS. Schachzabelbuch* compiled by Gerold Edlibach around 1490;[21] and as has been noted, the *Warnung* affords evidence that the argot was in use perhaps as early as 1422. For a handful of terms categorizing several vagrants it is possible to go back yet farther, to the *Notatenbuch* (c.1350) of Dithmar de Meckenbach, a canon and chancellor of the Duchy of Breslau under Charles IV (1346–1378),[22] who briefly catalogues the *maleficii* or evildoers of his time in terms which reappear in the rogue lists of the *Liber*. Behind this occurrence the trail becomes indistinct, perhaps not so much because records were not kept as because the language may not have existed much earlier.

According to Lazare Sainéan, the special languages of thieves, of which *Rotwelsch* and pedlar's French are representatives, appear to be a phenomenon of the late Middle Ages.[23] He observes that neither the classical literatures nor those of the earlier Middle Ages tell us whether such languages existed and that the lack of evidence in this matter amounts almost to a negative answer. What we call *jargon* or *argot,* he says, was not known in Europe until the end of the Middle Ages. The term *jargon* itself as used to designate a secret language occurs about the same time in the fourteenth century in the south and north of France (*gergon, gargon*). Some slight evidence exists to suggest that *argot* was used as

21. Thomas, p. 18. Thomas notes further that the *Rotwelsch Grammatik* apparently uses this word list, giving it first place in the text.

22. Ristelhuber, p. liv f. Thomas (p. 9) calls attention to the fact that grantners, voppers, and others were forbidden to enter Augsburg in 1342–43 and that the Constance *Ratsbuch* in 1381 gives the first inventory of rogues in the manner that Harman was later to make famous. Thomas finds also that *Blume der Tugend* (1411) by Vintner and *Das Teufels Netz* (c.1420) employ a few Rotwelsch terms.

23. *Les Sources de L'Argot Ancien* (Paris, 1912), I, p. 1.

early as the thirteenth century but no documents specifically illustrating any of the argots appear to occur before the sporadic examples in Dithmar de Meckenbach's *Notatenbuch,* and the first literary record with any pretence to fullness is that of the *Liber Vagatorum.* Each nation appears to have developed its own brand of argot. The Rotwelsch of Germany has Hebrew elements, but the French *jargon* contains no Hebrew but blends Old French terms with the patois of the north and the south. The French jargon influences and is influenced by the other Romance argots, namely the *Germania* of Spain, the *fourbesque* of Italy, and the *Calao* of Portugal, but is not influenced by Slavic argots, *Rotwelsch,* or the English cant (pedlar's French).[24]

Though neither the *maleficii* of Dithmar nor the vagabonds of Knebel's chronicle are identified as a special group, it is a curious fact that the notable increase in the number of vagabonds at this time, all accredited with knowledge of a private language, coincides, as we shall see later, with the first influx into Western Europe on a large scale of yet another people with a special language of their own, those very archetypes of the wandering life, the Gypsies. But, as Sainéan points out,[25] the jargon of France (and apparently this is true of the other argots as well) does not trace to Gypsy origins. Instead, the Gypsies are credited with assimilating the jargon of their beggar rivals without adding anything of their own to it. Up to the end of the eighteenth century the French jargon shows no Gypsy elements:

> Les rapports, frequent dès cette époque, entre les Bohemiens de France et les Gueux proprement dits temoignent que les premiers s'etaient assimilé le jargon de leurs rivaux sans rien ajouter de leur propre fonds: et en fait, le vocabulaire de l'argot ancien jusqu'à la fin du XVIII° siècle ignore tout trace d'élément tsigane.

And pedlar's French is similarly free, almost untouched by

24. L. Sainéan, *L'Argot Ancien (1455–1850)* (Paris, 1907), p. 2.
25. *Les Sources,* I, p. 45.

Romani.[26] Furthermore, though the Gypsies themselves employed pedlar's French in their activities, they maintained their own language essentially free of cant elements,[27] a singular fact in view of Romani borrowing from Greek, Slavonic, Roumanian, German, French, and other tongues.[28]

II
Pedlar's French: The Private Language of the English Vagabonds

The earliest recorded use of the common term designating the English cant occurs in John Palsgrave's definition in his lexicon in 1530:[29] "I speke a pedlars frenche, or a gyberishe, or any contrefait langaige, *Je jargonne,* prim. conj. They speke a pedlars frenche amongest them selfe: *ilz jargonnent entre eulx.*" Palsgrave's definition suggests that the term was already in general circulation at the time he wrote and that his readers would know something about the jargon itself.

Apparently no examples of the language date earlier than the beginning of the sixteenth century. An isolated phrase in *Cocke Lorelles Bote,* "couched a hogges heed" ("Some couched a hogges heed under a hatche") occurs as early as c.1510. Twenty-seven years later, Robert Copland's Porter speaks familiarly of the "bousy" (drunken) speech of the peddlers, their "pedlynge frenche," and even recites a pas-

26. See Note 9 of this chapter.

27. B. C. Smart and H. T. Crofton, *The Dialect of the English Gypsies* (London, 1875), p. xxii: "Most English Gypsies distinguish with great nicety between Romanes and the Cant Tongue, in the use of which latter the greater part of them are likewise proficient. 'That's not a *"tatcho lav"*' is a frequent Gypsy comment on hearing a canting phrase imported into a conversation which is being professedly carried on in their own proper dialect."

28. Franz Miklosich finds terms from all these languages in the dialect of Anglo-Scottish Gypsies (Smart and Crofton, p. xvii).

29. *L'Eclairçissement de La Langue Françoise* by John Palsgrave (Paris, 1852), p. 727. A facsimile of the 1530 title page reads: *Lesclar- / cissement de La Langue francoyse / compose par maistre / Jehan Palsgrave Angloys / natyf de Londres / et gradue de Paris. / . . . M.D. XXX.*

sage of verse written in it.[30] As already observed, beyond a few terms used in describing his rogues, Awdeley pays no attention to the language, perhaps because he was not familiar with it. Harman, however, is well acquainted with the "leud lousey language of these lewtering Luskes, and lasy Lorrels," and after defining 117 terms and phrases of it, illustrates their use in an imagined dialogue between an upright man and a rogue.

The Rotwelsch of the *Liber Vagatorum* and the "peddelars Frenche" in the *Caveat* are quite distinct from each other in the actual terms of their vocabularies, but they exhibit somewhat the same linguistic traits. As in *Rotwelsch,* certain terms in the English cant are formed by compounding descriptive adjectives with general terms such as *chete* (thing, derived from *escheat*), hence *smelling chete* (nose), *grunting chete* (pig); and *ken* (perhaps from *kennel,* OF *kenil*), as in *staulinge ken* (house receiving stolen wares), *bousing ken* (ale house). A few terms derive from Latin or French, such as *bene* (good), *commission* (shirt), *vyle* (town). Others are familiar words with new meanings: *cutte* (to speak), *the ruffian* (the devil), *stampes* (legs). Yet others are frankly imitative, such as *bufe* (dog), *quacking chete* (duck), or new coinages, such as *towre* (to see), *quaromes* (body). These terms, as Harman puts it, are "halfe myngled with Englyshe" (English function words) as in this sentence from the dialogue mentioned, "Why where is the kene that hath the bene bouse. Where is the house that hath the good drinke."[31]

The slender vocabulary set down by Harman appears to have been the only source of information on the subject that Thomas Dekker possessed, despite his claim that he derived his own word-list in *The Bellman of London* directly from the rogues and thieves themselves, for he adds no new terms. S. R. (Samuel Rid?), responding to Dekker's invitation to add new terms to the list, comes up with about a score in *Martin*

30. See p. 41 of this chapter.
31. *A Caveat,* sig. Giiii.

Mark-All, Beadle of Bridewell (1610).[32] And in due course, all writers of the Renaissance who use the terms get their information almost entirely from Harman or Dekker, that is, directly or indirectly from Harman. Dekker himself employs the cant extensively in *The Roaring Girl* (Middleton, his collaborator, does not show any specific knowledge of the speech elsewhere and almost certainly did not compose the cant scenes of this play).[33] Higgen, in Fletcher and Massinger's *Beggars' Bush,* uses one or two new terms (*clowes, twang*) in the ceremony of "stalling the rogue" or initiating Hubert into his fraternity of rogues.[34] In a much more elaborate use of rogue literature and cant in *The Jovial Crew,*[35] Richard Brome probably relies entirely on Dekker for his information.

The inventors of the cant, whoever they were, had imagination, and their inventions have color. It is therefore not surprising to find attempts at verse in the speech from the time of its earliest records down through its history. Thus, as remarked above, when Copland asks the Porter whether any peddlers come his way with their "bousy" speech, the Porter assents with an example of their speech in verse (Eiii^{v}):

> Ynow ynow / with bousy cove maund nace
>   Toure the patring cove in the darkman cace
> Docked the dell / for a coper meke
>   His watch shall feng a prounces nobchete
> Cyarum by salmon / and thou shalt pek my iere
>   In thy gan / for my watch it is nace gere
> For the bene bouse / my watch hath a wyn
>   And thus they babble tyll theyr thryft is thyn
> I wote not what / with theyr pedlyng frenche . . .[36]

32. S. R. claims to add 52 new terms, but about thirty of these are found in some form in Harman in compounds or in the text apart from the word list. The authors of the *English Rogue* (1665) add as many as fifty new expressions, but the currency of many of these is doubtful. See p. 151 of this text.
33. See p. 135.
34. See p. 164.
35. See p. 165.
36. B.M., C.57.b.30 (STC 5732): Title page missing; sig. Ai begins with the

This gallimaufry, apparently the earliest extended statement in the cant, was probably Copland's own attempt at verse in the speech.

Likewise, when Dekker wishes to illustrate the language with examples of verse, it is reasonable to assume that he composed them himself rather than that he had been supplied with them by a hypothetical patrico or frater, a claim that Dekker does not make. Dekker's several verses of this sort, with their matching translations, have a swing and naturalness that seem to qualify them as Dekker's invention.[37] One of these rhymes attains to unforgettable expression in at least four lines, as James Joyce realized:

> White thy fambles, red thy Gan,
> And thy Quarrons dainty is:
> Couch a Hogs-head with me than,
> in the Darkmans clip and kisse.[38]

III

The Ship of Fools and its Vagabonds and Knaves

The extensive literature developing the metaphor of the Ship of Fools also had its effect in shaping the tradition of the fraternity of knaves and unthrifts and imparted to it its own

---

title "The hye way to the Spyttell hous" above a cut of the Porter addressing Copland, with a beggar in the rear. Colophon: "Emprynted at London in the Fletestrete at ye Rose / Garland, by Robert Copland." This work was reprinted by E. V. Utterson in 1817; by W. C. Hazlitt, *Remains of the Early Popular Poetry,* 1856, IV, p. 17 f.; by Judges, pp. 1–25. For the words in the passage of pedlar's French (one that is frequently quoted) with its coarse meanings, the reader may refer to *OED* or Wright's *Dialect Dict.*

37. See p. 159.

38. See *English Villanies Six Severall Times Prest to Death by the Printers,* 1632, sigs. O2–O3 (see p. 157 for comment on this work). For the use by Joyce, see *Ulysses* (Paris, 1925), p. 47. Joyce fully appreciates rogue verses, as the paragraph preceding this verse indicates, a passage in which he describes the ruffian and his strolling mort: "Behind her lord his helpmate, bing awaste to Romeville . . . Buss her, wap in rogue's rum lingo, for O my dimber wapping dell." The verse quoted hardly needs translation, but Dekker's attempt at it (clearly inferior to his original) may be given for comparison: "White thy hand is, red thy lippe, / thy dainty body Ile not skippe; / To sleep, then downe ourselves lets lay / and cull i' the darke, and kisse and play."

special meaning. Though not the first to use the metaphor, Sebastian Brant has the honor of giving it international currency in his monumental satire, the *Narrenschiff*. As noted earlier, Brant appears to have made the first literary use of ideas and matter drawn from the *Warnung* of Basel in his chapter on beggars (lxiii), and his practice here of associating vagabondage with folly can be regarded as characteristic of the attitude of most writers in the Renaissance towards knaves and vagabonds. To Brant and his school of translators every human being who varies from pious rectitude is a fool, and fools never thrive: they are all unthrifts, and many, if not most, are knaves. What *A Mirror for Magistrates* was meant to be for princes and other rulers, the *Narrenschiff* was designed to be for the common man, a mirror in which he might see his every inclination to misconduct reflected, a work that crystallized the popular lore on folly.

This sprawling catalogue of the addicts of folly, superbly illustrated with emblematic woodcuts[39] which were doubtless hardly less influential than the text itself, was represented in Renaissance English by two versions, each based on adaptations of Brant's work and published in the same year, one written in clumsy prose by Thomas Watson, the other in labored but often vividly concrete Chaucerian stanzas by Alexander Barclay.

Watson's version,[40] thrice removed from the source in

39. Zeydel (see note 41 below) observes that these woodcuts, reproduced by Barclay, helped to make *The Ship of Fools* popular in England, and adds, "these cuts . . . were genuine 'emblems,' introduced by Barclay in England a generation before Alciati founded emblem literature."

40. Bibl. Nat.: Vélins 2368 (STC 3547): Title-page: *The shyppe of fooles.* / [woodcut of ship of fools]. Colophon: "Thus endeth the shyppe of fooles of this worlde. En- / prynted at London in Flete strete by Wynkȳ de Worde / . . . The yere of our lorde. M.CCCCC.ix. The fyrste ye- / re of the reygne of our soverayne lorde kynge Henry the / viii. The .vi. daye of Julu." A second edition followed eight years later: B.M., C.53.e.12. *The shyppe of Fools,* westminster, Wynkyn de Worde, 1517. For a full evaluation of this work and Barclay's in relation to their sources and influence, see Fr. Aurelius Pompen, O.F.M. (*The English versions of the Ship of Fools, A contribution to the His-*

Brant,[41] reaches occasional eloquence in its description of the knaves in the brief chapter (lix) "Of Beggers & of theyr vanytees," as in his sketch of the pardoners: "They make the poore folkes byleve moche gaye gere. They sel ye feders of the holy ghoost. They bere the bones of some deed body aboute the whiche paraventure is dampned. They shewe the heere of some olde hors / saynge that it is of ye berde of the innocentes." Sturdy rogues, he observes, prefer this life of vagrancy: "They be well at ease to have grete legges / and bellyes eten to the bones / for they wyll not put no medecynes therto for to hele them / but soner envenymeth them / & dyvers other begylynges of whiche I holde my pease."

Barclay's version, like Watson's, is also removed from Brant,[42] since he mainly followed the Latin version by Locher and apparently did not know Brant's text at all;[43] but his satire comes near to what Novalis calls mythic translation, a true rebirth of a work to suit another time and place. In his prologue Barclay sums up the moral intention of his work

---

tory of the Early French Renaissance in England, London, 1925); See also Zeydel's valuable bibliography of the translations and adaptations, pp. 24–31.

41. Fr. Aurelius Pompen (pp. 310–311) finds that Watson is following the second edition of Jehan Drouyn's shortened prose version (Lyons, 1499), which was adapted principally from Rivière. See also Edwin H. Zeydel, *The Ship of Fools by Sebastian Brant Translated into Rhyming Couplets. With Introduction and Commentary . . . and reproductions of the original woodcuts* (New York, 1944), pp. 27–31.

42. STC 3545: B.M., G.11593 (title page missing; publisher's note preceding table of contents: "This present Boke named the Shyp of folys of the worlde was translated i[n] the / College of saynt mary Otery in the counte of Devonshyre: out of Laten / Frenche / and Doche into Englysshe tonge by Alexander Barclay Preste: and at that tyme Chaplen in the sayde College traslated [*sic*] the yere of our Lorde god. M.CCCCC / viii. Inprentyd in the Cyte of London in Fletestre at the signe of Saynt George / By Richarde Pynson to hys Coste and charge: Ended the yere of our Saviour / M.d.ix. The xiiii day of December." A second edition appeared in 1570. The edition of 1509 was reprinted by Jamieson in 1874 in two volumes. My quotations are from the first edition.

43. Despite Barclay's profession of using "Doche" (the German of Brant) as well as the Latin and French versions, Pompen (p. 309) demonstrates that Barclay regularly follows Locher (principally) and Rivière.

(Fol. xi) in a way that shows that he fully appreciates the essential meaning of the original:

> Ye London Galants / arere / ye shall nat enter
> We kepe the streme / and touche nat the shore
> In Cyte nor in Court we dare nat well aventer
> Lyst perchaunce we sholde displeasure have therfore
> But if ye wyll neds some shall have an ore
> And all the remenaunt shall stande afar at large
> And rede theyr fauts paynted aboute our barge
>
> Lyke as a myrrour doth represent agayne
> The fourme and fygure of mannes countenaunce
> So in our shyp shall he se wrytyn playne
> The fourme and fygure of his mysgovernaunce . . .

Though Barclay's translation is free, "some tyme addynge and somtyme detractinge" from his source, it is still essentially faithful to the outlines of the original work. His own ambition, however, was to "redres the errours and vyces of this our Royalme of Englonde: as the foresayde composer and translaytors hath done in theyr Contrees . . ."; hence he freely omits whatever he regards as superfluous and inapplicable to English conditions as he knows them, and the result is a work distinctly more national in feeling than either Brant's or Locher's version.

Apart from the general conception of the universal ship of fools and the controlling theme of the motto, *Stultorum infinitus est numerus*, Barclay's work, like the original, has no unifying pattern of thought. The satire is directed mainly at unthrifts (the improvident, the ignorant, the careless, the lazy), but knaves and vagabonds rub shoulders with these, and frequently they tend to fuse into one picture, as in the attack on the folly of courtiers and gallants in following new fashions (fols. xix, xx). By devising new false styles for themselves, Barclay says, the masters deform the bodies God has made for them. The courtiers in their turn, seeing the masters deform their shapes, imitate them and are presently forced to steal and rob to maintain their pride. Many of these end on the gallows, with their garments offered for sale at Newgate, and their bodies wave with the weather while their necks hold.

In like fashion unscrupulous cleric and vagabond coalesce (cxxvii). The abbot, the prior, and their convent are so blind with greed that they continually devise new ways to add to their holdings. Some beg for brethren whom they pretend have been taken captive; some gain money from feigned miracles and fraudulent pardons (and drink all they gain at night in the alehouse); some beg for buildings or hoodwink country folk with false relics. As Barclay proceeds, we lose sight of the fraters and pardoners as, without transition, he speaks of strong young folk giving themselves over to sloth, smearing their legs and arms with blood and plasters and crippling along with sound legs falsely bound up (see Plate 6). Yet others, having disfigured their children, mangling their faces and breaking their bones to stir pity, shout pleas for alms and twist and distort their bodies. Such young people as give themselves to these practices, says Barclay, do so because they despise work and wish to live at the expense of others. And once they have taken the infection of vagrancy, they never change—and he echoes the familiar motif:

> if they a whyl have ron in the wynde
> And in theyr hande the staf some hete hath caught
> They never after shall leve the beggers craft

For a moment we catch a glimpse here of a vagabond crew, but we speedily lose them in the larger entourage: the company of fools is indeed almost infinite (cclxii):

> But to be playne / and speke as [I] [i]ntende
> All men ar folys that can nat them selfe gyde
> Thus all the worlde may I well comprehende
> Except a fewe: whom I may set asyde . . .

People of all lands come to the ship, but this ship has, very fittingly, no specific destination. It goes wherever fools are, and to English ports in particular (fol. v): "Where may we

Mēdicātes im
probi.

Tot mēdicoꝝ
cernis fraudeſ
ꝗ doloſqꝫ. Vt
merito hos fa
tuis grādibus
accumulē. Vtí
lius eſurienti
panis tollitur
ſi de cibo ſecu
rus iuſticiam
negligat q̄ eſu
riēti panis frā
gatur. vt iniu=
ſticię ſeduct⁹
acquieſcat.

C. mendi deba
li li.xi.v.q.v.
nō ois.xvii.di.
c.paſci.glo.ſup
math.

A Great company of folys may we fynde
Amonge beggers/whiche haue theyr hole delyte
In theyr lewde craft: wherfore I set my mynde
In this Barge theyr maners/brefely for to wryte
For thoughe that nede them greuously do byte.
yet is theyr mynde for all theyr pouerte
To kepe with them of children great plente

And though that they myght otherwyse well lyue
And get theyr lyuynge by labour and besynes
yet fully they theyr myndes set and gyue
To lede this lyfe alway in wretchydnes
The clerke/frere/or monke/whiche hath store of ryches
For all his lyfe. if he it gyde wysely.
Wyll yet the beggers offyce occupy

C. auaricie de
prebendis.
Prouer.xiiij.

Suche oft complayne the charge of pouerte
In garmentis goynge raggyd and to rent
But yet haue they of ryches great plente

PLATE 6. Barclay, *The Ship of Fools*. Of Beggars (Ch. 63). British Museum, G.11593.

best aryve? at Lyn or els at Hulle? / To us may no haven in Englonde be denayed!" In this aimlessness Barclay improves on Brant's more obvious plan to ship the fools to their own Utopia, Narragonia.

Interesting as Barclay's account of his beggars is, Brant's own chapter on the subject is more extensive; and, as Pompen observes, had Barclay followed it rather than Locher's resumé, both the author of *Cocke Lorelles Bote* and Copland might have added yet more pictorial details to their works. Thus Brant's clerical beggars who hoodwink the people with such supposed relics as a bone of Balaam's ass or the bridle of St. George's steed have color missing in Barclay. And though Harman does not give certain evidence of knowing either Barclay[44] or Brant, the chapter of the latter on the beggars is roughly parallel in structure to the *Caveat,* inasmuch as Brant mingles his description of beggar types with a brief illustration of *Rotwelsch,* the private jargon of these folk,[45] a procedure found in the *Caveat* and later rogue pamphlets. But Barclay's work, despite its shortcomings and obvious defects, has an impressive sincerity, and was to be deeply influential in English literature of the Renaissance; and though it was to be neglected thereafter, it has been a stimulus to some searching modern satire.

IV
Cocke Lorell and his Boat of Knaves

On the title page of his *Fraternitye of Vacabondes* in a verse dialogue between an upright man and Cocke Lorell,[46] Awdeley acknowledges the influence of that curious piece of

44. Harman in his opening "Epistle" speaks of repairing the "Shyp of knowledge" so that it may pass safely through all parts of the realm and his way of using the metaphor indicates some acquaintance with the purpose of the Ship of Fools. He probably knew Barclay's work.

45. Zarncke discovers over twenty Rotwelsch terms in the passage of fifteen lines representing the argot.

46. See Note 2, p. 23.

social satire, *Cocke Lorelles Bote,* in the shaping of his order of knaves and unthrifts. This satire is manifestly part of the Ship of Fools tradition, as was indicated by Wynkyn de Worde when he illustrated the text of the *Bote* with four woodcuts from Watson's *Shyppe of Fooles* (see Plate 7). But the author appears to have been inspired by Barclay, as Charles H. Herford has shown.[47] In the second stanza of his chapter "The universall shyp and generall Barke or barge" (cclxi), Barclay associates the crafts with knavery:

> Here shall Jack / charde / my brother Robyn hyll
> With Myllers and bakers that weyght and mesure hate
> All stelynge taylors: as Soper: and Manshyll
> Receyve theyr rowme: bycause they come to late
> The foulest place is mete for theyr estate
> A rowme for rascoldes hard by the pompe shall be
> That stynkynge placis and knaves may agre.

This passage, together with the following chapter, "The universall shyp of crafty men or laborers," seems to have been the literary inspiration behind *Cocke Lorelles Bote* (c.1508),[48] perhaps the most racy work in all the literature of knaves and rogues, not inferior to the *Tunning of Elinour Rumming* in its revelations of seamy types. Both Chaucer and Langland, to each of whom the author is indebted, would have enjoyed this cargo of rascals.

47. *Studies in the Literary Relationships of England and Germany in the Sixteenth Century* (Cambridge, 1886), pp. 346–347. Herford observes that Barclay follows Locher in fusing two widely separated chapters in Brant (48 and 108).

48. The unique copy of the first edition of this work, B.M., C.21.c.12, Garrick Collection (STC 5456), has no title-page; the colophon, sig. ciii^{v} reads: "*Here endeth Cocke Lorelles bote. Inprȳted / at London in the Flete strete at the sygne of / the sonne by Wynkyn de Worde.*" The first six pages of the poem are missing. Later editions were published in 1817 (Henry Drury, ed., for the Roxburghe Club); 1841 (Edinburgh); 1843 (Edward F. Rimbault, ed., Percy Society, XXX); and 1884 (J. P. Edmond, ed., Aberdeen).

Paul R. Baumgartner presents strong evidence that the poem was probably written between 1506 to 1508 ("The Date of *Cocke Lorelles Bote,*" *Stud. in Bibl.,* Bibl. Soc. of the Univ. of Va., IX (1966), 175–181.

Also it is graunted by our bulles of lede
That whan ony brother is dede
To the chyrche dogges shall cary hym
A ryche pal to lyon ẏ corse late fro rome is cōme
Made of an olde payre of blewe medly popley
For ẏ worshyppe of all ẏ bretherne. (hosone

PLATE 7. A Ship of Knaves. *Cocke Lorelles Bote*. British Museum, C.21.c.12.

Though the first six pages of the poem in the unique copy of the first and only early edition are lost, the author's intentions are clear. His poem falls roughly into six parts, an introduction (what is left of it, beginning on sig. B) describing in some detail thirteen members of the crew, the Pardoner's roll-call of knaves quartered on the boat (fifty specifically named wretches, not unlike those of Awdeley's *Quartern*), the Pardoner's explanation of the value of his pardon, the listing of craftsmen seeking passage, the preparations for sailing and for the voyage, and the conclusion with its wry comment on the disappointed religious orders who have missed the boat.

All the creatures of the poem, especially those of the introduction, are rascals claiming attention: one cannot easily forget Cocke's new laundress who is soft as a lamb when pleased, but a devil when vexed (if her husband calls her callat, she calls him knave, and will not die in his debt); or the butcher, gory with red blood, with his greasy hose, a breeding place for maggots, together with his unsavory companions. But the last three parts are especially pertinent. At the beginning of the fourth part, Cocke sees the streets thronged with people, one or more from every craft, seeking passage on his boat. The author here lists all the crafts he can think of, the most complete catalogue of the trades and means of livelihood that we have of the age, some 263 occupations, a list that atones for its monotonous length by suggesting to the imagination the remarkable scope of Tudor economics and industry. Nearly every possible craft and calling from harp-maker to arrow-header, horse-leech to rat-taker, tankard-bearer to smoggy collier, contributes its share of knaves. The writer apparently excepts only occupations relating to the courts of law, the clergy (save for the concluding irony), the nobility, and the King, and members of their establishments. Toward the end of his catalogue the author indiscriminately mixes with his craftsmen a score or more rascals and wantons such as thieves, bawds, flatterers, and drabs, ironically thus equating them with the craftsmen themselves (Ci):

> Of every crafte some there was
> Shorte or longe more or lasse
> All these rehersed here before
> In Cockes bote eche man had an ore

Though the accent is unpolished, we are not far removed from the satiric mood of John Gay:

> Through all the employments of life
> Each neighbour abuses his brother;
> Whore and Rogue they call Husband and Wife:
> All professions be-rogue one another.
> The Priest calls the Lawyer a cheat,
> The Lawyer be-knaves the Divine;
> And the Statesman, because he's so great,
> Thinks his trade as honest as mine.
>
> —*The Beggars' Opera*[49]

The preparations for sailing are lively and dramatic, with various members hoisting anchor, raising the sails, spreading standards, and couching a hogshead (sleeping) under a hatch.[50] They spread their sails and row forth with a "heve and howe rombelowe," from the port of "garlyke hede to knaves in," with intent to play between Tyburn and Chelsea:

> They banysshed prayer peas and sadnes
> And toke with them myrthe sporte & gladnes
> They wolde not have vertu ne yet devocyon
> But ryotte and revell with Ioly rebellyon

Cocke and his crew have sailed England through and through. As the author goes home to "mowe shame stere,"[51]

49. *The Poetical Works of John Gay* (London, 1926), p. 488.
50. This phrase "couched a hogges heed" appears to be the first example of pedlar's French in English (see p. 39).
51. No one appears to have identified this place, and my reviews of the maps and studies bearing on the time and earlier and later have been fruitless. Could the writer be referring to a hamlet no longer existing in the vicinity

he meets a company of hermits, monks, friars, and other members of religious orders seeking passage on the boat, all of whom are distressed at arriving too late; but they can sail another year. It is a merry thing, the author observes, when knaves meet, and Cocke has a great rout of them, every third person in England.

Cocke Lorell himself, manifestly a fiction, a name for an imagined leader of knaves, still mirrored the actuality of Elizabethan knavedom enough to foster a new legend. Casual references to him occur from time to time, and when the author of *Martin Mark-All, Beadle of Bridewell* (1610), attempts ostensibly the first history (purely fictive) of English vagabondage, he tries to establish Cocke as a once-living rogue who governed the English vagabonds for almost twenty-two years until 1533 and organized the Quartern of Knaves.[52]

---

of Moulsham, Essex? In manuscript, *Moulsham* might easily be read as *mowes ham,* which with the suffix *-ster,* could account for the name. *Moulsham* itself had its abbey and nunnery that could have provided such a procession as that visualized by the author.

In response to my query in *TLS,* 29 Feb. 1968, Miss M. McLachlan of Cheadle, Cheshire, in a letter dated May 1 offers me evidence largely confirming the above conjecture. Noting that most of the place names in the *Bote* relate to the Home Counties (near London), she finds *Moulsham* the only probable reference. *The Oxford Dictionary of Place Names* offers variant spellings: *Mulesham, Molesham, Muleshamstede; Place Names of Essex,* along with other forms, lists *Mulesham, Musham, Mowsham* (1558), Mowlsham (1594). Her search of other place-name records revealed no other possible source. Though the *-stere* suffix remains unexplained, it appears that the author of the *Bote* lived in or near Moulsham.

52. See Chapter IV, Note 19.

II

The Crowded Highway to the "Spyttell Hous"

THE ANCIENT IMAGE that interprets man's life as a pilgrimage sees the road forking in two ways, one being the straight and narrow path, the *via recta,* beset with hardships and obstacles but leading to the Heavenly City, and the other the broad highway of many temptations, the deceptively alluring primrose path to the everlasting bonfire. If it can be said that the medieval mind was preoccupied with the former image, it is also equally evident that the humanistic Elizabethans and Jacobeans were more concerned with the latter. It was natural, therefore, that they should visualize the passengers on our Ship of Fools, after their disembarking and tarrying awhile at Knaves Inn (a symbol for the taverns that received their kind), as soon or late following the rest of the ship's crew along the crowded highway to the melancholy doors of the institutions provided for needy wayfarers and sturdy vagabonds.

There were four celebrated foundations of this sort (though not so admirable as the four of Amaurote) in Tudor London, St. Bartholomew's, Bethlehem, Bridewell, and Newgate, each having its own special function. Hardly less famous than these in the time of Elizabeth was the Savoy, but its history in general is more variable.[1] Of these institutions, St.

1. The Savoy, as it was commonly known, originally a palace built in 1245 by Peter, Earl of Savoy and Richmond, was given by him to a fraternity of

Bartholomew's, the oldest and perhaps the most important to our study, will be considered last. Bethlehem Hospital, founded in 1247 by Simon Fitz-Mary, a Sheriff of London, as a priory of canons, through its mendicant brothers early administered to the poor and sick, but after 1377, with the probable transfer of the insane from Stone House at Charing Cross, seems to have become the principal institution for the mentally diseased, the asylum of the Bedlam beggars.[2] The history of the genuinely mad folk of Bethlehem mingles closely with that of the knave Bedlamites; it was hard for the people of the time to distinguish between Poor Tom the knave and Poor Tom the fool.

Bridewell Hospital, at one time the palace of Henry VIII and subsequently of imperial ambassadors, was granted by Edward VI to London in 1553 and finally turned over to the City in 1556. From this time a workhouse for the poor and a house of reformation for vagrants, thieves, and dissolute women arrested by the beadles and constables in their rounds and in the periodic attempts to reduce vagabondage, Bride-

---

Montjoy. In 1505 it was endowed by Henry VII as a hospital for one hundred poor, but was suppressed in 1552 and its equipment given to Bridewell and St. Thomas's Hospital. It was reendowed by Queen Mary and maintained as a hospital until the time of Queen Anne, 1702. William Fleetwood, Recorder of London, in 1569 in a letter to Lord Burghley speaks of the Savoy as the "chieff nurserie of all these evell people" and asks for its reformation. See H. B. Wheatley and Peter Cunningham, *London Past and Present* (London, 1891), III, 217–218; Henry Ellis, *Original Letters Illustrative of English History* (London, 1824), II, 283–286.

There were of course several other hospitals that cared for the poor and wandering. Of these, specially deserving mention is St. Thomas's in Southwark, founded in 1213 by Richard, Prior of Bermondsey, as an almonry, and taken over by the citizens of London as a hospital for poor and impotent people in 1552; and St. Giles, originally a hospital for lepers, founded in 1101 by Matilda, Queen of Henry I. At this hospital prisoners on their way to Tyburn were presented with a large bowl of ale as their last refreshment. See Wheatley and Cunningham, III, 373; II, 113.

2. Wheatley and Cunningham, I, 171–172 ff. See also Edward G. O'Donoghue, *The Story of Bethlehem Hospital* (London, n.d.), p. 67. For a detailed study of the influence of this hospital on Jacobean drama, see Robert R. Reed, Jr., *Bedlam on the Jacobean Stage* (Cambridge, Mass., 1952).

well became a synonym for *house of correction* and was to furnish the name and pattern for about two hundred Bridewells in the British Isles.[3] Newgate, mentioned as a prison as early as 1188, was given by Henry IV to the City in 1400. It was rebuilt sometime between 1414 and 1430 at the recommendation of Sir Richard Whittington and with money provided in his will (hence "Whittington College").[4] In its long history it lodged citizens and nobles as well, but was the main prison for rogues and knaves. In time its name became, as Nashe calls it, "a common name for all prisons, as homo is a common name for a man or a woman."

But the great refuge for the helpless indigent and the wayward in distress was St. Bartholomew's Hospital, whose ministrations had begun with the founding of the Priory of St. Bartholomew by Rahere in 1123, had continued through the Middle Ages, and apparently had become the responsibility of the City shortly after the dissolution of the Priory in 1536. Though the Hospital (now one of the most renowned of medical institutions) still occupies the site chosen for it by Rahere, the original buildings have all disappeared. Some faint idea of what it looked like in late medieval times may be gleaned from the picture of the fight with axes between John Astley and Philip Boyle held in front of it in January, 1441–1442 (see Plate 8).[5] Committed from the beginning to the care of the diseased, it seems to have been shelter also for vagrants in need as is suggested by a report published

3. Edward G. O'Donoghue, *Bridewell Hospital, Palace, Prison, Schools* (London, 1923), p. 5. The Bridewell of Westminster was used by Fielding in *Amelia*. See also Wheatley and Cunningham, I, 240–244. For a review of documents relating to the acquisition of Bridewell by the City, see Thomas Bowen, *Extracts from the Records and Courtbooks of Bridewell Hospital* (London, 1798), pp. 1–11.

4. Wheatley and Cunningham, II, 589–590. For a more extensive account, see Arthur Griffiths, *The Chronicles of Newgate* (London, 1884), I, 22, 62–95, 144; also Charles Gordon, *The Old Bailey and Newgate* (London, 1902), pp. 3, 24.

5. Sir D'Arcy Power, *A Short History of St. Bartholomew Hospital* (London, 1923), pp. 3–13; Gweneth Whitteridge, *The Royal Hospital of St. Bartholomew* (London, 1952), pp. 3–9; Wheatley and Cunningham, I, 117–118.

PLATE 8. Combat in front of St. Bartholomew's Hospital, January, 1441–1442. Hastings MS., M.775, Fol. 277v. The Pierpont Morgan Library.

by the Hospital in 1552, *The ordre of the hospital of S. Bartholomewes in West-smythfielde in London.*[6] In the preface the writer credits King Henry VIII with erecting a hospital in West Smithfield (presumably rebuilding and adding to the earlier institution) for the "continual relief & help of an C. sore and diseased" and endowing it with an annual grant of five hundred marks, with the provision that the City raise a like sum, as it did. But these sums, we learn, were insufficient; it was discovered that the hospital was inadequately equipped, having only "so much of housholde ymplementes and stuffe towarde the succouryng of this hundred poore, as suffised thre or four harlottes, then lieng in chyldbedde, and no more, yea, barely so muche, if but necessary cleanliness were regarded." The citizens, therefore, moved by compassion to not only their "own poore and afflicted, but to all other sore and diseased which dayly out of all quarters of the Realme resort to the Citie (as to a cõmune receipt and refuge of their miserie)," added almost a thousand pounds to the endowment to remedy these defects. Meanwhile, the author reports, the hospital has cured eight hundred of "pocques, fystules, filthie blaynes and sores" and taken care of 172 who have died "in their intollerable miseries and griefes, might otherwise have stõcke in the eyes & noses of the Citie

6. B.M., C.58.a.21(2) (STC 21557): *The ordre of / the Hospital of S. Bar- / tholomewes in West- / smythfielde in / London. / . . . Anno 1552;* colophon: "Imprinted at London by Ry- / charde Grafton, Printer to the Kinges maiestie." Power (p. 8) remarks that the hospital was originally planned to give relief for "every kind of sick person and homeless wanderer." Miss Whitteridge (p. 7) also remarks this fact: "In medieval times the Hospital of Saint Bartholomew was more than a house for the care of the sick poor . . . Besides being a hospital in the modern sense of the word, it was also an hospice and an almshouse, caring for the aged, for orphans and foundlings, and for the passing stranger or homeless wanderer." This condition of affairs seems to have continued well into the Renaissance. Miss Whitteridge observes further (p. 9) that though the Priory was suppressed in October 25, 1539 [Stowe], the Hospital seems to have continued to function, though in difficult circumstances. On December 27, 1546, Henry VIII gave the "late hospital of St. Bartholomew" to the City, and on January 13, endowed it with lands and properties to compensate for those seized at the Dissolution.

. . . if thys place had not vouchedsaufe to become a poompe alone, to ease a commune abhorryng." The governors hope to enlarge the benefits from a hundred to a thousand poor, and appeal to all other houses of alms to make a like endeavor. The report describes the duties and charges of the governors and other officers, the latter including the hospitaler, renter clerk, butler, porter, matron, twelve sisters, eight beadles, and a minister known as the Visitor of Newgate.

We have a lively picture of the host of unthrifts and knaves that probably sought shelter within the walls of this hospital in Robert Copland's verse narrative of over a thousand lines, *The hye way to the Spyttell hous* (c.1536–1537),[7] of all the works of rogue literature perhaps the most widely read in the Tudor and Jacobean periods and justly praised by Furnivall as the most valuable picture of the beggars and unthrifts of the time (see Plate 9).[8] It is indeed a marvellous parade of the people of our study.

The narrative begins with a highly didactic prologue in rhyme royal explaining at length that the author does not despise poverty but is writing against those who live in idleness by preference. This is followed by a description of the setting, in which we are told that about a fortnight after Hallowmass, Copland had stopped under the porch of a hospital (almost certainly St. Bartholomew's)[9] to await the passing of a stormy shower (see Plate 10):

> For it had snowen and frosen very strong
>   With great ysesycles on the eves long
> The sharp north wynd hurled bytterly
>   And with blacke cloudes / darked was the sky
> Lyke as in wynter / some days be naturall
>   With frost and rayne / and stormes over all.

7. See Chapter I, Note 36. In evaluating Copland's influence on later literature, I have drawn upon my survey of the subject, "Shakspere and the Fraternity of Unthrifts," *Harvard Stud. and Notes in Philol. and Lit.*, XIV (1932), 35–50.
8. *Jyl of Breyntfords Testament, by Robert Copland, Boke-Prynter, The Wyll of the Devyll and his Last Testament*, etc. (London, 1871), p. 4.
9. See Judges, p. 491.

¶ The hye way to the Spyttell hous.

¶ Copland and the porter.

¶ Who so hath lust, or wyll leaue his thryft
And wyll fynd no better way nor shyfte
Come this hye way, here to seke some rest
For it is ordeyned for eche vnthrifty gest.

PLATE 9. *The hye Way to the Spyttell hous.* Title page. British Museum, C.57.b.30(2).

As Copland waits he talks with the Porter of the house about the weather and presently inquires about the great flock of people whom he sees seeking entrance to the hospital, a most pitiful crew (Aiii[v]):

> With bag and staf / both croked / lame / and blynde
> Scabby & scurvy / pocke eaten flesh and rynde
> Lowsy and scalde / and pylled lyke as apes
> With scantly a rag / for to cover theyr shapes
> Brecheles / bare foted / all stynkyng with dyrt
> With .M. of tatters / drabblyng to the skyrt
> Boyes / gyrles / and luskysh strong knaves
> Dydderyng & dadderyng / leaning on their staves
> Saying good mayster / for your moders blyssyng
> Gyve us a halfpeny / toward our lodgyng
> The porter sayd what nede you to crave
> That in the spyttell shall your lodgyng have
> Ye shall be entreated / as ye ought to be
> For I am charged / that dayly to se
> The systers shall do theyr observaunce
> As of the hous is the due ordynaunce.

In the ensuing dialogue the Porter informs Copland that all sorts in general are admitted, but that some persons are shut out. Copland observes that he has seen at different hospitals many lying dead outside the walls for lack of succor. Every night he sees people, whether whores or thieves, lying under the stalls, in porches and doorways, in sheepcotes and hay-lofts, in Saint Bartholomew's church door and even by this hospital wall. When these people see Copland, presumably carrying out his citizen's duties as watchman, they run: "But oftymes whan that they us se / They do rēne a great deale faster than we." The Porter responds that these are michers, or petty thieves, who are refused entrance.

When Copland asks him what classes specifically are admitted, the Porter lists all sorts of unfortunates, particularly those unable to work and friendless, sick old people, poor women in childbed, wounded or diseased men, honest folk fallen into poverty by mischance, wayfaring men and maimed

Here begynneth the casualyte
Of the entraunce in to hospytalyte

To wryte of Sol in his exaltacyon
Of his solstyce or declynacyon
Or in what sygne, planet, or degre
As he in course is vsed for to be
Scorpio, pisces, or sagyttary
Or whan the moone her way dooth contrary
Or her eclypse, her wane, or yet her full
It were but lost, for blockysh braynes dull
But playnly to say, euen as the tyme was
About a fourtenyght after Halowmas
I chaunced to come by a certayn spyttell
Where I thought best to tary a lyttell
And vnder the porche for to take socour
To byde the passyng of a stormy shour
For it had snowen and frosen very strong
With great ysesycles on the eues long
The sharp north wynd hurled bytterly

PLATE 10. A "Spyttell hous" Scene, *The hye Way to the Spyttell hous,* Aiii. British Museum, C.57.b.30(2).

soldiers; but, he qualifies, "not every unseke stoborne knave / For than we shold over many have" (Bi).

Copland then inquires about the prating beggars who line the way to St. Paul's. One of these, a stubborn slave, accosted him for the sake of his companions (and the prating is as good as any we shall meet later):

> Now mayster, in the way of your good spede
> To us all four / behold where it is nede
> And make this farthyng worth a halfpeny
> For the fyve ioyes of our blyssed lady
> Now turne agayn for saynt Erasmus sake,
> And on my bare knees here a vow I make
> Our ladyes psalter thre tymes even now
> Now turne agayn / as god shall turne to you
> Now mayster, do that no man dyd this day
> On yone poore wretch / that roteth in the way
> Now mayster for hym that dyed on tre
> Lete us not dye for lacke of charyte.

Presently, after an honest serving-man came by and gave his alms, Copland saw the beggar show eleven pence to his fellows and exclaim: "se what here is / Many a knave have I called mayster for this / Lete us go dyne / this is a symple day / My mayster therwith shal I scantly pay." The Porter says that no such beggars are admitted to the hospital. They have houses to which they resort for gaudy cheer in the Barbican, Turnmill street, Houndsditch, behind Fleet prison,[10] and

10. According to Wheatley and Cunningham, the Barbican, a section of the street leading from Smithfield to Finsbury Square, between Aldersgate and Red Cross street and Golden Lane, was still infamous for lewd living as late as Dryden, who uses the street as the scene of *MacFlecknoe*. The same writers list Turnbull (or Turnmill street, between Clerkenwell Green and Cow Cross) as noted for disorderly people (Falstaff talks about Shallow's boasting of his conduct on Turnbull Street, *II Henry IV,* III.ii.326–331). Houndsditch street, between Aldgate and Bishopsgate, named for the moat along the City wall, was notorious for filth of the City, brokers, and from early to recent times, old clothes sellers. The Fleet, named for Fleet Ditch, a prison on Farringdon street, dating from Norman times, was burned in the fire of 1666. This prison, the end of the highway for Falstaff, was noted for its eminent prisoners. See Wheatley and Cunningham, I, 104–107; II, 56–60, 236–238; III, 411.

twenty places more. There they sing, "fyll the pot fyll / go fyll me the can / Here is my peny / I am a gentylman," and revel and quarrel through the day and night. Some of these beggars keep their own servants and apprentices in their craft, some dissemble at fairs and markets, begging with bloody clouts on their legs, some counterfeit leprosy, and others put soap in their mouths to produce foam and fall down as victims of St. Cornelius's evil. These are hale enough in their time, but when sickness overtakes them, they too come to the hospital.

Copland next wonders about the reception of masterless men that have served the king overseas and are now without wages. Surely they deserve alms? The honest ones do, agrees the Porter, but most are vagabonds wearing soldiers' clothing. Of these there are two sorts. One kind is the common vagabond who cannot be trusted in service; when weary of toil, he runs away, taking whatever he can carry off with him (Bii^{v}). The other kind he calls "nyghtyngales of newgate," those who pretend to have been taken prisoners in France for seven years and are now trying to get enough money to return to their homes. They lie at every crossroad and prate, or rob lonely passersby and afterwards meet with their kind in secret hostels[11] and houses of bawdry where they don their swords, bucklers, and short daggers and swagger as unthrifty braggarts, swearing their horrible oaths. When they can no longer succeed by begging, they steal and presently tumble on the gallows. Copland observes that there is an act of Parliament

11. The resemblance between Copland's lines here and those of Bolingbroke painting Hal as his "unthrifty son" (*Richard II,* V.iii.1–9) is probably more than a coincidence:

> Can no man tell me of my unthrifty son?
> 'Tis full three months since I did see him last . . .
> Inquire at London, mongst the taverns there,
> For there, they say, he daily doth frequent,
> With unrestrained loose companions,
> Even such, they say, as stand in narrow lanes
> And beat our watch and rob our passengers . . .

(References to Shakespeare in this study unless otherwise specified are to the text of G. L. Kittredge, *The Complete Works of Shakespeare,* Boston, 1936.)

to restrain such behavior if it were only enforced;[12] but even guiltier than the thieves themselves are the "bawdy brybrous knaves" who lodge them, the corrupt innkeepers.

Passing from these "soldier" vagabonds (listed later by Harman as "fresh water mariners"), Copland asks if the rogers (fraters), who sing and pray *Ave regina* and *De profundis* and claim to come from Oxford and Cambridge and lack friends to keep them at learning, come to his doors. Yes, says the Porter, they arrive daily and are doomed to come to this house in old age since they refuse to resort to virtuous work. The Porter next describes in picturesque detail the activities of some of the pseudo-scholars who practice as false doctors and prey on the illness of poor folk; such charlatans pretend skill in physic and palmistry, surgery, soothsaying, and physiognomy, by means of which they are able to prescribe for any malady. The hospital is not for them, but they daily come by the gate. Next Copland asks about the pardoners, and the Porter tells him that the pardoners are now known as proctors; "Subtilte is theyr father / & falshood theyr mother." When their juggling tricks fail, they run ashore and come hither.

At this point Copland wearies and asks the Porter to tell him shortly of all the folk who come to the hospital. The Porter answers with a lengthy account of the multitudinous faults in people that bring them to this refuge. He will keep no order (Copland is aware of this problem) because the wanderers come like scattered sheep, without reason or rule. Here as will be seen, Copland is drawing upon sources different from those of the preceding part of the work, and though he translates his material freely, this section of the narrative lacks the color of the first part and the conclusion of the poem

12. Judges notes (p. 491) that Copland has in mind an act in 1531 (22 Henry VIII, c.12), and observes that Copland's failure to comment on the provisions of the act specifying that sturdy rogues caught begging were to be tied naked from the waist up at the end of a cart and whipped till their bodies were bloody, indicates that these stringent penalties were not commonly enforced.

where he is qualifying his sources richly with his own observation and invention. All, as in the *Ship of Fools* and *Cocke Lorelles Bote,* who are guilty of folly or variance from the accepted norm of good conduct find their way to the hospital: unbelievers, those who do not reverence their parents, vicious priests and clerks, wastrels, unthrifty landlords, careless husbandmen, self-willed people who lack judgment, meddlers, foolish merchants, corrupt tavern-keepers, young folk that wed too soon, tailors that cut their clothes with jags and holes, henpecked husbands, old folk who give away their goods, lechers, adventurers, swearers, those guilty of the seven deadly sins, hypocrites, haters, and husbands with spendthrift wives. The very devil in hell, the Porter exclaims, could not have more pain: "By good fayth, the very devyll of hell / I trowe to my mynd hath not muche more payne." But he continues his categorizing at length until Copland asks whether he receives any peddlers with packs on their backs. And the Porter's answer incorporates, as we have seen, the first extensive example of pedlar's French; he also remarks the ancestors of Autolycus, perhaps the earliest allusion to cony-catching: "And with them comes gaderers of cony skynnes / That chop with laces / poyntes / nedles / & pynes."[13]

Copland then indicates one of his sources of inspiration: "Come ony maryners hyther of Cok lorels bote." Yes, says the Porter, and with them come also the fraternity of unthrifts, the twenty-four orders of knaves,[14] and the unnumbered order of fools. Finally Copland wonders why the Porter has not

13. *Cony-skynnes:* the manner of reference here suggests the type of person Greene was to name a conycatcher (1591). Greene is credited with the earliest recorded uses (*OED*) of *cony* in the sense of dupe or gull (*Art of Connycatching,* 1592), cony-catch (1592), and *cony-catcher,* 1591 (*A Notable Discovery of Coosnage*).

14. See Awdeley's "XXV Orders," p. 28. Copland possibly could have been influenced by Lydgate's well known Order of Fools, with its sixty-three types, none of which can ever prosper ("they shal never the"), but if so the debt is one of theme, not of particulars. Another poem of this sort, incorporating the twenty-five orders of Awdeley, with the theme of the unthrift fool is Timothy Granger's *XXV Orders of Fooles* (c.1569).

told about women vagrants, and the latter summarily observes that of all the sorts mentioned before there are plenty of women—the whole sisterhood of drabs, sluts, and callats, all partners of the confraternity of ill husbandry.[15]

Since the shower is over and he must leave, Copland thanks the Porter for his good talking. The Porter concludes:

There be a .M. mo than I can tell
But at this tyme I byd you farwell.

The poem ends with an envoy in which Copland asks pardon of those whom he has put in his book. His purpose has been to eschew vice, not to "disdain" any creature: "I were to blame yf I them forsoke / None in this world, of welth can be sure."

Copland appears to have been acquainted with most of the rogue literature extant in English at his time. Though he owes no debt of any substance to *Cocke Lorelles Bote,* his stanza on Cocke Lorell and his mariners, the fraternity of unthrifts, and orders of knaves and fools makes it reasonably clear that he was familiar with the poem. Possibly this stanza may even sum up the missing pages of the introduction of the *Bote.* The two allusions to a voyage may be an echo of either the voyage of the *Bote* or that of *The Ship of Fools* or both. Copland's debt to *The Ship of Fools,* presumably Barclay's version, is perceptible in occasional details, though not extensive. At times the relationship is sharply clear, as when he writes of horrid swearers, folk full of ire, and those who quench fires destroying another's house when their own are burning. Though these ideas were doubtless in common currency, Barclay provides the text and pictures that made them current in England. This may even be said of the almost proverbial metaphor of the lure of the beggar's staff[16] which one encounters here also (Bii^{v}):

15. Harman apparently follows Copland here in dealing summarily with women at the end of his listing of names.

16. See the use of this metaphor in Barclay, and in the *Liber Vagatorum,* pp. 35, 46 of this study.

For yf the staf in his hand ones catche heat,
Than farwell labor & hath suche delyte
That thryft and honesty fro hym is quyte

Much more elaborate is Copland's use of Robert de Balsac's *Le chemin de lospital,*[17] from which he derives his title, and the structural outline and much of the content of the second part of the poem. Even here, however, Copland is much livelier than his source. Balsac's prose is a dry, humorless listing of about one hundred and forty categories of people guilty of folly who are destined, as he asserts with unending monotony, to take the road to the hospital. Of these Copland employs less than a third, almost never translating directly, but modifying and frequently enlivening his categories. Thus Balsac's seventh category, "Marchãs q^e achaptẽt chier & a bon marche & a credit," becomes in Copland (ciiii^v):

Marchaunts that beyond the see bye dere
And lend it good chepe whan they be here
And be never payed / but by the lawe
Here have no beddyng / but lye on the strawe.

17. B.M., C.57.c.36: *Le chemin de lospi / tal. Et ceulx quien / sont possesseurs & heritiers.* Colophon: *Cy fine le chemin le hospital Imprimé a Lyon par Claude nourry Lan. Mccccc. & cinq.* This work is also available in B.M., C.97.bb.1(2): *La nef des princes . . .* by Robert de Balsac (Lyons, 1502); B.M., 12331.b.33.1–5 (no. 2): *Le Grand chemin de L'Hopital* (Lyons, 1635?); and M. P. Allut, *Étude Biographique & Bibliographique sur Symphorien Champier* (Lyons, 1869), pp. 119–126; also Tamizey de Laroque, in *Revue des Langues Romanes,* 1886, pp. 276 ff. (a faulty version). Allut (p. 117) doubts whether Balsac is the author of this work.

Fr. Pompen (p. 194f.) seems to have been the first to observe Copland's debt to this work. W. G. Moore ("The Evolution of a Sixteenth Century Satire" in *A Miscellany of Studies in Romance Languages & Literatures Presented to Leon E. Kastner,* ed. Mary Williams and James A. de Rothschild, Cambridge, 1932, pp. 251–360) analyzes the relationship in detail. Like Allut, Moore doubts the authorship of Balsac (p. 351), "a boisterous seneschal of the Agenais" and Gascony in 1469. Moore shows that Copland probably knew also Jacques d'Adonville's *Les Moyens d'eviter merencolie soy conduire et enricher en tous estatz par l'ordonnance de Raison* (1530). See also Moore's "Robert Copland and his Hye Way," *RES,* VII (1931), 404–418; and T. de Laroque, "Notice sur Robert de Balsac," *Revue des Langues Romances,* XXIX (1886), 281.

But the very act of assessing Copland's debt to his sources makes one aware of the superiority of his work. Despite his manifest faults as a writer of verse, Copland's sense of the picturesque and the dramatic, his very real gift of narrative and descriptive phrasing, make his work the richest of all the literature devoted specifically to rogues and unthrifts in his time. It is no wonder, then, that Tudor and Jacobean satirists, poets, and dramatists found it stimulating.

I
The *Hye Way* and Thomas Nashe

Perhaps the first to appreciate its usefulness was Thomas Nashe, whose acquaintance with penury at first hand is attested through most of his works. In at least two of these, *Pierce Penilesse his Supplication to the Divell* and *Summers last will and Testament,* he profits from Copland's devices.[18] In *Pierce Penilesse* (1592), Nashe uses Copland's work as a partial foundation for his satire on the abuse of learning in a crassly Philistine world. Copland's influence is one of several that help to shape the first part of the work, the supplication itself, together with Nashe's own observation of conditions in London, but the conception of the hospital and its inmates seems basic to his satire.

In the introduction to his supplication, musing on his poverty and comparing his fortunes with those of cobblers and hostlers, Nashe (in the guise of Pierce) asks: "have I more wit than all these . . . ? am I better borne? am I better brought up? yea, and better favored? and yet am I a begger?"[19] Scriv-

18. Gabriel Harvey (*Foure Letters and certaine Sonnets,* Bodley Head Quartos, ed. G. B. Harrison, N.Y., 1923, p. 44) charges that Nashe plagiarizes Tarleton's "famous play of the seaven Deadly sinnes" (now lost), a charge that Nashe denies (R. B. McKerrow, *The Works of Thomas Nashe,* reprint, ed. F. P. Wilson, Oxford: Basil Blackwell, 1958, I, 304, 20, IV, 79). In any event, since it is clear that Nashe knew Copland's work, it is probable that his debt to Copland is direct.

19. B.M., C.40.c.67 (STC 18371): *Pierce Penilesse his / supplication to the / Divell / Describing the over-spreading of / Vice, and suppression of / Vertue.*

eners, he finds, are better paid than scholars, and "men of arte must seek almes of Cormorants." Brooding on his misfortunes, he conceives of a possible remedy, a supplication to the Devil—if he can find him. He seeks him out among the lawyers at Westminster Hall and among the merchants at the Exchange, at last finding his agent, a Knight of the Post, at St. Paul's, who agrees to carry his petition to Hell. The supplication opens with a plea that Pierce be given sufficient money for his maintenance and that gold should be liberated from prison and restored to the needy. This hospital where gold lies prisoner will not accept the poor: "Famine, Lent, and dessolation sit in Onyon skind iackets before the doore of his indurance, as a *Chorus* in the Tragedy of Hospitality, to tell hunger and povertie thers no releife for them there."[20] Greediness, the apparent Porter, who stands ready to devour all who enter, is attended by Dame Niggardize, his wife. Nashe imparts order to his list of inmates by following the traditional order of the seven deadly sins (these are all represented in Copland's hospital indiscriminately).

In the court of the house sits Pride, appareled in the spoils and ruins of young citizens, represented by a crew of upstarts pretending to nobility, Italianate wits and travellers, would-be statesmen, unthrifty heirs, and scholars renouncing the faith. The would-be statesman "goes ungartred like a malecontent Cutpursse, & weares his hat over his eies lyke one of the cursed Crue; yet cannot his stabbing dagger, or his nittie love-locke, keepe him out of the Legend of fantasticall cockscombes."[21] Other inmates claimed by Pride are Mistress

Pleasantly interlac't with variable de- / lights: and pathetically intermixt / with conceipted reproofes. / written by Thomas Nash Gentleman. / [Device] */ London, / Imprinted by Richard Ihones, dwelling at / the Signe of the Rose and Crowne, nere Holburne Bridge. 1592,* see sig. B^v; this copy differs in slight details from the Britwell Library copy of the same date, used by McKerrow, as will be seen from a collation of the passages quoted. For the passage quoted here, cf. McKerrow, I, 158.

20. Sig. C^v; cf. McKerrow, I, 166.

21. Sig. C3; McKerrow, I, 169–170.

Minx, a merchant's wife who eats cherries only when they are twenty shillings a pound, upstart gallants raised from the plough, and drudges (serving noblemen) who lord it over others. Thus, says Pierce, "doe weedes grow up whiles no man regards them, and the Ship of Fooles is arrived in the Haven of Felicitie . . ."[22] Pride is further represented by examples of the separate vices of pride in various nations. Antiquaries who dote on worm-eaten antiquity end the list of Pride's retinue. Some of these are brothers of the fraudulent pardoners or proctors of Copland and Watson: "I know one sold an old rope with four knots on it for foure pound, in that he gave it out, it was the length and bredth of Christs Toomb. Let a Tinker take a peece of brasse worth a halfpenie, and set strange stampes on it, and I warrant he may make it more worth to him of some fantasticall foole, than all the kettels that ever he mended in his life."[23]

Envy is next summoned to appear (one is reminded that Copland's Porter says that the hospital of the envious is the deep pit of hell) before the great "Muster-maister of hel," and is even more picturesque in himself than Pride. Wrath, swearing by St. Tyburn and making all his words adjectives modifying Newgate, is illustrated by several anecdotes, including the story of a foul-mouthed knave called Charles the Friar, whose face is parboiled with men's spitting on it and whose back has been often knighted in Bridewell.[24]

Gluttony, Drunkenness, Sloth, and Lechery follow with equally vivid pictures. Pierce blames the Devil that the stall-fed cormorants of the land, the English bellygods "bung up all the welth of the Land in their snap-haunce bags, and poore Scholers and Souldiers wander in backe lanes and the out-shiftes of the Citie, with never a rag to their backes," like Copland's pseudo-soldiers loitering in the lanes and the supposed scholars from Cambridge and Oxford, but Pierce

22. Sig. D^{v}; McKerrow, I, 175.
23. Sig. E; McKerrow, I, 183.
24. Sig. E4; McKerrow, I, 187, 190.

hopes that the belly-gods will have unthrifts as heirs to spend in a week their life-time extortions.[25] Pierce inveighs against drunkenness in terms that are to be echoed in *Hamlet,* as Kittredge notes:

> A mightie deformer of mens manners and features, is this unnecessarie vice of all other. Let him bee indued with never so many vertues, and have as much goodly proportion and favour as nature can bestow uppon a man: yet if hee be thirstie after his owne destruction, and hath no ioy nor comfort, but when he is drowning his soule in a gallon pot; that one beastly imperfection, will utterly obscure all that is commendable in him: and all his good qualities sinke like lead downe to the bottome of his carrowsing cups, where they will lye like lees and dregges, dead and unregarded of any man.[26]

This indulgence, Pierce observes, will bring men in "olde age to be companions with none but Porters and car-men, to talke out of a Cage, rayling as dronken men are wont, a hundred boyes wondering about them . . ."[27] The allusion is to the porters of the hospitals and to the cart men who carried offenders from the hospitals and cages to Newgate or the gallows. In presenting his drunkards as talking out of cages with curious boys listening, Nashe adds a colorful detail not touched on by Copland or Harman, reminding us that cages for the temporary confinement of rogues and other vagrants were common in London from 1503.[28]

At the very end of his supplication to the Devil, Pierce concludes:

> *Lais, Cleopatra, Helen,* if our Clyme hath any such, noble Lord warden of the Wenches & Anglers, I commend them with the rest

25. Sig. G2^{v}; McKerrow, I, 204.
26. Sig. G3; McKerrow, I, 205. Cf. *Hamlet,* I.iv.17–38. Shakespeare generalizes on Nashe's particular theme, but the basic vice is drunkenness and the formula is essentially the same. Professor G. Blakemore Evans finds that this passage is Shakespeare's specific source ("Thomas Nashe and the 'Dram of Eale,' ") *N&Q,* 198(1953), 377–378.
27. Sig. G4; McKerrow, I, 208.
28. McKerrow, IV, 131 (citing Stow's *London,* ed. Strype, V, 127).

> of our uncleane sisters in *Shorditch*, the *Spittle, Southwarke, Westminster,* & Turnbull streete to the protection of your Portership: hoping you will speedily carry them to hell, there to keepe open house for all yonge devills that come, and not let our ayre bee contaminated with theyr six-penny damnation any longer.[29]

That the sisters referred to here as in the "Spittle" were the relatively free agents of the region outside Bishopsgate known as the Spittle,[30] rather than some of the inmates of Saint Bartholomew's is probable in view of the sense of the passage, but in any event, all these sisters are commended to the care of the Porter of Hell who himself keeps open house for all that come, as did Copland's Porter.

Nashe's second use of the *Hye Way*, much less oblique, occurs in *Summers last Will and Testament*, written, it is conjectured, two or three months after *Pierce Penilesse*, in September, 1592.[31] As the title implies, Nashe's inspiration for the device of the will (and little else) is possibly borrowed from Copland's notorious *Jyll of Brentford,* a verse satire on unthrifts (Copland borrows the basic device from Chaucer). But Nashe's main debt is to the *Hye Way,* whose vagabonds are new-fashioned here into an apparent satire on the new learning and poetry. The play itself, as Nashe confesses in his Prologue, delivered by a fictive Will Summers (modelled on the famous jester of Henry VIII, and a prototype of Falstaff), is "no Play neyther, but a shewe."[32] A masque of the seasons, with set speeches describing its characters rather than presenting action, it becomes, as Will Summers expresses it at one

29. Sig. H4; McKerrow, I, 217. The reading "Wenches & Anglers" in the B.M. copy here fits our subject more sharply than the Britwell copy's "witches and iuglers" and is presumably the manuscript reading.

30. McKerrow, IV, 138.

31. McKerrow, IV, 417–418.

32. B.M., C.34.d.50 (STC 18376): *A Pleasant / Comedie, called / Summers last will and / Testament. / Written by Thomas Nash /* [Device] / Imprinted at London by Simon Stafford, / for Water [Walter] Burre. / 1600, sig. B2; McKerrow, III, 235. Subsequent references are to McKerrow's text of the B.M. copy.

point, "a filthy beggerly Oration in the prayse of beggery," written, he adds, by "a beggerly Poet." As we read the play, though various characters take on the role of commentator on society, we gradually become aware of Will Summers as the main commentator, serving as Nashe's own Porter, interpreting the scenes before him to the audience.

Nashe is never far from the theme of vagabondage from beginning to end of the masque. Summer, represented as monarch of the seasons, summons Ver to give tribute, and Ver enters, singing with his train Nashe's sweetest song, beginning,

> Spring, the sweete spring, is the yeres pleasant King,
> Then bloomes eche thing, then maydes daunce in a ring,
> Cold doeth not sting, the pretty birds doe sing
> Cuckow, iugge, iugge, pu we, to witta woo.

which elicits Will Summers' admiring praise: "By my troth, they have voyces as cleare as Christall: this is a pratty thing, if it be for nothing but to goe a begging with." And Ver is little more than a vagabond. When asked for a reckoning of the use he has made of Summer's gifts, he brings in a hobby horse and a set of Morris dancers. A "monstrous unthrift," he has spent the flower of his youth on sports and good fellowship: "The world is transitory; it was made of nothing; and it must to nothing: wherefore if wee will doe the will of our high Creatour (whose will it is, that it passe to nothing), wee must helpe to consume it to nothing" (ll. 256–259). As he continues, Ver dispraises gold and exalts beggary:

> I will prove it, that an unthrift, of any, comes neerest a happy man, in so much as he comes neerest to beggery. Cicero saith, *summum bonum* consistes in *omnium rerum vacatione,* that it is the chiefest felicitie that may be, to rest from all labours. Now who doeth so much *vacare a rebus?* who rests so much? who hath so little to doe, as the begger?
>
> Who can sing so merry a note,
> As he that cannot change a groate?

Ver observes that all the poets, alchemists, and philosophers were beggars, and on his knees he thanks Heaven that has made him an unthrift (ll. 320–321).

Solstitium, who is summoned next, with his glasses measuring day and night, redresses the balance for right living, though Will Summers, like Falstaff (as viewed by Hal), has no use for hourglasses except those that call to supper.[33] Neither Solstitium nor Sol nor Orion who follow pursue the subject of beggary, but Harvest, who is accused variously of being a grain-hoarder, a conycatcher, a robber, and purse-taker, seems to have the marks of a member of Cocke Lorell's crew. He denies all guilt, brazenly; he is merely a good husbandman.

The subsequent dubbing of Will Summers with a black-jack and a pot of beer by Bacchus is akin in spirit to the ceremony of the installation of the rogue found in Harman. But it remains for Winter to borrow from the *Hye Way* in detail in a vehement satiric diatribe on scholars and poets. Autumn, says Winter, is a bankrupt ass that consumes all he has. He and Spring are the favorites of scholars, a thriftless crowd whom he renounces in metaphors drawn from Copland. First he excoriates the drunken parasites called poets who praised to the skies any city that forbore to whip or imprison them: Musaeus, Homer, and Orpheus were of this sort (ll. 1267–1283). Next come the philosophers:

> Next them, a company of ragged knaves,
> Sun-bathing beggers, lazie hedge-creepers,
> Sleeping face upwards in the fields all night,
> Dream'd strange devices of the Sunne and Moone;
> And they, like Gipsies, wandring up and downe,
> Told fortunes, iuggled, nicknam'd all the starres,
> And were of idiots term'd Philosophers . . .
> (ll. 1285–1291)

33. McKerrow, III, 247; cf. *I Henry IV,* I.ii.6–8. Also cf. Lauren Desmoulins, *Le Catholicon des Maladvisez* (Paris, 1513): "Pour leurs cloches ilz ont voirres & potz . . . Lodeur des matz est lensens delectable" (Biii^v). This work, as W. G. Moore (p. 355) remarks, is an imitation of Balsac's *Le chemin.*

All these, including such men as Pythagoras, Thales, and Diogenes, professed wretched poverty. All sorts of vices sprang up from the idle contemplation of philosophy. Like idle soldiers who walk in melancholy, cozen merchants and young heirs, and rob churches, these word-warriors, lazy stargazers, engender a thousand sects who are only "cunning shrowded rogues" like those, he says, of the present time. Some are grammarians, and they are like the beggars who use pedlar's French; some are tattered poets selling ballads in the streets; others are historiographers who, like lazars on the highway, will call knaves gentlemen for a penny. Just as Spittle-houses write their founders' names over their gates, these rogues in hope of gain record the benefactors of learning in the prefaces of their books. Orators, or lawyers as they are now known, actually swashbucklers and ruffians, for twelve pence will cause men to fight for straws. Sky-measuring mathematicians, gold-breathing alchemists, and pale physicians end the list: "Vaine boasters, lyers, make-shifts, they are all . . ." And Winter sums up his charge:

> Innumerable monstrous practises
> Hath loytring contemplation brought forth more,
> Which t'were too long particular to recite:
> Suffice, they all conduce unto this end,
> To banish labour, nourish slothfulnesse,
> Pamper up lust, devise newfangled sinnes.
> Nay I will iustifie there is no vice
> Which learning and vilde knowledge brought not in,
> Or in whose praise some learned have not wrote.
>
> (ll. 1388–1396)

The works of Machiavelli, Ovid, Aretine, Epicurus, Erasmus, and Aristotle are cited as justifying or parading vices. Only theology escapes the general condemnation of the "damned snares" of Latin, logic, and philosophy.

In response Summer very mildly repudiates the attack (ll. 1484–1488), but instead of attempting a refutation of the accusations, immediately rewards the obscurantism of Winter by making him the overseer of Autumn.

This despondency comes to a great lyric statement in the song anticipating Summer's death, with its lament for the perennial death of beauty:

> Beauty is but a flowre,
> Which wrinckles will devoure,
> Brightnesse falls from the ayre,
> Queenes have died yong and faire,
> Dust hath closde *Helens* eye.
> I am sick, I must dye:
> Lord, have mercy on us.
> (ll. 1588–1594)

Even in this, his finest moment, Nashe cannot quite forget the imagery of the world of rogues:

> Wit with his wantonnesse
> Tasteth deaths bitternesse:
> Hels executioner
> Hath no eares for to heare
> What vaine art can reply.
> I am sick, I must dye:
> Lord, have mercy on us.

The masque has yet other figures to present, the sons of Winter, namely Christmas, a newfangled Puritan, a scurvy knave, as Will Summers calls him, who reprehends revelry and mirth as the breeder of rogues and unthrifts; and Backwinter, a snarling rogue who hates the world and must be kept confined in a dark cell.

Thus Copland's hedge-creepers and unthrifts serve Nashe as an extended symbol of the nature and condition of poetry and learning in general as seen by Winter. That Winter expresses Nashe's own disillusionment growing out of his own impoverished living seems very likely. But this misgiving about the moral value of art and learning, if indeed seriously entertained by him, was not to last. A year later, almost as if to retract the sentiments of Winter, he accepts the orthodox view:

> Humaine Artes are the steppes and degrees Christ hath prescribed and assign'd us, to climbe up to heaven of Artes by, which is

> Divinity. He can never climbe to the toppe of it, which refuseth to climb by these steppes. No knowledge but is of God. Unworthy are wee of heavenly knowledge, if we keepe from her any one of her hand-maydes. Logique, Rethorique, History, Phylosophy, Musique, Poetry, all are the hand-maides of Divinitie. She can never be curiously drest or exquisitely accomplisht, if any of these be wanting.[34]

II
The *Hye Way* and Shakespeare

Most of the leading dramatists of the Renaissance period, especially Shakespeare, Dekker, Webster, and Jonson, were also to find the *Hye Way* useful when writing about knaves and knavish people. Though some of these doubtless influenced one another in using this material, there is no reason to suppose that any of them did not know the curious work itself.

Discounting his several references to unthrifts in his sonnets which may trace to various sources,[35] we find that Shakespeare makes his first significant use of Copland's work in *Measure for Measure* to point up the meaning of the play and to bring out its theme of compassionate justice derived from the Sermon on the Mount (Matthew, vii.1–2): "Judge not, that ye be not judged. For with what judgment ye judge, ye shall be judged; and with what measure ye mete it shall be measured to you again." Where Copland was concerned with giving an almost photographic record of the pageant of knaves, Shakespeare dramatizes the predicament of these

34. (STC 18366) *Christs / Teares Over / Ierusalem. / Wherunto is annexed, a comparative admonition / to London. / A Iove Musa. / By Tho. Nashe. /* [Device] */ At London, / Printed by Iames Roberts, / and are to be solde by Andrewe / Wise, at his shop in Paules Church- / yard, at the signe of the Angel. / Anno. 1593;* McKerrow, II, 125–126.

35. See Sonnets 4(1); 9(9–10); 10(1–2, 7–8); 13(9–13). Shakespeare may well have been inspired by Copland in these metaphors, but the influence of Nashe is also to be considered, as well as that of Marlowe; see Gertrud Lazarus, *Technik und Stil von Hero and Leander* (Bonn, 1915, p. 95; see also Janet G. Scott, *Les Sonnets Elizabethains* (Paris, 1929), pp. 259-261.

knaves as people in conflict with authority and its "strict statutes and most biting laws" (I.iii.19).

In opening Scene iii in Act IV, Pompey Bum as Deputy Hangman assumes briefly the role of Copland's Porter in listing the knaves and unthrifts who have found their way to the prison-house.[36] His soliloquy here is not merely the idle rumination of a knave turned hangman, now an agent of law. Through this device Shakespeare extends the world of offenses to which the theme of the play applies (in the course of the play Shakespeare dramatizes principally one of these offenses, lechery). With his sampling of knaves in the play and with Pompey's quick catalogue of offenders and its reminder of forty more such creatures, Shakespeare gives us an impression of a world of knavery. Pompey himself, his bawd Madam Overdone, and Barnardine the Bohemian (Gypsy) dramatically represent this low world of knaves, and in doing so serve as ironic counterpoint to the higher social world[37] in which, despite the efforts of good men, knavery also rears its Hydra head, a world of pious seemers and hypocrites often seen in places of power.

In the limits of the play Shakespeare has time to dramatize only one such rogue, the "Angel," the pious-seeming

36. It seems most likely that Copland's catalogue suggested the idea to Shakespeare, even though George Whetstone in his knave-laden *Promos and Cassandra* (Shakespeare's main source) offers a parade of six prisoners about to be hanged. Shakespeare's manner in the listing is distinctly more reminiscent of the Copland tradition than that of Whetstone. This is not to gainsay Shakespeare's general debt to Whetstone. Though Shakespeare as usual greatly transforms his sources, Lucio owes something to Phallax in origins, Pompey is Rosko magnified, and Abhorson has some kinship with the Hangman. Even the remarkable Barnardine seems to have a partial genesis in the "poore Roge" of this scene.

37. Herbert Weil, Jr., observes that the comic subplot with its various parallels helps to establish Shakespeare's "dominating comic intention" for the play ("Shakespeare's Comic Control in *Measure for Measure:* Subplot as Key to Dramatic Design" [unpub. diss., Stanford Univ., 1962]); and A. P. Rossiter likewise sees the subplot as "a commentary on the difficulty of applying *law* (a reasoned thing) to matters of *instinct*" (*Angel with Horns and other Shakespeare Lectures,* ed. Graham Storey, New York, 1961, p. 155).

Angelo. Even the wise Escalus, convinced of Angelo's probity, does not know how to counter his administration of unrelenting justice. Only the Duke with his all-seeing eyes knows Angelo fully; though even he cannot know in advance how Angelo will rule as his vicegerent, he surmises that Angelo is a seemer (I.iii.54), and with his wise prescience forestalls each of Angelo's sinister intentions. Isabella finally denominates him for what he is, in part or in intention, a man forsworn, a murderer, adulterous thief, hypocrite, and virgin-violator (V.i.38–42). How can one judge petty rogues when the world cannot see the great hidden rogues in high places unless they are unveiled by some inscrutable wisdom, some "Duke of dark corners" like Vincentio? In a like chaotic world of instincts warring with vice and each other, King Lear exclaims, "None does offend, none—I say, none!" In *Measure for Measure* Shakespeare anticipates this position in his revulsion against sanctimonious hypocrisy and in his espousal of a judgment that, while intent on righting wrongs, is ever merciful and bent on the reform of the misdoer. Indeed the whole play breathes with sympathy for the "wearisome condition of humanity, Born under one law, to another bound."

In *Macbeth* Shakespeare puts his knowledge of the *Hye Way* to a different but not less telling use. Here the device of the Porter commenting on the admission of unthrifts into his hospital serves as a brief allegory illuminating the destiny of two great criminals, Macbeth and his Lady. We recall that Copland's Porter visualized his hospital with its misery as very like hell (Dii^{v}); and Copland reinforces the image later, as we have seen, speaking of a special hospital for the envious: "As for the envyous I lete them dwell / For theyr hospytall is the depe pyt of hell" (Eii^{v}). We have seen also that this image appears to have been appropriated by Nashe in *Pierce Penilesse* for his own hospital of hell. That Shakespeare knew this work of Nashe seems attested by his apparent borrowings from it. But as is equally evident, he seems to have known

Copland's *Hye Way,* and in his turn he seizes upon the image supplied by Copland to put the great "quell" of the Macbeths in its proper light. Shakespeare's Porter, aroused from a drunken torpor by the knocking on the gate, visualizes himself as the porter of hell gate, admitting knaves and unthrifts, each in his way suggestive of Macbeth. Here is a farmer who hanged himself in expectation of plenty,[38] just as Macbeth is destroying himself because of the promises of the Weird Sisters; here is an equivocator who has committed treason, but cannot equivocate to Heaven (and equivocating Macbeth has just realized that *Amen* stuck in his throat when he most needed blessing); and here is a curious thief, an English tailor convicted of "stealing out of a French hose" and Macbeth too has stolen and is assuming the fashion of kingship that is not his. Other candidates are arriving, and the Porter has in mind the whole concourse of knaves, but it is too cold for him to retain his illusion:

> But this place is too cold for Hell. I'll devil-porter it no further: I had thought to have let in some of all professions, that go the primrose way to th' everlasting bonfire. *Knock.* Anon, anon! I pray you remember the porter.

Bodenstedt, among others, remarks the effective ironic counterpoint of the scene:

> After all, his [the Porter's] uncouth comicality has a tragic background; he never dreams, while imagining himself porter of hell-gate, how near he comes to the truth. What are all these petty sinners who go the primrose way to the everlasting bonfire compared with those great criminals whose gate he guards?[39]

Through their murder of Duncan, a murder as unnecessary as it was wicked ("If chance will have me King, why chance may crown me"), Lord and Lady Macbeth have now joined the sorry procession of knaves and unthrifts on the highroad, and their hospital is truly the deep pit of Hell. Ross's exclamation against Malcolm and Donalbain applies

38. This farmer knave-unthrift has a possible father in Jonson's Sordido (*Every Man Out Of His Humour*).

39. *Macbeth* (*Variorum* ed.), 1873, p. 111.

with obvious irony to the Macbeths (II.iv.28–29): "Thriftless ambition that will raven up / Thine own life's means!" But this image of the Macbeths as unthrifts is central to the play, not pervasive as the unthrift image is in *King Lear,* as will be seen later.

Shakespeare apparently liked his Porter Scene well enough to repeat its basic feature, that of a porter commenting on a crowd seeking entrance into an institution, this time into the Palace Yard in London in *King Henry VIII,* Act V, scene iv (the episode seems certainly his). The occasion is one of joy, however, the crowd being composed of London citizens eager to greet the new princess on her way to her christening and her formal presentation to her father. But the marks of Copland's knave-scene are still apparent. The crowd has overwhelmed the guards and a man from the Larder (called a rogue by the Porter), a brazier (judging by his face), a "haberdasher's wife of small wit," a group of youths that "thunder at a playhouse and fight for bitten apples," some of whom the Porter has confined for the beadles, represent the swarming multitude waiting to see the infant Elizabeth. The Porter and his men are doing their best with staves and clubs to fend them off, but even so the Lord Chamberlain reprimands them as lazy knaves. The whole mob scene itself, the denominations of rascal, rogue, and knave, and the trick of cataloguing recall various impressions of the *Hye Way.* Shakespeare uses this material at once to secure comic relief, to dramatize the event as irrepressibly shared in by all England, and to prepare for the great prophecy of Cranmer about the princess who will control this tumultuous people so that each, in an ideal land, shall sing "The merry songs of peace to all his neighbours."

III
The *Hye Way* and Thomas Dekker

Shakespeare's use of this device from Copland was part of a vogue for such scenes, several of which, along with certain interrelationships, show at least traces of possibly direct acquaintance with Copland's work. Thomas Dekker found the device irresistible, and employed it several times,[40] most notably in the resolutions of both parts of *The Honest Whore,* the first part of which (1604) antedates *Macbeth* by about a year. Needing an amalgam to unite his unrelated plots of the courtesan turned saint and the testing of a patient man, Dekker chooses to end both plots within the walls of Bethlehem Monastery in Milan (read *London*). Dekker's use of the device, as Robert R. Reed, Jr. has pointed out,[41] seems to be its first employment on the English stage; and in addition to its service in lending both plots a certain unity, it carries a satiric meaning: the mad creatures in Bedlam are not the only madmen, practically all Milan [London] is mad. At the end of Act IV, scene iii, Candido is committed to Bethlehem by his wife, in a final vain attempt to break his patience. In the following scene, the Doctor, the counterpart of Friar Lawrence in *Romeo and Juliet,* has arranged for Hippolito to meet his Infelice at Bethlehem, and there, disguised as friars, they are to be wed by Friar Anselmo. Bellafront herself, disguised as a mad woman, is to discover the lovers to the Duke and win her own reward of marriage with that excellent example of a sturdy rogue, Matthew. Also in disguise, the Duke and his party, led to Bethlehem by an informer, have come as visitors to see the mad folk, and we are reminded that this was a current diversion.[42] We are prepared

40. In addition to his use of the device in both parts of *The Honest Whore,* Dekker, collaborating with Webster in *Northward Ho,* fuses the effects of the Bedlam and Bridewell scenes in *The Honest Whore* for the sake of a Chaucerian jest (Bellamont, victim of the jest, has to pay all that is spent by the way). Although the scene is certainly part of the history of Copland's influence, it adds nothing new and has no function save that of entertaining the audience with the popular device of a madhouse scene.

41. Reed, p. 29.

42. Reed (pp. 22–26) discusses the popularity of Bethlehem as a place of amusement for visitors, citing passages from various plays as evidence for the resort to it in Jacobean times. He adds further that the hospital had a revenue from this source of about £400 a year, representing about 96,000

for a pageant of mad creatures (mostly unthrifts in origin) by the conversation of Candido's wife with George the apprentice:

> *Wife . . . George,* are there many madfolkes, where thy Maister lives.
> *Geo.* O yes, of all contries some, but especially mad Greekes, they swarme.
>
> (V.i.4-8)[43]

But the display itself begins with the entrance of the Sweeper, acted by Towne, Dekker's variant for the Porter. The questions and answers distinctly echo the *Hye Way:*

> *Pioratto:* Sirra are all the mad folkes in *Millan* brought hither?
> *Sweeper:* How all, there's a wise question indeede: why if all the mad folkes in *Millan* should come hither, there would not be left ten men in the Citty.
> *Duke:* Few gentlemen or Courtiers here, ha.
> *Sweeper:* Oh yes? abundance, aboundance, lands no sooner fall into their hands but straight they runne out a their wits: Citizens sons and heires are free of the house by their fathers copy: Farmers sons come hither like geese (in flocks) and when they ha sould all their corne fields, here they sit and picke the straws.
> *Sin[ezi]:* Me thinks you should have women here aswel as men.
>
> (V.ii.120–130)

Though the scene is transferred from Saint Bartholomew's to Bethlehem, the imitation of Copland is patent and is sustained further by Friar Anselmo who replaces Towne as commentator and gives us a vivid picture of the mad folk and the psychology of the Elizabethan visitor to Bethlehem:

> But gentlemen I must disarme you then,
> There are of mad men, as there are of tame,
> All humour'd not alike: we have here some,

---

visitors in the years before the hospital was closed to the public in 1770 (Thomas Bowen, *An Historical Account of the Origin, Progress, and Present State of Bethlehem Hospital,* London, 1783, p. 11).

43. This and other passages quoted in the following pages from Dekker's plays are taken from *The Dramatic Works of Thomas Dekker,* ed. Fredson Bowers (Cambridge, 1955), II.

So apish and phantastike, play with a fether,
And tho twould greeve a soule, to see Gods image,
So blemisht and defac'd, yet do they act
Such anticke and such pretty lunacies,
That spite of sorrow they will make you smile:
Others agen we have like hungry Lions,
Fierce as wild Buls, untameable as flies,
And these have oftentimes from strangers sides
Snacht rapiers suddenly, and done much harme,
Whom if youle see, you must be weaponlesse.
(V.ii.154–166)

Instead, however, of a procession of madmen, Dekker selects three as characteristic of the inmates of the hospital. Each of these seems to have been drawn at least in part from observation of madmen, most likely from cases in Bethlehem. The First Madman, whom Reed identifies as a monomaniac, wears a fish-net; he has lost his wealth at sea and says he is fishing for his lost ships. The second, a victim of phrenitis, suffers from the cuckold-delusion. The malady of the third is not particularized enough for identification, but his behavior, like that of the others, seems based on reality. On the other hand, the first and second madmen represent also satirical tradition. The first, claiming the courtier Pioratto as his son, says, "I made him a scholar and he made himself a fool"; and the selection of an example of cuckold madness is an obvious use of an accepted convention. These representations, distasteful to us, are meant primarily for comic effect; the Duke and his courtiers laugh at them as did the Jacobean audience. But even so, Dekker is not lacking in sympathy, as he has the First Madman exclaim: "Do you laugh at Gods creatures? do you mock old age you roagues? is this gray beard and head counterfet, that you cry ha ha ha?" (V.ii.201–203). And the courtiers themselves are moved: "A very piteous sight." We are also reminded of the harsh therapy of the time, all the more grim as Father Anselmo is clearly meant to be a wise and good master:

Cast: Father, I see you have a busie charge.

Ans: They must be usde like children, pleas'd with toyes,
And anon whipt for their unrulinesse.
(V.ii.241–243)

After their tribulation of body and spirit in Bethlehem Candido and Bellafront deserve to live happily ever after with their spouses, but Dekker likes his creations and his curious device too well to let them lie unused. The reformed courtesan and the patient man must be tested again, and in *The Honest Whore, Part II,* their distresses continue, to be resolved only with their release in the last act from Bridewell. Once more Dekker uses the same device at the same structural point, but with fresh, if somewhat labored invention. He deliberately recalls the use of the device in Part I by the speech of Ludovico opening Act V, scene i: "Yonder's the Lord *Hipollito,* by any meanes leave him and me together: Now, will I turne him to a Madman." The news he bears is that Bellafront is wearing a blue gown and beating chalk—that is, she has been sent to Bridewell, "the Schoole where they pronounce no letter well but *O*". In Scene ii, the Duke commends the institution itself:

Your Bridewell? that the name? for beauty, strength,
Capacity and forme of ancient building,
(Besides the Rivers neighbourhood) few houses
Wherein we keepe our Court can better it.

And the First Master sums up its history, with an allusion to the audience of Henry VIII held there for the Cardinal Campeius (Campeggio) in 1528, and the gift of the palace to the City by Edward VI:[44]

Hither from forraigne courts have Princes come,
And with our Duke did Acts of State Commence,
Here that great Cardinall had first audience,
(The grave Campayne,) that Duke dead, his Sonne
(That famous Prince) gave free possession
Of this his Palace, to the Cittizens,
To be the poore mans ware-house: and endowed it

44. O'Donoghue, p. 5; see note 2 of this chapter.

With Lands to 'th valew of seven hundred marke,
With all the bedding and the furniture, once proper
(As the Lands then were) to an Hospitall
Belonging to a Duke of *Savoy*. Thus
Fortune can tosse the World, a Princes Court
Is thus a prison now.

The Master goes on with grim irony to explain how the seven hundred marks are used in his work house, recalling the practice of recruiting soldiers from these institutions and the recurring cycle of vagabondage:

Warre and Peace
Feed both upon those Lands: when the Iron doores
Of warres burst open, from this House are sent
Men furnisht in all Martiall Complement
The Moone hath through her Bow scarce drawn to'th head,
(Like to twelve silver Arrowes) all the Moneths,
Since sixteen hundred Soldiers went aboord:
Here Providence and Charity play such parts,
The House is like a very Schoole of Arts,
For when our Soldiers (like Ships driven from Sea,
With ribs all broken, and with tatterd sides,)
Cast anchor here agen, their ragged backes
How often do we cover? that (like men)
They may be sent to their owne Homes agen.
All here are but one swarm of Bees, and strive
To bring with wearied thighs honey to the Hive.
The sturdy Begger, and the lazy Lowne,
Get here hard hands, or lac'd Correction.
The Vagabond growes stay'd, and learns to 'bey,
The Drone is beaten well, and sent away.
As other prisons are, (some for the Thiefe,
Some, by which undone Credit gets reliefe
From bridled Debtors; others for the poore)
So this is for the Bawd, the Rogue, and Whore.

The Master thinks that justice is administered fairly and with the right civic purpose, the regeneration of knave and unthrift:

Nor is it seene,
That the whip draws blood here, to coole the Spleene

> Of any rugged Bencher: nor does offence
> Feele smart, on spitefull, or rash evidence:
> But pregnant testimony forth must stand,
> Ere Iustice leave them in the Beadles hand,
> As Iron, on the Anvill are they laid,
> Not to take blowes alone, but to be made
> And fashioned to some Charitable use.

The Duke is properly impressed by this description of an ideal (for the age) reformatory, the representation of which is a thinly disguised history of the English Bridewell, and complacently observes: "Thus wholsom'st Lawes spring from the worst abuse."

The action ensuing illustrates the working of these laws. The gentleman-rogue Mattheo, his supposed accomplice Orlando, and Bellafront, all garbed in Bridewell blue, are arraigned before the Duke, and the knaveries of Mattheo, as well as other elements of the situation, have their background in current rogue literature. Mattheo accuses Bellafront of setting the match for the robbery of the peddlers (as did the chamberlain in *I Henry IV*), and in his description of taking Bellafront and Hippolito in one nest he represents himself as taking the part of a crossbiter (described by Greene in *A Notable Discovery*).[45] Justice fails with the "blacke-mouthed Devill," Mattheo; he is freed at the intercession of his father-in-law Orlando. The much-tried Bellafront's troubles are gloriously ended for the moment, though her alliance with Mattheo will be a continuing cross.

Here the play cannot end, for Candido must not be left in Bridewell, whither he has been haled as a receiver of goods stolen from the peddlers. And Dekker cannot conclude the scene without more attention to the hospital and its inmates. To achieve this purpose he has the Duke suspend the examination of Candido while he queries the constable about new candidates for Bridewell who have just arrived. One of these, Lieutenant Bots, earlier revealed as a bawd or apple-squire,

45. See p. 112 of this study.

claims to have been a soldier, wounded significantly enough at the Groyne in the Low Countries. As Hippolito surmises (V.ii.234), he is not a soldier, and presently he is shown up as another of the pseudo-soldier rogues described by Copland and his successors as frequenting the highways as robbers or resorting to cozening and pandering in the city.

As the inmates are marshalled before the Duke, once more, as in *Part I,* the Duke and his courtiers pose as visitors, curious to see how the prisoners behave (V.ii.260). The procession is a sad even if diverting picture, as the masters, beadles, and constables bring in the prisoners one by one. First we have Dorothea Target, gay in attire, but followed by two beadles, one with a spinning wheel and the other with a blue gown for her; next, Penelope Whore-hound, "like a Citizens wife," with her beadles carrying a blue gown and a lump of chalk and a mallet; and finally Catryna Bountinall and Mistress Horsleach, the latter described by Catryna as having been seven times whipped, six times carted, nine times ducked, and searched by a hundred and fifty constables. The last two are preceded by a beadle beating a basin, in ironic mockery of their former houses of revelry (V.ii.533), and it is Penelope and these two who expose Bots as a panderer, who is consequently sentenced to be whipped at various stations in the city and then banished, a common penalty for rogues. These "Birds of Bridewell," however repulsive, are breathing creatures and doubtless drawn from life. Their very realism and the ever-present reminders of justice and the penalties of law make the scene more grim and pitiful than comic, an effect notably different from the revelry of the Boar's Head Tavern.

IV
The *Hye Way* and John Webster

It is further testimony to the popular appeal of the *Hye Way* or at least of its basic device that John Webster also employed it in his two best plays. It is not surprising to encounter it in *The White Devil,*[46] a play whose characters are mostly rogues and knaves of high station. The White Devil herself is truly a "glorious strumpet" (V.vi.208); Brachiano an unprincipled murderer and poisoner; Flamineo a panderer and knave with characteristics of the rogues of Copland and the fraters of Harman, an unthrift university student, making a profession of knavery (I.ii.310–320); and Francisco, a Machiavellian whose craft serves virtue only because of his lust for revenge.

Francisco is a machiavel even with those who sympathize with him, as is seen when he veils from Monticelso his intention of seeking vengeance for his sister's death (IV.i.4). He will not resort to open war against Brachiano, and will not indulge in treacherous action, he says. Putting by these unhappy thoughts, he would change the subject; he has learned that Monticelso has a book recording the names of all notorious malefactors lurking in the city. Monticelso admits owning such a book, called by some his black book (an allusion to Greene's projected black book[47] is very probable), and lets Francisco examine it. Its list comprises "a generall catalogue of knaves," including informers, panderers, pirates, "base rogues—that undo yong Gentlemen / By taking up commodities," politic bankrupts, crossbiters, bawds wearing men's clothes, usurers, corrupt lawyers and divines, and murderers, indeed, as Francisco says, the "company of knaves" (IV.i.80). Francisco commends Monticelso for his service to the state in discovering these knaves, and we are reminded of Harman's and Greene's claims to such service. He borrows the book, and after Monticelso's exit, comments further on its contents and his intention to use it to select a "list of murderers, Agents for my villany."

This listing of knaves could have been inspired by Copland or Harman or Greene or other such listings; but the

46. For references to *The White Devil,* see *The Complete Works of John Webster,* ed. F. L. Lucas (New York, 1937), I.
47. See p. 127 of this study.

manner suggests the *Hye Way,* and though the scene is not that of a hospital admitting rogues, Francisco ends it by dispatching a message to Vittoria at the house of convertites, a Roman Bridewell. Later on, the dying Brachiano resorts to the like device of listing: he visualizes the devil in a blue bonnet and breeches with a great codpiece (obviously befitting Brachiano), Flamineo dancing on ropes with balancing money bags, a lawyer in a velvet gown, Vittoria, her hair sprinkled with arras powder, a Divine, and six grey rats crawling up his pillow (V.iii.99–126). Brachiano dies, as Ludovico says, like a poor rogue; and Vittoria's exclamation fits the situation and also reminds us of the hospital where all these rogues are to arrive: "O mee! this place is hell" (V.iii.182).

But this scene of horror is tame compared to that fashioned by Bosola and Ferdinand in *The Duchess of Malfi.*[48] Except for the heroine and her husband, the main characters again are villains of high and low station, the scheming Cardinal, the greed-crazed Ferdinand, and the arch-rogue Bosola. A malcontent railing at his own desires, a poor scholar from Padua (like Flamineo), Bosola has already spent seven years in the galleys as a suborned murderer, and expects no better fortune than that of the discharged soldier, to spend his latter days "on an honourable pare of crowtches from hospitall to hospitall" (I.i.66–75).

In *Macbeth* the Porter imagines that he is warden of the hospital of hell; in both parts of *The Honest Whore,* the characters go to the hospitals. In *The Duchess of Malfi* the hospital is symbolically brought to the Duchess. With the pretext of curing her deep melancholy, Ferdinand arranges that a group of madmen be brought to the palace: the Pope had been cured by being obliged to laugh at the antics of madmen, and hence he says (through Bosola), the Duchess may be cured as well. A servant takes the part of the Porter,

48. See *Complete Works,* ed. Lucas, II.

and his list of knaves and unthrifts is at once suggestive of Dekker in that all these creatures are mad, and of Shakespeare in the manner of enumeration and, in a few examples, in choice of types:

> There's a mad Lawyer, and a secular Priest,
> A Doctor that hath forfeited his wits
> By jealousie; an Astrologian,
> That in his workes sayd, such a day o'th'moneth
> Should be the day of doome; and fayling of't,
> Ran mad: an English Taylor, crais'd i'th'braine,
> With the studdy of new fashions: a gentleman usher
> Quite beside himselfe, with care to keep in minde,
> The number of his Ladies salutations,
> Or "how do you," she employ'd him in each morning:
> A Farmer too, (an excellent knave in graine)
> Mad, 'cause he was hindered transportation,
> And let one Broaker (that's mad) loose to these,
> You'ld think the divell were among them.
>
> (IV.ii.49–62)

We recognize the tailor from *Macbeth* even if his garb is slightly altered, and the "excellent knave in graine" also reminds us fleetingly of the farmer who hanged himself in the expectation of plenty. The gentleman usher seems a relation of Malvolio. Dekker's Bethlehem would admit no lawyers, but one leads the list in Webster, and there are other creatures of Webster's own meditation. As suggested, however, Webster appears indebted to Shakespeare and Dekker for the basic device. Though Webster doubtless had visited Bethlehem, his creatures seem more contrived than those of Dekker. Reed finds that they exhibit "deliberately devised forms of monomania."[49]

Of the several madmen listed, only four are vaguely identified by their remarks in the ensuing scene, namely the astrologian (First Madman), the lawyer (Second Madman), the secular priest (Third Madman), the doctor (Fourth Mad-

49. Reed, p. 44.

man). Not so precisely as the creatures of Shakespeare's Porter, but to some degree these creatures with their mad chatter relate in sense and imagery to the main action. The spectacle is indeed designed to be a "corrasive" to the Duchess's heart. The allusions to doomsday, sleeplessness, and lust (Ferdinand's interpretation of the Duchess's love), have a glancing pertinence. The usual comic effects of such scenes are replaced by the grotesque, the unreal, and the sordid. The tone is set by the mirthless howling song which introduces the mad dialogue and dance and the dissonant music with which it concludes—truly a nightmare scene, meant to drive the Duchess to insanity, but her fine normality is untouched to the end: "I am Duchess of Malfi still." That the conception of the device and its success should breed madness in its inventor instead is suitably ironic.

V
The Porter of *Bartholomew Fair*

The writers of most of the plays thus far considered clearly make use of devices tracing directly or indirectly to Copland's *Hye Way*. Ben Jonson's more extensive use of comparable rogue and knave material in *Bartholomew Fair* (1614), on the other hand, is problematic and cannot be traced to Copland with any assurance. But the subject matter belongs in the same general category and may be examined here as a relatively independent development of the tradition.

In this play the use of this material does not take the form of a brief allegory as in *Macbeth,* but becomes the very plot. The scene is no longer a hospital, but the great sprawling world of Bartholomew Fair itself in Smithfield, in the very shadow of the great hospital of Copland's poem. The event, celebrated annually in the Renaissance period for a fortnight beginning on August 22, was famous almost from its institution in the twelfth century both for its merry making and for its concourse of knavery.[50] The plot develops slowly, as befits the panoramic view of this great Jacobean Vanity Fair, but its nature is made apparent at once in the introduction. The Stage-keeper speaking the Induction is a kind of Porter himself as he comments on the play and the characters. He even mentions the Hospital; Master Littlewit the Proctor "plays one o' the Arches, that dwels about the *Hospitall,* and hee has a very pretty part."[51] And the Stage-keeper deplores Jonson's inability to deal adequately with the material: "Hee has not hit the humors; he do's not know 'hem; hee has not convers'd with the *Bartholmew*-birds, as they say." Jonson was well aware that Greene, Dekker, and other writers of the time were closer students of traditional rogue literature than he. (In this play he was to prove at least their equal in observing actual rogue behavior.)

In Act I we meet representative London citizens and others who are to be diversely gulled and fleeced at the Fair, and a knavish gentleman named Quarlous who helps to engineer the major deceptions. They make an amusing crew: Littlewit, who considers himself a great wit, and his vain wife; Winwife, the estate-hungry suitor of the widow Dame Purecraft; Bartholomew Cokes, a country esquire, Grace, his unhappy betrothed, and Wasp, his steward; and Zeal-of-the-land Busy, the Puritan hypocrite, also suitor to Dame Purecraft. Dame Purecraft has just had her fortune told, has learned that she will never be happy unless she marries a madman within a week, and has been going to Bethlehem Hospital twice a day to find a mad gentleman suitor.

50. Henry Morley (*Memoirs of Bartholomew Fair,* London, 1859) lists the date of the beginning of the Fair as 1120 (see his index), three years before the founding of the Priory and Hospital (not eighteen years after that event, as stated in Herford and Simpson, *Ben Jonson,* X, 167). The first charter for the Fair seems to have been given by Henry I in 1133. See also Wheatley and Cunningham, I, 110–115.

51. *Ben Jonson,* ed. C. H. Herford, Percy and Evelyn Simpson (Oxford: Clarendon Press, 1938), VI, p. 13. In *The New Inne* (1631), the Host visualizes converting his inn into a "Spittle, / For lasars, or switch-sellers! . . . An Academy of Rogues" (I.v.35).

The plot proper centers around the figure of Justice Overdo, whose name reflects on the intricate problem of administering justice to the knaves and rogues of the time. Haroun al Raschid-like, Justice Overdo has decided to go to the Fair himself for the commendable civic purpose of discovering the enormities of knavery practiced in London. With motives like those of Harman and Greene, "in Iustice name, and the Kings; and for the commonwealth," he assumes first the disguise of a fool, though he knows of another worthy who had taken the guise of a porter or a carman for the same purpose. The "other worthy," as C. S. Alden has indicated,[52] was almost certainly Sir Thomas Hayes, Lord Mayor of London at the very time when this play was first produced, who had actually served as his own private detective in discovering the villainies and abuses of the city, as he himself tells us in a letter to the Lord Chamberlain dated July 8, 1614:[53]

> Right honorable my very good Lord my Dutie remembred, knowing yor Lordshipps honorable care for the good of the comon wealth I make bould in breef to certifie what courses I hold in Reforminge what I founde out of order in this cittie when I came into my place. First I begann to free the streetes of a swarme of Loose and idle vagrants men and women providing for the relief of all such as were not able to gett theire livinge and keeping them at worke in Bridewell, not punishinge any for begginge but settinge them on worke which was worse then death unto them. Secondlie when I understoode of many Lewde houses kept for wickednes and shoppes of synne, I informed my self by all due meanes of the truthe, usinge Spies hired for that purpose, to discover their corners and dissolute courses. And to be assured not to be abused by such instruments, I have gone my self disguised in person to divers badd houses. And finding those Nurseries of

52. C. S. Alden, *Bartholomew Fair by Ben Jonson, Yale Stud. in English,* XXV (New York, 1904), pp. 163–164.
53. MS. *Remembrancia,* III, 1614, No. 46, in Archives of the Records Office of the Corporation of London. This letter is summarized in *Analytical Index to the Series of Records among the Archives of the City of London* (London, 1878), pp. 358–359. See E. A. Horsman's review of this material in his edition of *Bartholomew Fair, Ben Jonson* (Cambridge, Mass., 1960), pp. xx–xxi.

> villanye I punished them accordinge to theire deserts, some by carting and whippinge and verie many by Bannishment from home, for that many houses stand emptie which causeth some exclamation against mee . . .

The letter continues at some length, telling of the Mayor's perception that these evils had their origin in the alehouses, whose number he finds to exceed a thousand, possessing a total of forty thousand barrels of strong, heady beer. He has abridged the number of the houses and introduced a system of licenses. One can easily understand how Jonson's play can be read as a satire on Hayes' over-assiduity in reforming these abuses.

Did Hayes, like Justice Overdo, take the guise of mad Anthony Bradley and subsequently of a porter to achieve his purpose? Possibly this was part of the oral tradition of the period; or possibly the use of the porter-disguise traces to the literary tradition of Copland's Porter.

The Justice has his own black book to record the enormities of the Fair, and he encounters enough of them, committed by creatures who are enormities themselves: Joan Trash, the gingerbread woman who sells wares made of stale bread, rotten eggs, musty ginger, and dead honey; Nightingale (compare Copland's "nightyngales of newgate"), related to Autolycus, selling his ballads with his secretary Zekiel, the cutpurse;[54] the remarkable Ursula, the pig-woman, bawd, receiver of stolen goods, the very "womb and bed of iniquity"; and Jordan Knockhum, the horse courser of Turnbull (actually a rogue or "cutpurse of the sword").

Immediately Justice Overdo is gulled by his informers into thinking that Knockhum is an honest horse-trader and Zekiel an innocent young man who is being seduced by bad

54. Jonson probably models Nightingale on Autolycus, and Shakespeare could have been his sole source for the cutpurse and ballad-singing episode. On the other hand, certain details suggest that he also knew the source of Shakespeare's apparent inspiration, the story of the ballad-singing cozeners in Greene's *Thirde and last Part of Cony-Catching* (see p. 244 of this study).

company. In turn he is mistaken by Wasp and beaten as being a patrico or "patriarch of the cutpurses" (Harman's attempt to discredit the existence of this type of knave could not cancel the myth). The quarreling of Knockhum and Quarlous; the pandering of Whit; the gluttony and hypocrisy of Zeal-of-the-land Busy; the gulling and robbing of Cokes even while he is singing the refrain of a ballad warning against pickpockets; the gulling of Overdo by the seeming madman, Troubleall; the stocking of Wasp, Busy, and Overdo; the fantastic transformation of Mistresses Littlewit and Overdo into apparent women of the game—all are part of the fast-shifting kaleidoscope of the great human circus of the Fair.

At the end, Jonson resorts to the familiar device of the Porter as observer and recorder of enormities, whatever his source for the idea. In Act V, scene ii, Justice Overdo comes in disguised as a porter to carry out his purpose of revealing and punishing knavery, and presently, in scene vi, he makes his revelation: exultantly he denounces in turn the particular knaves, panderers, bawds, and women of light virtue whom he has observed at the Fair. But at this moment of triumph he is baffled: Mrs. Overdo herself is introduced sick, apparently from too much liquor (she has been in the company of Whit the panderer); and the young man whose honesty he would protect is unmasked as the cutpurse who helped to secure him his beating and punishment in the stocks. Justice Adam Overdo must remember that he is but "Adam, flesh and blood." The play ends with Justice Overdo inviting the others, knaves and all, home to supper. He has learned that in this world in which it is difficult to distinguish between sanity and madness, between honesty and knavery, a world in which a thin line may mark the boundary between the accepted lady and the courtesan, one must not concentrate on punishing enormities. Instead, as is implied in *Measure for Measure,* the purpose of justice must be to reform, not to punish: "I invite you home, with mee to my house, to supper: I will have none feare to go along, for my intents are *Ad correctionem, non ad destructionem; Ad aedificandum, non ad diruendum:* so lead on."

One must believe that this play was not composed purely for the amusement of the King and the audience that first witnessed it. In the Induction, it is true, Jonson himself forbids his hearers to attempt to identify any person of the play with figures of the time, or to interpret it as a political allegory. But there is no mistaking his satire on the Puritans, whom Quarlous condemns in the familiar terms of knavery (V.ii.41 ff.): "Away, you are a heard of hypocriticall proud Ignorants, rather wilde then mad. Fitter for woods, and the society of beasts then houses, and the congregation of men. You are the second part of the society of *Canters,*[55] Outlawes to order and *Discipline,* and the onely privileg'd *Church-robbers* of *Christendome.*" And it is patent that this drama is a plea for human sympathy and understanding in dealing with the complexities of the social problems of knavery.

Like the attitude of Shakespeare in *Measure for Measure,* Jonson's view of his rogue world here is, on the whole, large-souled and tolerant, a sane, sophisticated view that recognizes the narrow distinction between knave and knavish citizen. Though he "hath not hit the humors" of the rogues of tradition, in many respects his creatures seem more real than those of the other authors of the time. Shakespeare's, which always hit the humors, always are larger than life.

* * *

Other examples of Copland's influence could be cited,[56] but those given are enough to show how his device of the Porter observing the rogues on the highway caught at the

55. This phrase, "the second part of the society of *Canters,*" possibly is an echo of the divisions that Awdeley establishes between his vagabonds and knaves, or it could be Jonson's proposal for an addition to the "orders" in Copland and Harman: a second set of Puritan knaves with Zeal-of-the-land Busy the "capitall Knave of the land" (V.ii.66–67).

56. One such example may be cited in Cyril Tourneur's *Revengers Tragaedie* (1607) in the episode in which Vindice enters the service of Lussorio (I.iii.53–87). Lussorio says, "Thou hast beene Scrivener to much knavery then?" And

imagination of Renaissance authors. With Nashe, his unthrifts and knaves of the seven deadly sins have already been received by the porter of their hospital of hell, and his scholars, philosophers, and poets are stigmatized as a company of ragged knaves, lazy hedge-creepers, "usde to no labour but to lowze themselves." In Shakespeare the device serves in *Measure for Measure* to extend the impression of a world of knavery inviting compassion in the place of harsh judgment; in *Macbeth* to illuminate as a central allegory the plight of the Macbeths; and in *Henry VIII* to prepare the way for a belated tribute to Elizabeth. In turn, Dekker for at least two of his plays could think of no device more apt to please his audience than visits with the madmen of Bethlehem and the

Vindice replies, using the tell-tale term *abundance* [Dekker's equivalent of Copland's "Ynow, ynow"]: "Foole, to abundance, sir . . ." and proceeds with a list of licentious actions associated with the unthrift waste of lands and heritage for lust (see *The Works of Cyril Tourneur,* ed. Allardyce Nicoll, London, 1929, pp. 90–91). A more vague yet entertaining example may be found in *The Pilgrim* (1621) by Fletcher. In this comedy the heroine, Alinda, is presented at the outset as celebrated for her charity: with her family Porter she "Relieves more Beggers than an Hospital." Act I, scene ii, is devoted to her ministrations to four of these beggars, and the Pilgrim, her lover in disguise. The drama contains the expected mad scene at a house where all sorts of lunacies are provided for, and whose mad people are perhaps drawn from observations of cases in Bethlehem and dim reminiscences of Webster and Dekker.

A more subtle example, based also on observation and related to Webster, Dekker, and Copland, occurs in John Ford's *The Lover's Melancholy* (1629). In this play after Corax, the physician to Prince Palador, has defined melancholy, Aretus asks, "There are sundry kinds / Of our affection?" And Corax answers: "Infinite: it were more easy to conjecture every hour / We have to live, than reckon up the kinds, / Or causes of this anguish of the mind" (*Dramatic Works of John Ford,* ed. Henry Weber, Edinburgh, 1811, I, 164–165, Act III, scene i). But Corax hopes to discover the cause of Palador's malady, and does so, in part through a masque ("The Mask of Melancholy," III, iii) in which seven stages of melancholy are depicted, such as lycanthropia, hydrophobia, delirium, phrenitis, hypochondria, St. Vitus's dance, and love melancholy. These cases seem to be based on Webster, Burton, and possible observation of actual Bedlamites, and the scene is functional in its relation to the love-melancholy of Palador. Later (IV.ii), Corax and the demented Meleander briefly philosophize after the fashion of Copland on the categories of a knavish world in which politicians thrive and fill lordships and in which none is wise "but unthrifts, bankrupts, beggars, rascals."

knaves and doxies of Bridewell, under the inspiration of Copland. Webster's great knaves of high places seem to make their own special uses of Copland's device and catalogue, and the white face of the Duchess of Malfi appears against this background. Most extensive of all is Jonson's apparent use of the device to help unify his world of *Bartholomew Fair* with its plea, like that of *Measure for Measure,* for a merciful justice in dealing with these wanderers of the highway.

III

Robert Greene, "Autor for Knaves," and his Conycatchers

OF ALL THE KNAVISH CRAFTS, cozening is the most ancient and durable, and with the increase in vagabondage in Renaissance England cozening burgeoned. Robert Copland makes what appears to be the first English reference to the special practices of the basic cozener in his *Hye Way,* where his Porter speaks in passing of "gaderers of cony skynnes / That chop with laces / poyntes / nedles / & pyns" (Eiv).[1] The unknown author (perhaps Gilbert Walker) of *A manifest detection of the moste vyle and detestable use of Diceplay* (c.1552)[2] seems to have been first to describe in Eng-

1. This curious reference to an Autolycus-like peddler appears to be the first record of the knavish peddler who barters his wares for conyskins and takes in his customers as well, who thus become conies.

2. Bodl., 8°K.3 Art.BS (STC 24961): *A manifest de- / tection of the most vyle and detestable / use of Diceplay, and other practises lyke / the same, a Myrrour very necessary for / all yonge Gentilmen & others soden- / ly enabled by worldly abūdāce, / to loke in. Newly set forth / for their behoufe.* Colophon: "Imprinted at London, in Paules / church yarde at the sygne / of the lamb, by Abra- / ham Vele." CBEL and STC list only this one edition (c.1580); but Aydelotte (p. 120) furnishes almost incontrovertible evidence, confirmed by Judges (p. 492), that an earlier edition was published by Richard Tottyl in 1552 (Judges finds more evidence for a yet earlier edition in 1545). This work, a source book for Greene and other writers, is ascribed to an otherwise unknown author, Gilbert Walker, on the uncertain evidence of a Ms. note in a volume of tracts formerly owned by Topham Beauclerc (see Aydelotte, p. 120). *A manifest detection* is a dialogue (perhaps inspired by

lish the shifts of the card- and dice-playing group of cheaters, known later as cozeners, and to define the term *cozen* (cheaters "cousin" their intended victims)[3] and the functions of the cheaters such as those of the taker-up, the verser, the barnard, and the rubber (rutter?),[4] together with other terms

---

Copland's *Hye Way,* of which there are a few apparent recollections) between R., a young gentleman, and M., an older friend and counsellor. R. tells of his encounter with a well-dressed gentleman in Paul's who invites him to dinner where he introduces him to a gay company of gallants who spend their leisure playing cards and dice. M. elicits the details of R's entertainment at the house and reveals to R. that he has fallen in to the company of cheaters (as they call themselves, juggling with the meaning of *escheat,* relating in law to waifs or strays confiscated by the lord). These cheaters dignify their various practices with the name of "law," such as sacking law, high law, and figging law (referring to cozening through lechery, robbery, and purse-picking respectively). M. explains at length how cheaters are made. After a young land-owner has been cozened of his wealth, the cheater may initiate him into the craft by instructing him in the art of dice play, involving as many as fourteen types of false dice, and in the devices used to entrap other "cousins," particularly by means of the barnard's law, in which four cozeners team together to fleece a victim.

Aydelotte (pp. 120–121, 175–177) has shown how Greene occasionally borrows from this work, and how Dekker and Samuel Rid use pages of it almost verbatim. *Mihil Mumchance* (1597) is, Aydelotte shows (pp. 129, 175), a plagiarized version.

3. *OED* speaks of the derivation of *cozen, v.* as uncertain, but generally associated with *cousin, sb.* It lists the use in Awdeley's *Fraternitye of Vacabondes* (1561), and suggests that the term may come from vagabond usage. But one may object that it is not found in pedlar's French. The author of *A manifest detection* (1552) uses it for the victim of the cheater, defining it as indicated presumably about eleven years before Awdeley, who seems to derive his information about cozeners from this source. Awdeley may be given credit for the earliest recorded use of *cozener* (cousoner). *A manifest detection* also seems to be first to use and define *cheater* as borrowed from law (*escheat*). The relation to pedlar's French *chete* is obvious.

4. *OED: "Verser:* One of a gang of cozeners or swindlers . . . c.1550 [1552] *Dice-Play A manifest detection:* He lightly hath in his company a man of more worship than himself, that hath the countenance of a possessioner of land, and he is called the verser."

Barnard: OED: "Obs. . . . [app. a variant of *Berner,* one who waited with a relay of hounds to intercept a hunted animal.] The member of a gang of swindlers who acts as a decoy; a lurking scoundrel, a sharper. Cf. *Barnacle* sb.[2] 3b."

Rubber: Apparently a ruffian or brawler who starts a fight to enable coz-

important in later works such as "sacking law" (cozening through lechery), "high law" (the craft of robbery), "figging law" (the craft of picking purses).

In his *Fraternitye of Vacabondes,* as we have seen, John Awdeley adds three cozeners to his fraternity, naming them "the company of Cousoners and Shifters." He lists and describes at considerable length three types, the courtesy-man, the cheater or fingerer, and the ring-faller. Though his courtesy-man bears some resemblance to the whipjack or freshwater mariner, his fawning reminds one of the cozeners of *A manifest detection.* Awdeley's description of the cheater or fingerer is likewise based on the practices of the cheaters of the same work, though the functions are not as sharply defined. His ring-faller, a descendant of the knave with the silver finger of the *Liber Vagatorum,* drops a supposedly valuable ring where it is sure to be picked up by a "cousin," claims half-share in the finding, and finally tricks his victim into buying his half at a price far above the value of the ring. In sum, these were not beggars but tricksters, confidence-men. Harman had no interest in these rascals; they were city knaves, not strolling vagabonds.

Awdeley's account is hurried and adapted from *A manifest detection.* The latter work is good in its sort, but its revelations could be amplified and illustrated with a fund of stories if a writer had access to the right sources for such material. Such a person apparently was Robert Greene, professedly something of a knave and certainly an unthrift, who,

eners to escape with their prize. *OED* lists *a rubber at cuffes* (1680) as a scuffle or fight in which only the hands are employed. The *rubber* of *A manifest detection,* who has a vague relationship to this meaning, antedates it by over a century.

Rutter: OED: "One of a party of swindlers . . . ;" derived ultimately from MDu. *rutter,* a cavalry soldier; first citation from Greene, 1591, *Notable Discovery.* This is Greene's very sensible substitution for the *rubber* of *A manifest detection,* a word which he probably did not understand. It is, of course, possible that Greene's copy of *A manifest detection* read *rutter* instead of *rubber* and that *rubber* was a misprint in the one extant copy.

whatever his motives, devoted much time in the last years of his life to the exposure of knavery.

We may suppose that Greene was more a knave in seeming than in actuality. His known sins, as Harold Jenkins argues,[5] appear to have been his own rather than those of a conycatcher, and he indicates more than once that he was an observer rather than a participant in the vices of his cozeners. Yet it seems that he associated with knavish characters and that he may have resorted to some knavish practices. To review the evidence, we must consider the almost too well known charges against him, which are summed up in the virulent *Foure Letters* of Gabriel Harvey.

The portrait of Greene that Harvey paints in his Second Letter[6] is that of the complete knave and unthrift, so embracive in its villainies that it might almost serve as a composite picture of all knavedom and worth quoting at some length for that very reason (B2–B3^{v}):

> Petty Cooseners are not woorth the naming: he they say, was the Monarch of Crosbiters, and the very Emperour of shifters. I was altogether unacquainted with the man, & never once saluted him by name: but who in London hath not heard of his dissolute, and licentious living; his fonde disguisinge of a Master of Arte with ruffianly haire, unseemely apparell, and more unseemelye Company: . . . his fine coosening of Iuglers, and finer iugling with cooseners: hys villainous cogging, and foisting; his monstrous swearinge, and horrible forswearing; his impious profaning of sacred Textes: . . . his infamous resorting to the Banckeside, Shorditch, Southwarke, and other filthy hauntes: . . . his imployinge of Ball, (surnamed, cuttinge Ball) till he was intercepted at Tiborne, to leavy a crew of his trustiest companions, to guarde

5. See Harold Jenkins, "On the Authenticity of Greene's *Groatsworth of Wit* and *The Repentance of Robert Greene*," *RES*, II (1935), p. 39.

6. B.M., C.40.d.14 (STC 12900): *Foure Letters / and certaine Sonnets: / Especially touching Robert Greene and other parties, / by him abused: / But incidently of divers excellent persons, / and some matters of note. / To all courteous mindes, that will vouchsafe the reading. /* [Ornament] */ London / Imprinted by Iohn Wolfe, / 1592.* See G. B. Harrison, *Gabriel Harvey Foure Letters and certaine Sonnets,* Bodley Head Quartos, No. 2 (N. Y. and London, 1923), pp. 28–41.

him in daunger of Arrestes: his keping of the foresaid Balls sister, a sorry ragged queane, of whom hee had his base sonne, *Infortunatus Greene:* his forsaking of his owne wife, too honest for such a husband: . . . He never envyed [annoyed?] me so much, as I pittied him from my hart: especially when his hostisse *Isam,* with teares in her eies, & sighes from a deeper fountaine, (for she loved him derely) tould me of his lamentable begging of a penny-pott of Malmesy: . . . and how his dublet, and hose, and sword were sold for three shillinges: and beside the charges of his winding sheete, which was foure shillinges; and the charges of hys buriall yesterday in the New-churchyard neere Bedlam, which was six shillinges, and foure pence; how deeply hee was indebted to her poore husbande; as appeered by his own bonde of tenne poundes: which the good woman kindly shewed me: and beseeched me to read the writting beneath: which was a letter to his abandoned wife, in the behalfe of his gentle host: not so short as persuasible in the beginning, and pitifull in the ending.

> *Doll, I charge the by the love of our youth, & by my soules rest, that thou wilte see this man paide: for if hee, and his wife had not succoured me, I had died in the streetes.*
>
> *Robert Greene.*

The whole pattern of his life, Harvey insists in his Third Letter, was "a terrible Caveat" for people of his sort, and he asks (D2): "Where should Conny-catchers have gotten such a Secretarie?" And he once more resumes Greene's nature, as he sees it:

> Loe a wilde head, ful of mad braine and a thousande crotchets: A Scholler, a Discourser, a Courtier, a ruffian, a Gamester, a Lover, a Souldier, a Travailer, a Merchaunt, a Broker, an Artificer, a Botcher, a Petti-fogger, a Player, a Coosener, a Rayler, a beggar, an Omnigatherum, a Gay nothing: a Stoare-house of bald and baggage stuffe, unwoorth the aunswering, or reading: A Triviall, and triobular Autor for knaves, & fooles: an Image of Idlenes . . .

To the judicial mind, the most important sentence in all this torrent of abuse is the confession, "I was altogether unacquainted with the man, & never once saluted him by name . . ." All the charges are based on hearsay, supplemented by Harvey's interpretation of what he had found in Greene's pamphlets, and reported after Greene's death, a report by a man then known and now chiefly remembered for his quarrelsome disposition.

In his retort to this invective, Thomas Nashe repays Harvey with comparable abuse, but does not unequivocally refute the charges that Greene had lived the life of a knave. Greene himself, Nashe says, would have answered Harvey vigorously if he had lived; but the way in which he imagines Greene would have answered is scarcely reassuring regarding Greene's conduct (C3^{v}): "Had hee liv'd, *Gabriel,* and thou shouldst so unarteficially and odiously libeld against him as thou hast done, he would have made thee an example of ignominy to all ages that are to come, and driven thee to eate thy owne book butterd, as I sawe him make an Apparriter once in a Tavern eate his Citation, waxe and all, very handsomly serv'd twixt two dishes."[7]

In summing up his merits, Nashe credits Greene with more virtues than vices, but even here his merits take on the color of vice (E4–E4^{v}):

> Hee inherited more vertues than vices: a iolly long red peake, like the spire of a steeple, hee cherisht continually without cutting, whereat a man might hang a Iewell, it was so sharpe and pendant.
>
> Why should art answer for the infirmitie of manners? He had his faultes, and thou thy follyes.
>
> Debt and deadly sinne, who is not subiect to? / with any notorious crime I never knew him tainted; (& yet tainting is no infamous surgerie for him that hath beene in so many hote skirmishes).
>
> A good fellowe hee was, and would have drunke with thee for more *angels* then the Lord thou libeldst on *gave thee in Christs Colledge;* and in one yeare he pist as much against the walls, as thou and thy two brothers spent in three . . .
>
> For the lowsie circumstance of his poverty before his death,

7. B.M., 96.b.16(3) (STC 18377): *Strange Newes, Of the intercept- / ing certaine Letters and a Con- / voy of Verses, as they were going Privilie to / victuall the Low Countries. / Unda impellitur unda. / By Tho. Nashe Gentleman. /* [Ornament] / *Printed 1592.* See *The Works of Thomas Nashe,* ed. R. B. McKerrow (Oxford, 1958), I, 271.

> and sending that miserable writte to his wife, it cannot be but thou lyest, learned *Gabriell*.
>
> I and one of my fellowes, *Will. Monox* (Hast thou never heard of him and his great dagger?) were in company with him a month before he died, at that fatall banquet of Rhenish wine and pickled hearing (if thou wilt needs have it so), and then the inventorye of his apparrell came to more than three shillings (though thou saist the contrarie). I know a Broker . . . shall give you thirty shillings for the doublet alone, if you can helpe him to it.[8]

Later in the same work Nashe touches once more on Greene's conduct, leaving the same ambiguous impression (L4^{v}):

> What *Greene* was, let some other answere for him as much as I have done; I had no tuition over him: he might have writ another *Galateo* of manners, for his manners everie time I came into his companie: I saw no such base shifting or abhominable villanie by him. Something there was which I have heard, not seene, that hee had not that regarde to his credit in, which had beene requisite he should.[9]

A curious defense indeed! An artist should not be held accountable for misconduct; every one commits deadly sin. Nashe knows of no serious crime that Greene has committed, but one who has had so many hot skirmishes could be pardoned for a taint of such a crime. As for his virtues, he had a jolly red beard and he was a good fellow with a great thirst. As for his poverty and the memorable writ, Harvey is a liar But whatever the worth of Greene's doublet as Nashe saw it, the "miserable writte" that Harvey read seems to have been piteously genuine, and we may assume that Nashe is wrong and that Harvey is right about Greene's death in poverty. Nashe helps to exonerate Greene of cozenage and knavery

8. McKerrow, I, 287–288.

9. McKerrow, I, 330. Nashe wishes to give the impression that his defense of Greene is not that of a friend and close associate. Thus he adds to the passage just quoted: "A thousand there bee that have more reason to speake in his behalfe than I, who since I first knew him about town, have beene two yeares together and not seene him." See also McKerrow, I, 303: ". . . neither was I *Greenes* companion any more then for a carowse or two."

("I saw no such base shifting or abhominable villanie by him"), but he leaves the doubt: "Something there was which I have heard, not seene . . ." And by his own testimony he saw him rarely.

Greene himself confirms the impression that there was something to the rumors about him, if we are willing to accept his testimony against himself as valid. In his at least partly autobiographical *Groatsworth of Witte,* one can easily perceive many likenesses between the baldly disguised Roberto Gorinius and Robert Greene. But some of the story is fiction. What parts of the following are we to accept as true?

> But *Roberto* now famozed for an Arch-plaimaking-poet, his purse like the sea sometime sweld, anon like the same sea fell to a low ebbe; yet seldom he wanted, his labors were so well esteemed. Marry this rule he kept, whatever he fingerd afore hand, was the certaine meanes to unbinde a bargaine, and being askt why hee so slightly dealt with them that did him good? It becoms me, saith hee, to bee contrary to the worlde; for commonly when vulgar men receive earnest, they doo performe, when I am paid any thing afore-hand, I breake my promise . . . His companie were lightly the lewdest persons in the land, apt for pilferie, periurie, forgerie, or any villainy. Of these hee knew the casts to cog at cards, coossen at Dice; by these he learnd the legerdemaines of nips, foysts, connycatchers, crosbyters, lifts, high Lawyers, and all the rabble of that uncleane generation of vipers: and pithily could he paint out their whole courses of craft: So cunning he was in all craftes, as nothing rested in him almost but craftines. How often the Gentlewoman his Wife labored vainely to recall him, is lamentable to note: but as one given over to all lewdnes, he communicated her sorrowfull lines among his loose truls, that iested at her bootlesse laments. If he could any way get credite on scores, he would then brag his creditors carried stones, comparing every round circle to a groning O procured by a painfull burden. The shamefull end of sundry his consorts deservedly punished for their amisse, wrought no compunction in his heart: of which one, brother to a Brothell hee kept, was trust under a tree as round as a Ball (E1v–E2).[10]

10. B.M., C.57.b.42 (STC 12245): *Greenes, / Groats-worth / of witte, bought with a / million of Repentance. Describing the follie of youth, the falsehood of*

A real cozener and knave if we take him at his word! No wonder that, if he really believed himself guilty of all these misdemeanors, he feared for his salvation, as revealed in his lament in what is supposed to be his last work, with its cony-catching title, *The Repentance of Robert Greene:*[11]

> Oh I feele a hell already in my conscience, the number of my sinnes do muster before my eies, the poore mens plaints that I have wronged, cries out in mine eares and saith, *Robin Greene* thou art damnd; nay the iustice of God tels mee I cannot bee saved. Now I do remember (though too late) that I have read in the Scriptures, how neither adulterers, swearers, theeves, nor murderers shall inherite the kingdome of heaven. What hope then can I have of any grace, when (given over from all grace) I exceeded all other in these kinde of sinnes? (B3)

As Professor Jenkins points out, Greene is not saying that he is guilty of all these sins, but rather of sins of this kind, which exclude the sinner from salvation. That he was guilty of adultery and blasphemy is probably true, but he almost certainly was not a murderer (Gabriel would not have missed this chance) and probably not a thief or cozener for all his possible association with them. Perhaps his most relevant confession is implied in his final appeal to the youth of England to "flie whoredome, drunkennes, swearing, blaspheming, contempt of the word, and such greevous and grosse sinnes" (C4ᵛ). These faults seem to be his special concern in this apprehensive hour; but there is no hint of conycatching as one of these sins (if we discount as vague his earlier refer-

make- / shifte flatterers, the miseries of the negligent, / and mischiefes of deceiving Courtesans, / Written before his death and published at his / dyeing request . . . London / Imprinted for William Wright. / 1592. See sig. E1-E1ᵛ. Greene tells us that he has been revealing his own life: "Heere (gentlemen) breake I off Robertos speach; whose life in most parts agreeing with mine, found one selfe punishment as I have done" (E2).

11. Bodl., Malone 575 (STC 12306): *The Repentance / of Robert Greene Maister / of Artes. / Wherein by himselfe is laid open his loose life, / with the manner of his death. /* [Printer's device] */ At London, / Printed for Cuthbert Burbie, and are to be sold at / the middle shop in the Poultry, under / Saint Mildreds Church. / 1592. Greenes Groatsworth* and *The Repentance* have been edited by G. B. Harrison, Bodley Head Quartos, No. VI.

ence to "the poore mens plaints that I have wronged"). Instead, he thanks God that he has been the means of exposing cozenage (C3^{v}): "But I thanke God, that hee put it in my head, to lay open the most horrible coosenages of the common Conny-catchers, Cooseners, and Crosse-biters, which I have indifferently handled in those my severall discourses already imprinted. And my trust is, that those discourses will doe great good, and bee very beneficiall to the Common-wealth of England."

Considering all the available evidence, however, we may assume that "Robin" Greene did know some knaves and wantons. He appears to have deserted his wife for a courtesan, sister to a presumably actual rogue named Cutting Ball, hanged at Tyburn. There was an ill-fated banquet of Rhenish wine and pickled herring attended by Greene, Nashe, and Will. Monox of the great dagger, which marked the beginning of Greene's last illness; and he died deserted by his friends (Nashe, a casual associate rather than a friend, was out of London because of the plague) and impoverished. It may be assumed that Greene knew much about roguery that he had not read in books, particularly about cozeners, to whom he gave a new name that became their most common sobriquet—conycatchers.[12]

How far can we rely, then, on the authenticity of his revelations about his conycatchers? Greene himself suggests the answer in his preface "To the Gentlemen Readers" in *Greenes Vision* (A4): "I have shotte at many abuses, over shotte my selfe in describing of some; where truth failed, my invention hath stood my friend."[13] Most of the stories prob-

12. See Chapter II, p. 66, Note 13.

13. B.M., C.40.c.36 (STC 12261): *Greenes / Vision: / Written at the instant of his / death. / Conteyning a penitent passion for / the folly of his Pen. / Sero sed serio. /* [Ornament] / *Imprinted at London for Thomas / Newman, and are to be sould at his shop / in Fleetestreete, in Saint Dunstones / Churchyard.* See Grosart, *Works*, XII, 195–196. John C. Jordan (*Robert Greene*, New York, 1915, p. 94) argues vigorously that Greene is a "literary liar," that however wicked his life may have been, there is little that is original in Greene's cony-

ably have bases in actual knavish incidents, but Greene has heightened their color freely with his invention.

I

Greene's conycatching pamphlets demonstrate that he had more than a surface acquaintance with knavery, and they represent at the same time a picturesque new approach to familiar subject matter. The *personae* of the literature, their functions and character, had been largely established by the author of *A manifest detection,* Copland, Awdeley, and Harman; Greene was to resume some of the earlier work and to refurbish it with new names and new illustrations. Unlike Harman, Greene is not interested in mere beggars and rogues: all his leading characters in these pamphlets have the spice of cozenage in them; even when they behave as robbers, as Harman's upright men do on occasion, they proceed according to ruses and have setters (like Gadshill) who *set a watch* (Shakespeare prefers *set a match*) as illustrated in "High Law" with its separate agents, namely the thief (high lawyer), the setter of the watch (the scripper), the spy for the watch (an oak), and the victim (the martin).[14]

With his personal experience with knaves and cozeners it was natural for Greene to turn to this subject matter. That he hoped that such writing might be remunerative is manifest, but at the same time he may well have been convinced, like Luther and Harman before him, that he would be serving his country by exposing the fraudulent practices of the

catching pamphlets; he believes that Greene knew little of the craft outside his literary sources. One thing seems certain: Greene adds many stories of knavish practices that are surely not invention and which have no known literary sources.

14. These terms seem to be based on Greene's fancy. *OED* lists *scripper* as cant and cites Greene's use in *Notable Discovery* (1591) as the first recorded example. The word appears to be based on *scrip* (wallet). *Oak* is not listed in this use in *OED*. It possibly is Greene's invention for a concealed watcher or spy (behind a tree). *Martin* (*OED*) is defined as *dupe* in this usage, possibly based on *martin* the bird; the first record is Greene's use in *Notable Discovery*. There seems to be no evidence that these terms were ever used by cozeners.

cozeners who preyed on the unwary citizens and people from the country, as he never wearies of maintaining in the titles and prefaces of his pamphlets. Thus his first pamphlet (see Plate 11) on its title page advertizes this motive:

> *A / Notable Discovery of Coosnage. / Now daily practised by sundry lewd per- / sons, called Connie-catchers, and / Crosse-byters. / Plainely laying open those pernitious sleights that hath brought many igno- / rant men to confusion. / Written for the general benefit of all Gentlemen, Citizens, Apprentises, Countrey Farmers / and yeomen, that may hap to fall into the company of such coosening companions. / With a delightfull discourse of the coosnage of Colliers. / Nascimur pro patria. By R. Greene, Maister of Arts.* / [cut of cony holding two cards, with a bowl and tankard on either side and dice at feet] / *London. / Printed by Iohn Wolfe for T. N. and are to be solde over / against the great South doore of Paules. 1591.*[15]

And his social purpose is further emphasized by the address of his preface, "To The Yong Gentlemen, Marchants, Apprentises, Farmers, and plain Countreymen," and by the body of the preface itself in which he appraises his fitness for his task. He is truly repentant for his earlier wanton days, but he intimates that (as with Prince Hal), there was a purpose in his misbehavior: "The odde mad-caps I have beene mate too, not as a companion, but as a spie to have an insight into their knaveries, that seeing their traines I might eschew their snares; those mad fellowes I learned at last to loath, by their owne gracelesse villenies, and what I saw in them to their confusion, I can forewarne in others to my countreies commodity."

His intention in this work is to reveal two chief abuses, the "Art of Conny-catching" and the "Arte of Crosbiting," two pernicious practices that have ruined unnumbered persons. He says further that he is publishing his pamphlet despite grave threats by those whom he is exposing: "Yet Gen-

15. B.M., C.27.b.20 (STC 12279). See *Robert Greene, M.A. A Notable Discovery of Coosnage 1591 / The Second Part of Conny-Catching 1592,* Bodley Head Quartos, No. I, ed. G. B. Harrison, London, 1923.

A

Notable Diſcouery of Cooſnage.

Now daily practiſed by ſundry lewd per-
ſons , called Connie-catchers, and
Croſſe-biters.

Plainely laying open thoſe pernitious ſleights that hath brought many ignorant men to confuſion.

Written for the generall benefit of all Gentlemen, Citizens, Aprentiſes, Countrey Farmers and yeomen, that may hap to fall into the company of ſuch cooſening companions.

With a delightfull diſcourſe of the cooſnage of Colliers.

Naſcimur pro patria. By R. Greene, Maiſter of Arts.

3

LONDON
Printed by Iohn Wolfe for T.N. and are to be ſold ouer
againſt the great South doore of Paules. 1591.

PLATE 11. *A Notable Discovery of Coosnage.* Title page. British Museum, C.27.b.20.

tlemen, am I sore threatned by the hacksters of that filthie facultie, that if I sette their practises in print, they will cut off that hand that writes the Pamphlet." But he does not fear them. He would even print a list of their names (as Harman did) if it were not that he hopes for their amendment.

In the text itself Greene justifies his claim that his conycatchers are much more subtle than those of *A manifest detection,* despite his obvious debt to that work. At the outset he seems to be simplifying the earlier barnard's law. Instead of the four knaves, the taker-up, the verser, the barnard, and the rubber, the art of conycatching requires only three, the rutter, the verser, and the barnacle.[16] The functions of these correspond to those of the like figures in the barnard's law. Greene's omission of the rubber at this point suggests that he is not dependent merely on *A manifest detection* for his information; though he makes use of its observations, he seems to be writing also from his own study of these practices. The outline of his information about card-playing and the basic device of the cozening are derived from *A manifest detection,* from which Greene borrows some passages almost verbatim, but almost everywhere he adds fresh substance to the outline. Thus the suggested devices by which the taker-up in the earlier work approaches his victim become greatly elaborated in Greene's account of the ways in which the setter deceives the cony; and the card tricks barely indicated in the earlier work are practiced before our eyes by Greene's conycatchers. Despite the fact that many of the practices are thus suggested or partially described earlier, Greene's work in nearly every way is more informative of the ruses of the city knaves who frequented Paul's and the inns and taverns of London.

16. *OED* finds *barnacle* possibly based on *barnacle* sb.[2], 2. "English name of the pedunculate genus of cirripedes, which attach themselves to objects floating in the water"; fig. (3), "a companion that sticks close." Greene's usage for a decoy swindler (*Notable Discovery,* 1591) is the first recorded example. Greene here is simply using his invention, replacing the *barnard* of the barnard's law, which he later summarizes as the "drunken barnards law," with his barnacle.

At the end of his exposition of the art of conycatching, Greene adds a table detailing the various "laws" practiced by knaves and rogues in general, giving the supposed cant names applied to the various persons needed for the practice of each law. He lists eight of these procedures, "lawes of villanie, leading the high way to infamie," which he briefly defines as follows (C4):

1. High Law	*Robbing by the high way side.*
2. Sacking Law	*Lecherie.*
3. Cheting Law	*Play at false Dice.*
4. Cros-biting Law	*Coosenage by whores.*
5. Conny-catching Law	*Coosenage by Cardes.*
6. Versing Law	*Coosenage by false gold.*
7. Figging Law	*Cutting of purses & picking of pockets.*
8. Barnards Law	*A drunken coosenage by cards.*

There are yet other laws, he adds in Latin, but it would take too long to write them down—a promise of things to come.

The "laws" are probably Greene's invention, based on the single barnard's law of *A manifest detection.* The fact that he later discredits some of them, and that at least one later writer challenges them, leads one to suspect that they have little foundation in reality. They presumably illustrate the general human passion for order even in disorder: since conycatching is highly schematized, so must be all the other devices used by knaves and rogues.

The table of laws is followed by an explanation of the art of cross-biting, which was supposed to complete the work, according to the scheme indicated in the preface. But he adds ten more pages detailing yet another type of cozenage, that of the "law of legering," entitled "A Pleasant Discovery of the cousenage of Colliers."[17]

17. This particular section clearly does not belong in *A Notable Discovery* as the work was first planned, but might well have been included in *The Second part.* Greene appears to have added it to *A Notable Discovery* to make the pamphlets of about equal length.

In his second knave pamphlet, *The Second part of Conny-catching,*[18] Greene extends the meaning of conycatching to cover almost all the arts ("laws") of the knave and rogue world. The title page itself promises to reveal all the cozenages not already revealed in the *Discovery,* namely, the black art (lock-picking), the vincent's law (cozening at bowling), the prigging law (horse-stealing), the curbing law (stealing through windows with a hook), lifting law (shoplifting), along with the arts of the foist and the nip. Each of these, we learn from a later analytic table (B1), is performed by crews of four or five knaves, known by supposed cant names. Certainly no such methodical division of these activities existed in such detail. Once more Greene addresses prefa-

18. Huntington, 61123 (STC 12281): *The / Second part of Conny-catching. / Contayning the discovery of certaine wondrous / Coosenages, either superficiallie past over, or / utterlie untoucht in the first. /*

As the nature of	*The blacke Art,*	*Picking of lockes.*
	The Vincents Law.	*Coosenage at Bowls.*
	The Prigging Law,	*Horse stealing.*
	The Courbing Law,	*Hooking at windows.*
	The Lifting Law,	*Stealing of parcels.*
	The Foist,	*The pickpocket.*
	The Nippe,	*The cut purse.*

With sundry pithy and pleasant Tales worthy the reading of all e- / states, that are ennemies to such base and dishonest practises. / Mallem non esse quam non prodesse patriae. / R. G. / [Printer's device] */ London. / Printed by Iohn Wolfe for William Wright, and / are to be sold at his shop in Pauls Church / yard, neare to the French schoole. / 1591.*

In the following year a second edition with a misleading title appeared: Bodl., Malone 575 (STC 12282): *The / Second / and last part of Conny-catching. / With new additions containing many merry tales of / all lawes worth the reading, because they are wor- / thy to be remembred. Discoursing strange cunning in Coosnage, which if you reade with- / out laughing, Ile give you my cap for a Noble. / Mallem nonesse quam non prodesse patriae. /* R. G. / [Cut of cony with connycatching devices]. */ London. / Printed by Iohn Wolfe for William Wright / 1592.* See Note 15 for G. B. Harrison's ed. In this edition Greene properly arranges the Table of Laws after the title-page. Then, following the preface, with no reference to order he opens with a brief "Tale of a Nip," and omits the discourse on conycatchers and the accompanying tale (a logical omission since this material is not provided for in the Table). Otherwise the contents are unchanged, and manifestly this is not the "last part" of the series.

tory remarks to the same audience for which he wrote the *Discovery,* and expresses his intention of attacking base villainies for the profit of his countrymen. The hazards of his task are seemingly more formidable than when he wrote the *Discovery:* the conycatchers now swear that they will massacre his bones and cut off his right hand as well. This danger is at least partly imagined and used for its sensational effect, since the *Discovery* and the *Second part* were apparently published within a few days of each other.[19] Later Greene elaborates on the success of his attack on the cozeners and their threats of reprisal: "Tush, it was so easie for the Setter to take uppe a Connie before I discovered the cosenage that one stigmaticall shamelesse companion amongst the rest, would in a braverie were parsly in his hat, and said he wanted but Aqua vitae to take a Connie with but since he hath lookt on his feet, and valed his plumes with the Peacocke, and sweares by all the shooes in his shop, I shall be the next man hee meanes to kill, for spoyling of his occupation" (B3).

The work shows marks of haste in planning and subject matter. The general scheme Greene ostensibly had in mind was to present the practices of each law in turn and illustrate each with one or more tales, but he found his material intractable. He begins with a discourse on the methods of horse-stealing, illustrated with one tale. Next he "discovers" the vincent's law, but fails to provide an illustrative story. At this point he inserts the "Table of Laws," which presumably he had originally intended to follow his preface. After the table he breaks the scheme with an anecdote revealing (as indicated above) the new problems faced by the conycatchers now that the conies have been warned by the first book; and he further advertizes the virtue of his book in the accompany-

19. The Stationers' Register (Arber) lists under the date December 13, 1591: "Entred for their copie under the handes of master Hartwell and [blank] *The Arte of Connye katchinge* . . . vj[d] [Edward White and Thomas Nelson]" and "Entred for his copie to be printed alwayes for him by Iohn Wolf *The second parte of Connye katchinge* under th[e h]andes of master Hartwell And / [blank] . . . vj[d]." See Judges, p. 504.

ing story. This narrative is followed by a story relating how some conycatchers were themselves cozened through a stolen horse, a story that might better have served as a second illustration of the prigging law. A semblance of order is restored in the next section, with the discourse on the nature of nips and foists, with three tales. The discussion of the lifting law following these has no illustrations, but the discussions of the curbing law and the black art have two and one respectively.

The work is thus erratic in scheme, but the contents are on the whole more lively and pleasantly varied than those of the *Discovery*. Greene is specially interested in the foists and nips whose chief walks are "Paules, Westminster, the Exchaunge, Plaies, Beare garden, running at Tilt, the Lorde Maiors day, any festival meetings, fraies, shootings, or great faires":

> In Paules (especiallie in the tearme time) between ten and eleven, then is their howers, and there they walke, and perhaps, if there be great presse, strike a stroke in the middle walke, but that is upon some plaine man that stands gazing about, having never seene the Church before but their chiefest time is at divine service, when men devoutly given doe go up to heare either a sermon, or els the harmonie of the Queere and the Organes: there the Nip, and the Foist as devoutly as if he were som zealous parson standeth soberlie, with his eies elevated to heaven when his hand is either on the purse or in the pocket, surveing everie corner of it for coyne, then when the service is done and the people presse away, he thrusteth amidst the throng; and there worketh his villanie (C4^{v}).

Recently the magistrates have taken effective measures to deal with them. When purses of great value are stolen, the victims complain to the magistrates who authorize the keepers of Newgate to arrest all known pickpockets and oblige them as a group to make good the theft (a proceeding not overlooked by Dekker who has Moll Cutpurse in *The Roaring Girl* use similar means in restoring a purse).[20]

20. *The Dramatic Works of Thomas Dekker,* ed. Fredson Bowers (Cambridge, 1958), III, p. 89 (V.i.242–279).

Greene not only knows the secrets of these rascals, but also about their meetings. Like Harman's rogues who have their assemblies, these pickpockets have an order of their own and Greene knows where they meet (despite his avowed intimacy with knaves, he does not claim ever to have met with them at any of their festivities):

> . . . they have a kinde of corporation, as having wardens of their company, and a hall: I remember their Hall was once about Bishopsgate, neere unto fishers follie, but because it was a noted place, they have remooved it to Kent-street, and as far as I can learne, it is kept at one *Laurence Pickerings* house, one that hath bene if he be not still a notable Foist. A man of good calling he is, and well allied, brother in law to Bull the hangman, there keepe they their feasts and weekely meetinges, fit for their company (D2^{v})

Perhaps Greene never attended such a meeting because he could not: as he doubtless knew, such organizations and appointed meetings were largely fictive, based on suggestions in Harman and Gypsy lore and chance, not organized, gatherings of small groups of knaves.[21] No evidence has been produced to show that the rogues and knaves of the Renaissance period had anything like the elaborate organization of various rackets and vice-rings of the present century.

The Second part of Conny-catching was originally conceived as the last of Greene's conycatching pamphlets, but even as he wrote it, new possibilities for other works dealing with these knaves were occurring to him. In his tale of the horse that cozened a conycatcher, he tells his readers again that he has learned that the conycatchers plan revenge because of his discovery of their secrets, and that they have secured a scholar to write an invective against him (C3–C3^{v}):

> Marry the good men Conny-catchers, those base excrements of dishonesty, they in their huffes report they have got one (   ) I

21. See Harman, *Caveat,* chap. 24, "Their usage in the Night"; also see the elaborate efforts of Samuel Rid and Dekker to extend this fiction, pp. 53, 153 of this study.

> will not bewray his name, but a scholler they say he is, to make an invective against me, in that he is a favourer of those base reprobats; but let them, him, and all know, the proudest peasant of them all, dare not lift his plumes in disparagement of my credit, for if he doe, I will for revenge onely appoint the Iakes farmers of London, who shall case them in their filthy vesselles, and carrye them as dung to manure the barrain places of Tibourne, and so for Conny-catchers an end.

Greene thus preludes the coming publication of *The Defence of Conny-catching,* which was entered in the Stationers' Register on April 21, 1592.[22] If, as seems probable, he was the author of this pamphlet, the deception he practiced is perhaps his chief feat as a cozener, for he has led many scholars into accepting the work as an attack on him by an anonymous author.[23] In any event, it belongs with the other pamphlets as an exposure of knavish behavior.

Far from being an invective against Greene, the *Defence* is a testimony to the influence that his work has had in

22. B.M., C.40.b.6 (STC 5655): *The Defence of / Conny catching. / Or / A Confutation of those / two iniurious Pamphlets published by R. G. against / the practitioners of many Nimble-witted / and mysticall Sciences. / By Cuthbert Cunny-catcher, Licentiate in Whittington Colledge / Qui bene latuit bene vixit, dominatur enim / fraus in omnibus.* / [Cut of cony with buckler] / *Printed at London by A. I. for Thomas Gubbins / and are to be sold by John Busbie, 1592.* See *Robert Greene The Blacke Bookes Messenger 1592 / 'Cuthbert Conny catcher' The Defence of Conny-Catching, 1592,* ed. G. B. Harrison, Bodley Head Quartos, No. X (London, 1924).

23. Professor Harrison apparently believes that "Cuthbert Cunny-catcher" is an assumed name of an actual friend of the conycatchers (*Robert Greene . . . The Defence of Conny-catching,* pp. vi–vii). J. C. Jordan is inclined to believe that Greene himself is the author. On the other hand, McKerrow, in a review of Jordan's study (*MLR,* XI, 1916, 233–235) defends the traditional view: "In view . . . of the very definite charge made in it against Greene in connection with *Orlando Furioso,* it seems to me that the evidence is against Dr. Jordan's view. The charge, even if, as Dr. Jordan suggests, it is untrue, is at any rate a serious one, and it seems unlikely that Greene would make it in order merely to give an air of verisimilitude to the attack." Recently E. V. Miller has presented strong textual evidence that the *Defence* is by Greene (*N & Q,* Nov. 24, 1951, Oct. 11, 1952), though he sees Nashe as a possible collaborator ("The Relationship of Robert Greene and Thomas Nashe," *MP,* XXXIII, 1954, 353–367).

exposing conycatching and putting citizens on guard against its snares. In the introduction we are told that the anti-hero, Cuthbert Conny-catcher, "Licentiate in Whittington College" (Newgate),[24] and most proficient of all students in the "Foolosophie" of his art, has wandered all over the country happily practicing his mystery in cards, dice, and theft, but recently has been circumvented by two "peevish Pamphlets." It is no longer possible to fleece a cony, since even country farmers know Greene's books. This has determined him to challenge Greene and prove that whereas conycatchers that live by dice and cards are trivial offenders, other professions in England are the great conycatchers. In the *Defence* itself, Cuthbert admits that Greene has played the part of a good subject in anatomizing the secrets of the cozeners, but this is the Iron age in which all estates live by their wits: "Hee that cannot dissemble cannot live, and men put their sonnes now a dayes Apprentises, not to learne trades and occupations, but craftes and mysteries" (A4^v). Greene is straining at gnats and missing elephants. How about the fox-furred gentlemen who practice usury: why not write about them? And as Greene does in the earlier pamphlets, the author examines some of the devices used by usurers and "Mounser the Miller with the gilden thumbe," illustrating each type with stories.

But all professions, Cuthbert continues, are knavish: consider the butcher puffing up his meat to please the eye, the draper shadowing the dye of his cloth, the lawyers with

24. Though Whittington College was originally an alms-house endowed by the famous Dick Whittington (see *Sir Richard Whittington, Lord Mayor of London,* by Walter Besant and James Rice, London, 1894, p. 188), the name was used in Renaissance times as a euphemism for Newgate, which had been rebuilt in connection with provisions of Whittington's will. Greene uses the term probably in this sense in *The Thirde and last Part of Conny-catching* (see intro., p. 1), S. R. (Samuel Rowlands?) warns those sucking poison out of his *Greenes Ghost-haunting Conie-Catchers* (1602) lest they become bachelors in Whittington College. Samuel Rid defines "Whittington" as "Newgate" in his canting dictionary in *Martin Mark-All* (1610). Dekker also in his *Belman of London* (1608) makes the identification (see the end of the section on figging law).

their quiddities, the gentlemen-travellers who boast of their experiences abroad but who have never travelled a foot out of England, the "crew of terrible Hacksters in the habite of Gentlemen" who prey on ale-houses (like Awdeley's courtesy-men), amorous men in general, and tailors with their enormities of fashion. Men who counterfeited epilepsy or wore bloody plasters were not what they seemed; but even well-dressed gentlemen might prove frauds, and worse still, men in honorable professions might employ the devices of learning and religion to cheat those who trusted them.

Most noteworthy of all these accusations is the one against Greene himself: "Aske the Queens Players, if you sold them not *Orlando Furioso* / for twenty Nobles, and when they were in the country, sold the same Play to the Lord Admirals men for as much more. Was not this plaine *Conny-catching* Maister R.G.?" (C3–C3v). Greene's only possible excuse for this knavery, namely that players measure honesty by gain, is the same one, Cuthbert says, that conycatchers use in fleecing their farmers, whom they strip of their gains secured by robbing or cheating the poor. This accusation has been accepted as perhaps the strongest proof that Greene did not write the *Defence,* on the ground that it is unlikely that Greene would make so serious an accusation against himself simply for the sake of verisimilitude. On the other hand, the charge was probably current, and its use here would help to mislead readers who but for its presence might have suspected Greene to be the author.

But while the attention of this author (whether Greene or another) is thus drawn to conycatching in the trades and the professions, Greene continues to be primarily interested in the genuine city knaves, those who, as he says in the Epistle to *The Thirde and last Part of Conny-catching* (1592), (see Plate 12),[25] "beare outward shew of civill, honest, and gentle-

25. Bodl., Malone 575 (STC 12283): *The / Thirde / and last Part of Conny- / catching. / With the New Devised / knavish Art of Foole-taking. / The like Cosenages and Villenies never before / discovered. / By R. G. /* [Cut of cross-

THE

THIRDE

and last Part of Conny-
catching.

WITH THE NEW DEVISED
knauish Art of Foole-taking.

*The like Cosenages and Villenies neuer before
discouered.*

By R. G.

Imprinted at London by *Thomas Scarlet* for
Cutberd Burbie, and are to be solde at his shoppe in the
Poultrie, by S. Mildreds Church. 1592.

Not in Ames's H. of Printing –

PLATE 12. *The Third and last Part of Conny-catching.* Title page. Malone 575, Bodleian Library.

manlike disposition, but in very deed their behaviour is most infamous to be spoken of. And as now by their close villanies they cheate, cozen, prig, lift, nippe, and suche like tricks now used in their *Conie-catching* Trade, to the hurt and undoing of many an honest Citizen, and other: So if God should in iustice be angrie with us . . . and (as the Lord forfend) our peace should be molested as in former time, even as they did, so will these be the first in seeking domesticall spoile and ruine . . ." ($A3^v$).

In his first two works on conycatchers, Greene had disclosed all that he had learned from earlier rogue and knave pamphlets and from his own observation about the various devices and tricks of the cozeners. In the *Thirde and last Part* he contents himself with telling more tales about their practices. For his stories this time, he tells us, he has had recourse, not as in the past, to his own professed experience, but to that of an aged gentleman of grave speech. This gentleman, whom he met at a supper where the conversation dealt with the villainies of the world in general and conycatching in particular, admitted that Greene's books had informed him of many things, but he himself as a commissioner of the peace had learnt through observation and report of others much information which he would gladly have given to the author had he known him. This is doubtless another of Greene's fictions; and the gentleman commissioner of the peace is most likely the shade of Harman. Within a fortnight the gentleman sent him his notes, out of which he has compiled the nine stories of this pamphlet.

These stories, though the reader's attention lags because of the repetition of similar devices by faceless characters,

---

biter and courtesan holding a skinned cony] / *Imprinted at London by Thomas Scarlet for / Cutberd Burbie, and are to be solde at his shoppe in the / Poultrie, by S. Mildreds Church. 1592.* See *Robert Greene M.A. / The Thirde & Last Part of Conny-catching / A Disputation Between a Hee Conny-catcher and a Shee Conny-catcher,* ed. G. B. Harrison, Bodley Head Quartos, No. III (London, 1923).

are hardly less ingenious than those of the earlier pamphlets. Of curious interest both for itself and as the apparent begetter of a notable series of scenes in Renaissance drama is the tale of the cozening ballad-singers, who charm their audience while their fellows pick their purses.

Autolycus was a more clever knave than these "Fooltakers"[26] and consequently gets away with the purses himself while singing his ballads; but Greene's narrative could serve with slight changes as a stage direction for the famous scene (recently praised by Edmund Wilson) in *Bartholomew Fair* where the foolish gull, Bartholomew Cokes, has his purse cut while Nightingale, the ballad singer, sings his song against cutpurses and his "secretary" Zekiel pursues his craft. And one is also reminded of the similar incident in Jonson's *Metamorphosed Gypsies* in which a mass purse-stealing occurs.[27]

Even with *The Thirde and last Part of Conny-catching* Greene had by no means mined all his ore. There were other possible approaches, and two other works, *A Disputation Betweene a Hee Conny-catcher, and a Shee Conny-catcher* (1592)[28] and *The Blacke Bookes Messenger* (1592) exploited the material in new ways that promised an indefinite continuance of pamphlets on the subject if death had not ended the series.

The *Disputation*, the liveliest and most entertaining of all the group, falls into two parts, the *Disputation* itself and

26. This new "art of fool-taking" obviously has some connection with the "Foolosophie" of the *Defence* (and of course Barclay) and suggests again that Greene may have been the author of the *Defence*.

27. See pp. 244, 282 of this study for the uses of this material by Shakespeare and Jonson.

28. Bodl., Malone 574 (STC 12234): *A Disputation, / Betweene a Hee Conny-catcher, and a / Shee Conny-catcher, whether a Theefe or a Whoore, is / most hurtfull in Cousonage, to the Com- / mon-wealth. / Discovering the Secret / Villa- / nies of alluring Strumpets. / With the Conversion of an English Courtizen, reformed / this present yeare, 1592. / Reade, laugh, and learne. / Nascimur pro patria. / R. G. /* [Cut of a female and a male conycatcher in debate] */Imprinted at London, by A. I. for T. G. and are to be solde at / the West ende of Paules. 1592.* See also Note 25.

a separate account of the conversion of a courtesan.[29] In the conventional form of a debate, the *Disputation* presents a dialogue between Lawrence, a foist, and Nan, a courtesan, on the subject whether a harlot or a thief is more injurious to the public welfare. Despite some ambiguity, Lawrence, the anti-hero, appears to be Lawrence Pickering, whom Greene has introduced to us earlier as a famous pickpocket, brother-in-law to Bull the hangman, though nothing is known to confirm Greene's story that he actually existed. Fair Nan is identified only as a courtesan with a thief and pickpocket for a husband. The debate is an exemplification of the timeless theme that the wiles of women exceed the wit of men. At first Lawrence offers some opposition, marked by a masculine patronizing tone, but he is speedily subdued not only by the overwhelming force of Nan's stories, but by the torrent of her speech (her part in the dispute takes approximately twenty-four of the thirty-five pages). With her vivacity and wit, Nan, who comes in treading daintily on her tiptoes, almost emerges as a living character. As it is, she is a good addition to the gallery of portraits of autem-morts and doxies. The illustrative stories (one by Lawrence, three by Nan) match the quality of the tales of the earlier pamphlets, but the interest lies principally in the debate and the manner of the irrepressible flow of Nan's revelations.

At the end of the *Disputation,* Greene gives his readers a further account of his personal relationship to the knave world of London. Mistress Nan and others have vowed his death, and recently a crew of them have attacked him at supper (C4^{v}–D):

> . . . mistresse Nan . . . hath sworne to weare a long Hamborough knife to stabbe mee, and all the crue have protested my death, and to proove they ment good earnest, they belegard me about in the

29. This part, "The Conversion of an English Courtizen" comes to the expected yet surprising climax of the progression from dark to darker rooms which effects the conversion. McKerrow has pointed out that Greene is retailing a story from Erasmus's *Colloquia* (*MLR,* XI [1916], 235); but Greene has richly expanded the story.

> Saint Iohns head within Ludgate beeing at supper, there were some fourteene or fifteene of them met, and thought to have made that the fatall night of my overthrowe, but that the courteous Cittizens and Apprentises tooke my part, and so two or three of them were carryed to the Counter, although a Gentleman in my company was sore hurt.

The number of these rascals is diminishing, however, since the publishing of his book, and he now plans to give them the *coup de grace* in another pamphlet, with a new set of "laws," and more important still, the names of all such knaves in London (D):

> I cannot deny but they beginne to waste away about London, and Tyborne (since the setting out of my booke) hath eaten up many of them, and I will plague them to the extreamitie, let them doe what they dare with their bilbowe blades, I feare them not: and to give them their last adue, look shortly Countrimen for a Phamphlet against them, called *The blacke Booke,* containing foure new Lawes never spoken of yet, *The creeping Law* of petty-theeves, that rob about the Suburbes. *The lymitting Lawe,* discoursing the orders of such as follow Iudges, in their circuites, and goe about from Fayre to Fayre. *The Iugging Law,* wherein I will set out the disorders at Nyneholes and Ryfling, how they are onely for the benefite of the Cutpurses. *The stripping Lawe,* wherein I will lay open the lewde abuses of sundry Iaylors in England. Beside, you shall see there what houses there bee about the Suburbes and townes ende, that are receyvers of Cut purses stolne goods, Lifts, and such like. And lastly, looke for a Bed-roll or Catalogue of all the names of the Foystes, Nyps, Lifts, and Priggars, in and about London: and although some say, I dare not doe it, yet I will shortly set it abroach, and whosoever I name or touch, if hee thinks himselfe greeved, I will aunswere him before the Honourable privie Counsayle.

These claims seem real enough: several courtesans in London might have been insulted by the story of Nan, and Greene's life might well have been in danger from the conycatchers, who were not merely creatures of fiction. Moreover, the idea of publishing a list (to match Harman's earlier list of vagabonds) of well-known conycatchers, at least all that were known to him or that he might learn about by consulting the keepers of the hospitals and prisons, might have occurred to him as a profitable enterprise both for himself and for the common good. That he may have compiled such a work in part is quite possible, but his intentions of completing it and publishing it were not to be fulfilled, and the world thus lost what might have been a very curious and exciting document.[30]

Some time before his fatal banquet, Greene had planned the last of his conycatching pamphlets, a work originally entered in the Stationers' Register on August 21, 1592 as *The Repentance of a Cony catcher / with the life and death of* [ ] *MOURTON AND NED BROWNE, twoo notable cony catchers / The one latelie executed at Tyborne the other at Aix in Ffraunce.*[31] But at the last moment Greene altered his intention and omitted the story of Mourton, and the work appeared as *The / Blacke Bookes / Messenger. / Laying open the Life and Death / of Ned Browne . . .* (London, 1592).[32] In his address "To the Curteous Reader," Greene

30. G. B. Harrison believes that the book existed: "There can be little doubt that the real *Blacke Booke* was actually written, as Chettle, who was likely to know the truth about Greene's affairs, in his *Kind-Harts Dreame* makes 'Greene's Ghost' remark: 'For my Bookes of what kind soever, I refer their commendation or dispraise to those that have read them. Onely for my last labours [*i.e.,* the conycatching pamphlets] affirming, my intent was to reprove vice, and lay open such villanies, as had been very necessary to be made knowne, whereof my *Blacke Booke* if it ever see light, can sufficiently witnesse.'

"But the Conny-catchers had the last word, and the manuscript of the *Blacke Booke* disappeared" (*The Blacke Bookes Messenger 1592,* etc., Bodley Head Quartos, No. X, London and N. Y., 1924, p. viii.).

31. *Transcript of the Stationers' Registers,* E. A. Arber, II, 292. Harrison, *The Blacke Bookes Messenger,* p. vii.

32. Bodl., Malone 575 (STC 12223): *The / Blacke Bookes / Messenger. / Laying open the Life and Death / of Ned Browne one of the most notable Cutpurses. / Crosbiters, and Conny-catchers, that / ever lived in England. / Heerein hee telleth verie plea- / santly in his owne person such strange pranks and / monstrous villanies by him and his Consorte / performed, as the like was yet never / heard of in any of the former / bookes of Conny- / catching. / Read and be warnd, / Laugh as you like, / Judge as you find. / Nascimur pro Patria. / by R. G.* [Printer's device] / *Printed at London by John Danter, for Thomas / Nelson dwelling in Silver streete, neere to the / signe of the Red-Crosse. 1592.* See also Note 30.

observes that he would have completed his *Blacke Booke* had he not fallen ill; it will be the first thing he will publish on his recovery. Meanwhile he sends them this Messenger to his *Blacke Booke,* "a Fayring, discoursing *Ned Brownes* villanies, which are too many to bee described in [his] *Blacke Booke.*" He explains that he has omitted "The Repentance of a Conny-catcher" because of its difference in character from the story of Ned Browne. The explanation is not convincing; it seems probable that Greene omitted the Mourton story for the sake of the profit of its separate sale or that, as with the *Blacke Booke,* he had only conceived, not written it.

That the basic story of Ned Browne, stripped of accretions that it gathered in Greene's fancy, was that of an actual rogue and cutpurse may well be true; that the confession of Browne is Greene's fiction seems self-evident. Ned Browne is a sophisticated rogue, a conycatcher version of Copland's and Harman's soldier rogues:

> Hee was in outward shew a Gentlemanlike companion attyred very brave, and to shadowe his villany the more would nominate himselfe to be a Marshall man, who when he had nipt a Bung or cut a good purse, he would steale over in to the Lowe Countries, there to tast three or foure stoapes of Rhenish wine, and then come over forsooth a brave Souldier: But at last hee leapt at a daysie for his loose kind of life, and therefore imagine you now see him in his owne persone, standing in a great bay windowe with a halter about his necke ready to be hanged, desperately pronounsing this his whole course of life and confesseth as followeth (A3v).

The confession, thus vividly advertized, is unhappily disappointing. For all Greene's avowed experience with the lowest elements of the underworld, Browne has no new revelations to make and only a few not too new stories to tell. But there are some touches that give promise of new material: Browne becomes a high Lawyer or highway man, riding freebooted in the country "like a Cavalier on horsebacke." On such a ride into Berkshire ("A merrie tale how Ned Browne used a Priest"), he subtly tricks a priest out of twenty nobles and his capcase stuffed with crowns for purchasing land. This clever thief on horseback affords a prototype for the exploits of Gamaliel Ratsey, the most celebrated of thieves in the decade following.[33] At the end, we learn that Browne had grown odious in London for his filching, foisting, and crossbiting, and that, going over to France as a soldier, he had robbed a church and was consequently hanged, as Bardolph was to be in Shakespeare's world for stealing a pax.

II

The possibilities that Greene's experimentation had introduced were immense, and if he had lived a few years longer he probably would have composed numerous I-confess pamphlets based on the experiences of knaves and other rascals easily available at the hospitals and prisons or to be had for a penny from the lips and imaginations of passing conycatchers and doxies. Others were quick to perceive these possibilities, and a series of conycatching pamphlets began to appear, several in direct imitation of Greene, though often making use of earlier writers as well. The most important of these in continuing the tradition are Henry Chettle's *Kind-Harts Dreame* (1592),[34] *Greenes Ghost Haunting Conie-*

33. Bodl., Malone 651(3) (STC 20753): No title page; sig. A2 heading: "The / Life and Death of Gamaliell Ratsey, a famous theefe of Eng- / land, executed at Bedford the 26. / of March last past, 1605." See also STC 20753a: *Ratseis ghost or the Second part of his madde prankes. V.S.*[ims], 1605. M [Rylands Library]. The latter work has been reprinted in the John Rylands Facsimiles, No. 5, Manchester Univ. Press, and reviewed, with attention to the figure in general, in "Ratsey and his Ghost," *TLS.*, March 16, 1933.

34. B.M., C.14.a.6 (STC 5123): *Kind-Harts / Dreame. / Conteining five Apparitions, with their / Invectives against abuses raigning. / Delivered by severall Ghosts unto him to / be publisht, after Piers Peniless Post / had refused the carriage. / Invicta Invidia. / by H. C. /* [Ornament] */ Imprinted at London by William Wright.* This pamphlet, published about three months after Greene's death, presents five apparitions, including the ballad singer Anthony Now-Now (identified by Mrs. Celeste T. Wright ["Munday and Chettle in Grub street," *Boston Univ. Stud. in English,* V (1961), 134–135] as Anthony Munday), the jester Richard Tarleton, the physician Dr. Burcot, William Cuckoe the juggler, and Robert Greene himself, "a man of indifferent yeares, of face

Catchers (1602)[35] by S. R. (probably Samuel Rowlands), *Martin Mark-All, Beadle of Bridewell* (1608)[36] by S. R. (apparently Samuel Rid), and Thomas Dekker's *Belman of London* (1608), with its revised editions, including the variant edition entitled *O per se O* (1612). *Martin Mark-All* and the pam-

amiable, of body well proportioned, his attire after the habite of a schollerlike Gentleman, onely his haire was somewhat long." The apparition of Greene is primarily interesting for his apologia for Greene's works (he emphasizes the moral intention of his conycatching pamphlets). But the other apparitions are mainly concerned with knavish abuses of their callings. Anthony Now-Now attacks idle youths singing wanton ballads. Dr. Burcot inveighs against cozeners in medicine, citing as one example, the misleading of a tin-melter's wife, who "to breake her husbandes colde, when he sate sleeping in his chaire, videlicet two ounces of pure Tinne put in an iron ladle, melted in the fire, and poured at an instant downe the throat" (p. 29). Richard Tarleton satirizes those who abuse plays and players, showing how bawds resent the exposure of their practices. But a richer document in knavery is William Cuckoe's exposure of the devices of jugglery, including several illustrations as vivid as Greene's best stories. Chettle is drawing upon a special art of cozening law: the tradition of the juggler as a deceiver is as old as the art itself. One of the first literary examples in English is *Jack Juggler* (perhaps by N. Udall); Samuel Rid's *Art of Juggling* (though largely plagiarized from Reginald Scot and *A manifest detection* as Aydelotte demonstrates) best represents the cozening tricks of the craft.

Interesting also in the history of cozening is Chettle's pamphlet, *Piers Plainness: Seven Years Prenticeship,* in which Piers, a shepherd of Thessaly, becomes in turn an apprentice of an upstart courtier, a broker, a usurer, and a customs officer, learning knavish tricks from them all. The main design of the work is obviously borrowed from *Lazarillo de Tormes,* but the material on knavery closely follows the conycatching tradition.

35. B.M., C.40.d.40 (STC 12243): *Greenes Ghost / Haunting Conie- / Catchers. / Wherein is set downe, / The Arte of Humouring. / The Arte of Carrying Stones. / Will. St. Lift. / Ia. Fost. Law. / Ned Bro. Catch. and / Blacke Robins Kindnesse. / With the conceits of Doctor Pinch-backe a / notable Makeshift. / Ten times more pleasant then any thing yet / published of this matter. / Non ad imitandum, sed evitandum. /* [Device] */ London, / Printed for R. Jackson, and I. North, / and are to be solde in Fletestreete, / a little above the Conduit. / 1602.* Edward D. MacDonald ("An Example of Plagiarism among Elizabethan Pamphleteers," *Indiana Univ. Stud.,* 1911) shows that S. R. (Samuel Rowlands) borrows heavily from Greene (most of the pamphlet), the *Defence of Conny-catching,* Lodge's *Wits Miserie,* Nashe's *Summers last will,* and other sources.

36. See p. 150 of this book.

phlets by Dekker, unifying the materials of Harman, Greene, and others will be considered in the following chapter.

One other pamphlet, the inventive though often scurrilous *Greenes Newes both from Heaven and Hell* (1593)[37] by B. R. (Barnabe Rich) deserves brief attention for its attempts to describe the fortunes of Greene in the other world. Rejected by St. Peter because of his partiality in exposing only the petty conycatchers rather than the fox-furred knave-gentlemen (as in the *Defence*), Greene is finally rejected also by Lucifer because of the protests lodged against him by the conycatchers. He is thrust out of hell gates and doomed to wander the world as a restless walking spirit. He warns his friends to beware in their night walks, for he will be the maddest Goblin ever abroad in the Moonshine. Sometimes he will be a spirit of the Buttery and mislead those who frequent his haunts so that they will mistake their way to bed. Sometimes he will be Robin Goodfellow and frighten wanton wenches in dark corners, and sometimes show dreams and visions to women as they sleep that will induce them to cuckold their husbands when awake. Sometimes he will transform himself into divers shapes and walk through all occupations, always bent on mischief.[38] This goblin is much more wanton and malicious than his cousin in *Midsummer Night's Dream*, but his love for mischief is the same, and it is interesting to note this formulation of the behavior of this character a year before the probable date of Shakespeare's creation of his

37. B.M., C.40.d.39 (STC 12259): *Greenes / Newes both from / Heaven and Hell. / Prohibited the first for writing of / Bookes, and banished out of the last for / displaying of conny- / catchers. / Commended to the Presse / By B. R.* / [Ornament] / *At London, / Printed, Anno. Domini. / 1593.*

38. Sig. H2–H3. See also E4: '(and I thinke there is no corner betweene thys and Hell that I have lefte unsearched: and were it not for thys holy Candle, whose vertue is able to defende me from the inchauntment of anie spirit or devill, I would thinke I were *Goblyn* lead, I have wandered so farre aboute . . ." The tortuous wanderings of the man with the candle and the horned miller in the dim regions between Heaven and Hell have a dream-quality not unlike that of the maze in which the lovers are lost in *Midsummer Night's Dream*, but the basic image is archetypal, a part of every man's dreams.

more personable sprite and to fancy that there may be a faint touch of Robin Greene in his Robin Goodfellow.[39]

But more important than all these pamphlets imitating Greene or influenced by him is the continuing even if shadowy influence of Greene's conycatchers as seen in the works of Jonson and Shakespeare. Though, as has been remarked earlier, Jonson was an observer of knavery himself, one must believe that his crafty cozeners Brainworm, Face and Subtle, Volpone and Mosca, are somehow related to and descended from Greene's conycatchers. As for the works of the "upstart crowe beautified with our feathers," in addition to their borrowings of source materials, they too owe a debt to Greene not easily analyzable but felt from time to time. The greatest of human cozeners, Iago, with his simple gull Roderigo and his power to cozen even the wisest, is far beyond the imagination of Greene, but Greene's cozeners are still part of his lineage. Sir John Falstaff's cozening of Shallow and his exploits in *The Merry Wives* also owe something to this lore.[40] More easily tied down, as will be seen,[41] is Shakespeare's debt to Greene for the basic conception of his Autolycus, even though Shakespeare as usual soars away with his borrowed plumage when the larger figure of his creation is contemplated.

39. Shakespeare doubtless derived his ideas about Robin Goodfellow from many sources, of which several have been listed in the *Variorum* and Arden editions and other works. This use in Rich's work, which appears somewhat closer to Shakespeare in its massing of ideas than those remarked thus far, may have been suggestive to him.
40. See p. 185.
41. See pp. 240, 244.

IV

Thomas Dekker, Bellman of London, and his Tradition

OF ALL ELIZABETHAN and Jacobean authors, Thomas Dekker, who was bailed out of the Counter in the Poultry by Henslowe and who spent almost seven years in King's Bench prison,[1] would appear to have had the best opportunity to become intimately acquainted with rogues and knaves, but his several rogue books and his plays all indicate that his literary sources were yet more instructive to him than his own observation of rogue ways. Though he embellishes the patterns afforded him by Copland, Harman, and Greene, he is clearly using their designs and materials, and, in part, his additions appear pure invention. This fact is not altogether surprising, since his imprisonment was presumably for debt, and in prison he probably spent most of his time in the company of other indigents, not necessarily knaves or rascals.

I

Though we might expect more actual observation of rogue life from Dekker than his several treatments of the subject afford us, these treatments, beginning with his plays and continuing in his essays, are more numerous and varied than those of any other writer, and they offer a lively social com-

1. W. W. Greg, *Henslowe's Diary* (London, 1904), I, 83; Mary Leland Hunt, *Thomas Dekker, A Study* (New York, 1911), pp. 79–80, 165–167.

mentary on the rogues and unthrifts of his time. Of his plays, *The Honest Whore, Parts I* and *II,* present, as we have seen, striking examples of the rogue tradition;[2] and the plots of *Westward Ho* and *Northward Ho,* written in collaboration with Webster, extensively employ the devices of cozening. Justiniano neatly sums up the action of *Westward Ho* when he exclaims: "Am not I (gentlemen) a Ferret of the right haire, that can make three Conies bolt at a clap into your pursenets? ha? little do their three husbands dreame what coppies I am setting their wives now? . . ." (II.iii.34–38).[3] Hardly less knavish are the intrigues devised in *Northward* Ho by Greenshield and Fetherstone in deluding Mayberry, as well as the devices used by Mayberry in overwhelming retaliation. In such society gentlemen may well beware gentlemen: "The world's a stage from which strange shapes we borrow: / Today we are honest, and ranke knaves tomorrow" (I.ii.101–102). These are knave-citizens, and good citizens playing the parts of knaves; but the *bonae robae* who assist them in their intrigues, Birdlime and Doll Hornet, are relations of the creatures of Harman and Greene, though more vivid, creatures of blood and bone. The devils of *If This Be Not A Good Play, The Devil Is In It,* Rufman, Shacklesoule, and Lurchall, though disguised respectively as a courtier, a friar, and a merchant, also practice their deceptions like cozening rogues.

More specially important in the tradition of knavery is *The Roaring Girl* (1612) (see Plate 13), written in collaboration with Middleton. In view of Dekker's greater knowledge of rogue literature, Fleay and Professor Bowers are almost surely right in assigning a substantial part of the play to Dekker;[4] certainly the canting and cutpurse scenes are Dekker's and very likely the whole concept of Moll and her activities is

2. See p. 83 of this book.
3. *The Dramatic Works of Thomas Dekker,* ed. Fredson Bowers (Cambridge, 1958), III, 346. My quotations from the plays of Dekker are from this text.
4. Bowers, III, 8.

The Roaring Girle.

OR

Moll Cut-Purse.

As it hath lately beene Acted on the Fortune-stage by *the Prince his Players.*

Written by *T. Middleton* and *T. Dekkar.*

Printed at *London* for *Thomas Archer*, and are to be sold at his shop in Popes head-pallace, neere the Royall Exchange. 1611.

PLATE 13. *The Roaring Girl.* Title page. Ashley 1159, British Museum.

his contribution. In his portrait of the "wench / Cal'd *Mol*, mad *Mol* or merry *Moll*," Dekker is supposedly sketching the activities of a real doxy of the time, Mrs. Mary Frith, a creature no less celebrated than the well-known Long Meg of Westminster, whose life and pranks and idealized feminine knight-errantry appear to have been his principal source of inspiration.[5] As the title of the play implies, Moll belongs to a special classification of roguery, that of the roaring girl, the female counterpart of the roaring boy.[6] In the prologue the author tells us that there are many of this type: one such creature "roares at midnight in deepe Taverne bowles, / That beates the watch, and Constables controuls," and another roars in the daytime but sells her soul to lust. These two are Suburb-roarers. There are also City-roarers who consume their husbands' estates with pride and feasting and leave their husbands roaring behind prison bars. But Moll flies with more lofty wings.

The thin romantic main plot is devised primarily to permit Moll to strut the stage in male attire, exposing the ways

5. Hunt, p. 110. The legend of this Mrs. Frith is presented in (B.M., 1079.b.11) *The Life and Death of Mrs. Mary Frith, Commonly called Mal Cutpurse. Exactly collected and now Published for the delight and recreation of all Merry disposed persons* (London, 1662). Meg of Westminster was the heroine of a play bearing her name in 1594 (Henslowe [*Diary*, ed. Greg, I, 21] lists "long mege of westmester" as of February 14, 1594). Jonson employs her in *Fortunate Isles*. Her activities are depicted in a pamphlet, B.M., C.44.b., (STC 17782) *The / Life and Prankes / of / Long Meg / of Westminster / Imprinted / at London for Abra- / ham Veale, dwellinge in / Paris Church yearde at / the signe of the Lambe*. The colophon gives the date 1582. In fashioning his Moll Cutpurse, Dekker seems to have been more inspired by Long Meg than by Moll herself, as will be seen by a comparison of Meg's behavior toward a soldier whom she fights in Tuttle-fields and Moll's duel with Laxton in Gray's Inn Fields (Act III.i), as well as other incidents.

6. This type of rogue is described at great length by Samuel Rowlands in *A Pair of Spy-Knaves*, "A Roaring Boyes Description," as a complete rogue, one that abounds in all villainies, spending his days and nights in idleness, drink, and play, a blasphemer, consort of thieves and cozeners, panderers, cutpurses, and robbers, a fantastic in styles with a nitty love-lock. Falstaff's roarings at Gadshill and Pistol's rantings, along with the actual existence of such creatures, probably helped in the naming of the type.

of rogues and exhibiting her own marked nobility of character, her heart of gold. And thick and fast the themes and images of roguery begin to take shape, with the notable picture and the flower below it in Sir Alexander Wengrave's gallery serving as a symbol of the action and the story:

> Nay when you looke into my galleries,
> How bravely they are trim'd up, you all shall sweare
> Y' are highly pleased to see whats set downe there:
> Stories of men and women (mixt together
> Faire ones with foule, like sun-shine in wet wether)
> Within one square a thousand heads are laid
> So close, that all of heads, the roome seemes made,
> As many faces there (fill'd with blith lookes)
> Shew like the promising titles of new bookes,
> (Writ merily) the Readers being their owne eyes,
> Which seeme to move and to give plaudities,
> And here and there (whilst with obsequious eares,
> Throng'd heapes do listen) a cut purse thrusts and leeres
> With haukes eyes for his prey: I need not shew him,
> By a hanging villanous looke, your selves may know him,
> The face is drawne so rarely. Then sir below,
> The very flowre (as twere) waves to and fro,
> And like a floating Iland, seemes to move
> Upon a sea bound in with shores above.
>
> (I.ii.14–32)

But after this touch of art, the effects of the rogue allusions are more prosaic. The gist of the main plot can be reduced to a sentence: Sir Alexander's son, Sebastian, in order to win his poor but beautiful love, Mary Fitz-Allard, as his wife, teases his father into submission to his wishes by pretending to woo Moll Cutpurse. Sir Alexander attempts to foil his son's apparent purpose by enlisting the aid of Ralph Trapdore, a conventional example of a rogue, who promises to ensnare Moll and boasts in an equivocal sentence, "A Roaring Boy, the Roaring Girle puts downe" (I.ii.251).

After Moll has put down several swaggerers, including Master Laxton, a would-be seducer, and Trapdore himself, she takes part in an elaborate exposure of knavery, almost certainly of Dekker's composition, based as it apparently is on his rogue pamphlets. Trapdore enters, in a familiar rogue disguise, "like a poore Souldier with a patch o're one eie, and Teare-Cat with him, all tatters" (V.i.56). The two rogues tell Moll and her friends a tale, familiar in its pattern, that they have been wounded in Hungary against the Turk, taken prisoner in the Venetian galleys, and wandered begging all over Italy. Teare-Cat is Dekker's necessary Dutchman, and is a ruffler accompanying the upright man, Trapdore. Both qualify as whipjacks, as Moll points out (V.i.120–144):

> A meare whip-Iacke, and that is in the Commonwealth of rogues, a slave, that can talke of sea-fight, name all your chiefe Pirats, discover more countries to you, then either the Dutch, Spanish, French, or English ever found out, yet indeed all his service is by land, and that is to rob a Faire, or some such venturous exploit: *Teare-Cat,* foot sirra I have your name now I remember me in my book of horners, hornes for the thumbe, you know how.
>
> *T. Cat.* No indeed Captaine *Moll* (for I know you by sight) I am no such nipping Christian, but a maunderer on the pad I confesse, and meeting with honest *Trapdore* here, whom you had cashierd from bearing armes, out at elbowes under your colours, I instructed him in the rudements of roguery, and by my map made him saile over any Country you can name, so that now he can maunder better then my selfe.
>
> *Iac. Dap.* So then *Trapdore* thou art turn'd souldier now.
>
> *Trap.* Alas sir, now there's no warres, 'tis the safest course of life I could take.
>
> *Moll.* I hope then you can cant, for by your cudgels, you sirra are an upright man.
>
> *Trap.* As any that walkes the hygh way I assure you.
>
> *Moll.* And *Teare-Cat* what are you? a wilde rogue, an angler, or a ruffler?
>
> *T. Cat.* Brother to this upright man, flesh and bloud, ruffling *Teare-Cat* is my name, and a ruffler is my stile, my title, my profession.

This incident is a dramatization in effect of details from Harman's *Caveat* through the medium of the *Belman of Lon-*

don. Moll and Trapdore indulge in a canting conversation with terms borrowed from the rogue pamphlets, ending with a canting song. After the rogues have been dismissed, a gallant cutpurse enters, and Moll obliges him to return a stolen purse,[7] an action which enables her to justify herself as an observer, not an agent of that craft:

> I must confesse,
> In younger dayes, when I was apt to stray,
> I have sat amongst such adders; seene their stings,
> As any here might, and in full play-houses
> Watcht their quicke-diving hands, to bring to shame
> Such rogues, and in that streame met an ill name:
> When next my Lord you spie any of those
> So hee bee in his Art a scholler, question him,
> Tempt him with gold to open the large booke
> Of his close villanies: and you your selfe shall cant
> Better than poore *Mol* can, and know more lawes
> Of cheaters, lifters, nips, foysts, puggards, curbers,
> With all the divels blacke guard, then it is fit
> Should be discovered to a noble wit.
> I know they have their orders, offices,
> Circuits and circles, unto which they are bound,
> To raise their own damnation in.
>
> (V.i.285–301)

Moll is no cutpurse, but a friend of law and order, a female knight-errant like Long Meg, and the proper person to resolve the hero's difficulties by helping him in his plot to convert his father.

II

As Dekker experimented with his knaves in his plays, it must have occurred to him often that a new version of the earlier pamphlets on rogues and cozeners might afford one way of meeting his debts and making a living. In *The Won-*

7. V.i.242–278. This action is reminiscent of the practice of the keepers of Newgate who required cutpurses as a group to make good particular thefts (Greene, *The Second and last part of Conny-catching,* "A Discourse . . . Laying open the Nature of the Cutpurse and Pickpocket," Harrison, p. 36).

derfull yeare. 1603, the picture of one notable rogue gives a foretaste of what is to come. Dekker here tells of a tinker who was "none of those base rascally Tinkers, that with a ban-dog and a drab at their tayles, and a pike-staffe on their necks, will take a purse sooner then stop a kettle: No, this was a devout Tinker, he did honor God Pan: a Musicall Tinker, that upon his kettle-drum could play any Country dance you cald for, and upon Holly-dayes had earned money by it, when no Fidler could be heard of."[8] This Tinker is employed by the host of a country inn to dispose of a Londoner dead of the plague, and in doing so, boldly strips the body to save its clothes and to take its purse of seven pounds, buries the body, and returns to the frightened village singing out: "Have yee any more Londoners to bury, hey downe a downe dery, have ye any more Londoners to bury . . ." And in *Iests to make you Merrie* (1607)[9] Dekker, if it may be assumed that this portion of the work is largely his, makes possibly his first essay at warning London and England about the dangers from knaves, thieves, and conycatchers, but the work is limited in scope, the hasty work of a journeyman in the subject. In the following year, however, he published the first of an ambitious series of pamphlets, less original than Greene's, but in their own right entertaining contributions to the literature of roguery.

Like Luther, Harman, and Greene before him, Dekker

8. B.M., E.1940(3) (STC 6534): *The / Wonderfull yeare. / 1603. / Wherein is shewed the picture of London, ly- / ing sicke of the Plague. / At the end of all (like a merry Epilogue to a dull Play) cer- / taine Tales are cut out in sundry fashions, of purpose / to shorten the lives of long winter nights, / that lye watching in the darke for us. / Et me rigidi legant Catones. /* [Ornament] / *London / Printed by Thomas Creede, and are to be solde / in Saint Donstones Church-Yarde / in Fleete-streete.* See sig. F2v.

9. *Iests to make you Merrie: With / the Coniuring up of Cock Watt, (the / walking Spirit of Newgate). To tell Tales. / . . . Written by T. D. and George Wilkins. / London 1607.* It is debatable whether this material is Dekker's since it makes use of terms that are not encountered later in his rogue literature (and it is obvious that Dekker reprints his rogue material as often as possible).

makes much of his service to the state in revealing the mischief of his knaves. The title-page of his pamphlet (see Plate 14), like those of Greene, advertizes this service: *The Belman / of London. / Bringing to light the most notorious / villanies that are now practised / in the Kingdome. / Profitable for Gentlemen, Lawyers, Merchants, Citizens, Farmers, / Masters of Housholds, and all sortes of servants, to marke, / and delightfull for all men to Reade. / Lege, Perlege, Relege. /* [Cut of Bellman, with lantern, staff, bell, and dog.] / *Printed at London for Nathaniel Butter. 1608.*[10] And he emphasizes his civic purpose with more vehemence even than Greene in the Introduction (A3):

> At your *Gates* the *Belman* of London beateth, to awaken your eies, to looke back after certaine *Grand* and *common Abuses,* that dayly walke by you, keeping aloofe (in corners) out of the reach of Law . . . I chuse you as *Patrons* (not to my booke) but to defend me from those Monsters, whose dennes I breake open in this my discovery. More dangerous they are to a State, then a *Civill warre,* because their villanies are more subtile and more enduring . . . In this blacke shore of mischiefe have I sailed along, and beene a faithfull discoverer of all the Creekes, Rockes, Gulfes, and Quicksands, in and about it: Be you therefore as second adventurers, and furnish men armed with Iustice, and well furnished in all points with a desire to Conquer these Savages, and send them to set strong and fearefull footing amongst them . . . For my owne part, I vowe, that as I *Dedicate* these my labours to your hands, so will I *Devote* my life to the safetie of my countrey, in defending her from these Serpents.

Dekker begins his treatise with an essay considering the beauty of solitary places and life in the country as offering peace and stability not to be found in the city and the hurtling world of change. Wandering in the country, he comes to an earthly paradise which reminds him of that of our great

10. B.M., C.40.c.20. (STC 6480). Though this work appears anonymously, as Judges points out (p. 510), Dekker's authorship is established by the fact that *Lanthorne and Candlelight,* published seven months later, carries his signature after the dedicatory letter. Judges notes that the *Belman* was immediately successful and was revised three times in 1608.

THE BELMAN OF LONDON.

Bringing to light the moſt notorious villanies that are now practiſed in the KINGDOME.

Profitable for Gentlemen, Lawyers, Merchants, Citizens, Farmers, Maſters of Houſholds, and all ſortes of ſeruants, to marke, and delightfull for all men to Reade.

Lege, Perlege, Relege.

Printed at London for NATHANIEL BVTTER. 1608.

PLATE 14. *The Belman of London*. Title page. British Museum, C.40.c.20.

grandsire, and he plans to make it the temple of his thoughts: some of his hours will be spent in speculation about the heavens, some on the earth and its creatures, some on satires against the wickedness of the world, some in chanting roundelays in praise of country life, and the rest in providing for his body. But while meditating thus, he sees far off clouds of smoke, and on investigating, finds a lonely cottage with a strangely low door. Such is the setting Dekker provides for his account of his knaves and vagabonds. With better fortune than Greene—and his choice of a beginning is a credit to his dramatic sense, he has come by chance on one of the feast days of the rogues, and is permitted by the beldam hostess of the remote inn to watch the festivity. Presently the guests arrive at the rendezvous:

> . . . This is the *Ragged Regiment: Villaines* they are by birth, *Varlets* by education, *Knaves* by profession, *Beggars* by the Statute and *Rogues* by act of Parliament. They are the idle *Drones* of a Countrie, the *Caterpillers* of a Common-wealth, and the *Ægyptian* lice of a Kingdome. And albeit that at other times their attire was fitting to their trade of living, yet now were they all in hansome cleane linnen, because this was one of their *Quarter dinners,* for you must understand, that (as afterward I learnt by intelligence) they holde these solemne meetings in foure severall seasons of the yeare at least, and in several places to avoid discoverie (B4^{v}).

After their assembly, Dekker witnesses the ceremony of stalling the rogue (the initiation of a novice). At the ceremony, described first by Harman[11] but more dramatic here, the upright man pours a quart of ale on the head of the kneeling candidate and grants him the right to cant (use pedlar's French and beg). In the charge delivered to the new rogue, the upright man makes clear his duties and the rights of seniority among rogues. After a wild feast ("their teeth made a noise, as if so many Mils had beene grinding"), the Speaker of the house makes an address in praise of the beggar life, summing up as follows: "The life of a *Begger* is the life of a

11. *Caveat,* leaf 8 (Viles and Furnivall, p. 34).

souldier: he suffers hunger and cold in Winter, and heate and thirst in Summer: he goes lowsie, he goes lame, he's not regarded, he's not rewarded: here onely shines his glorie: The whole Kingdome is but his *Walke,* a whole *Cittie* is but his *Parish,* in every mans *kitchin* is his meate drest, in every mans *Seller* lyes his beere, and the best mens pursses keepe a penny for him to spend" (C2^{v}).

After the meeting has dispersed, Dekker inquires from the beldam about her guests and she describes each type. At this point Dekker's invention ends, and most of the rest of the first part of the pamphlet is his revised version of the works of Awdeley and Harman.[12] Since he does not acknowledge his sources (a habit of the times: even Harman merely speaks of an old brief), and since he follows his authors fairly closely in plan and subject matter, Dekker is commonly accused of plagiarizing his sources. But he possibly thought of himself as free to use this encyclopedic material, and he skillfully rewrites most of what he takes from each work. Except for his omission of Harman's story illustrations, which do not fit his scheme, he almost always improves on his sources. He corrects at the outset an error in sense: Harman's ruffler, who becomes in time an upright man, should not in logic be first in the fraternity; hence Dekker ranks the upright man first.[13] He freely amends Harman, adding details from Awdeley, including the Irish toyle and restoring the jackman and patrico to regular standing. And his style is livelier, more fluid, though less richly detailed as may be seen in the following sentences:

Harman: These [priggers of prancers] have also theyr women, that walkinge from them in other places, marke where and what they see abrode, and sheweth these Priggars

12. Mary L. Hunt suggests (p. 137) that Dekker may have used the *Groundwork of Cony-Catching* instead of Harman, but Dekker ignores the opening new material with which this reproduction of Harman begins, a fact which suggests that Dekker is following Harman (and Awdeley) directly.

13. It is curious that Dekker follows the order of Harman (with slight modifications from Awdeley) in his list of rogues in *Lanthorne and Candlelight.*

therof, when they meete, which is wythin a weeke or two. (C4v).

Dekker: These have their female spyes that survey medowes and Closes, and long onely for horse flesh.

At the end of the beldam's discourse, Dekker, now disgusted with the vices of the country, returns to the city. There he meets the Bellman of London with his lantern, staff, and dog. They talk together and the Bellman reveals what he has seen of the vices of the city. These vices Dekker now describes to the reader in the second part of the pamphlet in which he sums up all the information he could find in the various works on city knaves available to him. From *Mihil Mumchance his Discoverie of the Art of Cheating in false Dyce play* (1597), as remarked earlier a slightly altered version of *A manifest detection,*[14] he borrows largely word for word his material for the cheating law (cozening with false dice). Troubled by conflicting reports in Greene regarding the barnard and the barnacle and Rowlands' claim that up-to-date cozeners denied the use of such terms and the name *conycatching* as well and urged the adoption of a new set of terms under the name of *batfowling,*[15] Dekker reconciles the conflict by giving each a place. But he tends to slight conycatching as limited to the cozening of gulls or conies from the country. From the *Second part of Conny-catching* he derives his vincent's law, the black art, curbing law, prigging law, lifting law, and figging law. For good measure Dekker adds "The Five Jumps at Leapfrog," his metaphor for five cozening tricks borrowed from Rowlands' *Greenes Ghost Haunting Conie-Catchers.*[16] As in the first part of his pamphlet, Dekker summarizes and condenses, eliminating all but a few illustrative stories.

14. See p. 102. Cf. *Mihil Mumchance* (1597), title page ("The names of false Dyce") and sig. B4v with *Belman,* E3. Aydelotte demonstrates this plagiarism, pp. 129, 175–176.

15. *Greenes Ghost Haunting Conie-Catchers,* A4.

16. *Greenes Ghost Haunting Conie-Catchers,* B3–C1 (Aydelotte calls attention to this debt, p. 130). See also p. 131 of this study.

Dekker's moral purpose is emphasized in the general design of his work in which nearly all the tales which amused the readers of the earlier pamphlets are stripped away, leaving only the presumed facts about the rogues and knaves and their practices; and at the end he expresses anew his distress at these evils (I): "Who would imagine that in a Kingdome so fertill in all sorts of wholesome discipline, there should grow up such ranke and such pestilent beds of Hemlocke? that in the very heart of a state so rarely governed and directed by good lawes, there should breede such loathsome and such ulcerous impostumes? that in a City so politike, so civill, and so severe, such ugly, base, and bolde impieties dare shew their faces?" He prays that the state may devise stratagems and laws to raze the rebels. And he ends with an echo of the familiar ship metaphor; all these wretches are destined for the gallows, "where I leave them, as to the haven in which they must cast anchor, if *Derricks* Cables doe but hold (and unlesse they amend.) Give thankes to the Bel-man of London if either profit or pleasure bee gained by this Discovery."

The warm reception given the *Belman* encouraged Dekker to continue his efforts, and in the same year he brought out another pamphlet entitled *Lanthorne / and Candlelight. / Or, / The Bell-Mans second Nights-walke. / In which / Hee brings to light, a Broode of more strange Villanies, / then ever were till this yeare discovered. / Decet novisse malum; fecisse, nefandum.* / [Cut of Bellman] / *London / Printed for Iohn Busbie, and are to be sold at his shop in / Fleet street, in Saint Dunstans church-yard / 1608.*[17] In his introduction Dekker mixes the Bellman metaphor with that of an army representing "Law, Iustice, Order, Ceremony, Religion, Peace, and that honorable Title of Goodnesse," arrayed against the army of evil, and visualizes the Bellman as the leader of the forces of goodness. Among the verses commending the author is a sonnet by "Io: Da" (John Davies?)

17. B.M., C.38.d.24 (STC 6485). A second edition was printed for Busby in 1609.

which defends Dekker's efforts against the criticisms that his revelations may help to breed the vices that they attack.

Up to this time, Dekker has neglected pedlar's French, possibly because he did not see how to improve on Harman's word-list, but now he attacks the problem boldly in his first chapter, "Of Canting." He intimates that he writes from extensive knowledge of the subject: "it is impossible to imprint a Dictionary of all the Canting phrases, I will at this time not make you surfet on too much, but as if you were walking in a Garden, you shall onely pluck here a flower, and there another, which (as I take it) will be more delightfull then if you gathered them by Handfulls" (B4). Next he introduces some canting rhymes, of which most curious is the familiar one derived from Copland, which he invites the reader to translate by means of the vocabulary he presents. Since the vocabulary does not include some of Harman's terms, one has the uneasy feeling that Dekker himself could not translate the passage. Dekker's word-list has one advantage over Harman's in that it is alphabetical; otherwise he adds nothing new, a fact which indicates that his knowledge of these rogues is mainly literary rather than one of personal contact. At the end of the list he invites any one "more rich in this *Canting* commodity" to lend him his store, an indirect admission of his lack of any intimate association with rogues.

Moreover, Dekker's information about pedlar's French has little to do with most of the rogues that he is exposing in this pamphlet. We are prepared for the change of venue in the second chapter, "The Bel-Mans Second Nights walke," in which, as earlier in Nashe's *Pierce Penilesse,* we are given a view of term-time in Hell, a satire upon procedures in the law courts. The actions tried in Hell relate to the professions on earth, these actions being brought against courtiers, soldiers, scholars, and others for characteristic sins. These trials are interrupted by a post bringing a letter warning Lucifer and Hell that the Bellman of London in revealing all the tricks of knavery is making it impossible for knaves to pursue their trades. To meet this menace, the infernal court decides to send up a shape-shifter to entice new victims with new deceptions, and Pamersiel, the chosen agent, leads us to view the new cozening in the ordinaries and other places frequented by gentlemen. The knaves we now meet are knavish gentlemen, not the rogues of Harman, in station a step above the gentlemen-knaves of Greene. The tricks they play are for the most part familiar, but the agents of Dekker's "gull-groping" or the cheating of gentlemen at ordinaries are more sophisticated than the cozeners of the barnard's law. At the outset of their games they disarm the gull by detecting and disposing of faulty dice and burning defective cards. The fourth chapter, Ferreting, or the undoing of gentlemen by taking up commodities, is likewise an advanced form of conycatching, one that "pulles down Parkes, layes open forrests." The fifth chapter introduces a new type of knavery, that of the Falconers, who fleece gentlemen by dedicating to them as patrons books or pamphlets hastily patched together; Dekker resorts to verse in his indignation against these "*Theeves of wit, Cheators of Arte! traitors of schooles of Learning*":

> One booke hath seaven-score patrons: thus deseart
> is cheated of her due: thus Noble art
> Gives Ignorance (that common strumpet) place,
> Thus the true schollers name grows cheap and base.

Dekker shows considerable knowledge also of various other gentlemen knaves, such as Rank-riders (Chapter VII), who cozen inn-keepers into believing they are gentlemen of substance; Jacks in a box, or devils in men's shape who win merchants' confidence by leaving forty pounds in gold in pawn for forty pounds of silver and presently return counterfeit coin for the borrowed silver (Chapter XI). But most contributive of all are his chapters on Moon-men (Chapter VIII), the best verbal picture that the time affords of the Gypsies,[18] and the Infection of the Suburbs (Chapter IX). In the latter, the devil's agent visits the suburbs where he finds

18. See p. 267 of this book.

more alehouses than taverns in Spain, and the wide-open doors of brothels with painted harlots in taffeta gowns serving as signposts. Dekker asks if constables, churchwardens, bailiffs, beadles, and other officers are not "parcell-Bawds to winck at such damned abuses, considering they have whippes in their owne handes, and may draw bloud if they please?" Some of these officers take money of these bawds, money earned by lust. The suburbs are the breeding places of crime: "Would the Divell hire a villaine to spil bloud? there he shall finde him. One to blaspheme? there he hath choice. A Pandar that would court a matron at her praiers? he'es there. A cheator that woulde turne his owne father a begging? he'es there too: A harlot that will murder her newborne Infant? Shee lies in there" (H4).

In the final chapter the Devil's knight-errant, wandering after dark, sees bankrupts emerging and squandering other men's money, and lechers and crossbiters at their activities; but he takes special interest in the way ostlers wean horses—by greasing their teeth so that the poor jades cannot eat and hence saving their provender. At the end, after observing many abuses under the cover of night, he encounters the Bellman and, since it is a moonlit night and the Bellman is without his lantern, mistakes him for one of his own fellows and reveals all his island voyage to him.

Dekker's invitation in this pamphlet to add to his canting dictionary is quickly accepted by S. R. (probably Samuel Rid), the author of *Martin Mark-All, Beadle of Bridewell* (1610).[19] S. R. first attacks Dekker for claiming originality in

19. B.M., C.27.b.24 (STC 21400). *Martin / Mark-All, / Beadle of / Bridewell; / His defence and Answere / to the Belman of / London. / Discovering the long concealed Originall and Regi- / ment of Rogues, when they first began to take head, and how they / have succeeded one the other successively unto the sixe and twentieth / yeare of King Henry the eight, gathered out of the Chro- / nicle of Crackeropes, and (as they term it) / the Legende of Lossels. / By S.R. / Oderunt peccare boni virtutis amore, / Oderunt peccare mali formidine poenae. / London / Printed for Iohn Budge, and Richard Bonian. / 1610.* Aydelotte's study (pp. 135–136) makes it fairly certain that Samuel Rid (not Samuel Rowlands) wrote this pamphlet.

his *Bellman* (which, he indicates, is merely Harman in a new dress). Then he presents the rogues of the land as meeting at the Swan with Five Necks in King's street[20] where a Cocke Lorell type of jury is called to try the Bellman for his attacks on vagrants; he should instead, as was argued in *The Defence of Cony-catching,* have concentrated on the enormities of the fox-furred gentlemen (S. R. strangely ignores Dekker's attempt to accomplish this very purpose in the second part of *Lanthorne and Candlelight*). The Bellman makes an eloquent defense, expropriated at length from Sir John Cheke,[21] defining a loiterer as "a sucker of honie, a spoyler of coine . . . a Baseliske of a comon wealth, which by companie and sight doth poyson a whole countrey and stayneth honest minds with the infection of his venome. . . ." (B3^v), but before the case can be resolved, a messenger from Don Purloiningo of Theivingen arrives, bringing a letter promising all the rabble protection; all are to sail thither (as in Brant) on the next wind. The highway (as in Copland) and the places of abode on the way fit the latitude of Great Britain and the whole world (as in Barclay), and the allegory of this land of lust and crime is vividly drawn. Following this fantasy (the writer gives no specific examples of knavish behavior), he brings the Harman-Dekker canting dictionary up to date, adding about a score of new terms,[22] his one substantial contribution to knave-lore, and concludes his remarkable document with a full "history" of the regiment of rogues, all of it, despite the insertion of a few historical names and dates, patently fiction.

In 1612 an edition of *Lanthorne and Candlelight* with

20. Judges (p. 515) notes that King Street, running from Charing Cross to the royal palace in Westminster, was famous for its taverns and that the Swan with Five Necks (more accurately, he suggests, Five Nicks) was perhaps the Swan in King Street visited later by Pepys (*Diary,* ed. Wheatley, II [1893], 30; VI, 3). But see also Wheatley and Cunningham on the Swan Tavern at Charing Cross, famous in Tudor times and frequented by Ben Jonson.

21. See p. 11 of this study.

22. S. R.'s claim of adding fifty or more terms is not valid; see p. 41 of this book.

an added section containing some arresting new material appeared under the title *O per se O or A new cryer of Lanthorne and Candle-light.*[23] The text is the same as that of *Lanthorne and Candle-light* except for the added material described in the title. This added matter is largely an independent contribution to the literature of roguery, and so different in tone and scheme from the rest of Dekker's work that doubt arises whether the material is Dekker's.[24] The author begins by criticizing the Bellman's work (L2):

> In that Map of Villanies, which you have drawne in Print already, I like the handling of your Pensill, but not the laying on of your colours: they are smooth enough, but you have not given them their true Sweetning, Heightning, and Shadowing. But I cannot blame you, because *nocte latent mendae,* Women, Horses and Colours are not to be chosen by candle-light: and you (Gaffer Bell-man) having no better guide, it is a wonder you stumbled no more, considering you walked i'th darke.

In this work the writer does heighten his colors, presumably because, as he claims, with his spectacles (perhaps a symbol of the title *O per se O*), he saw these things more clearly

23. B.M., C.27.b.19 (STC 6487): *O per se O / or / A new cryer of Lanthorne and / Candle-light. / Being an Addition, or Lengthening, of the Bell- / mans Second Night-walke. / In which, are / Discovered those Villanies, which the Bell-man (because hee went / i'th darke) could not see: now laid open to the world. / Together / With the shooting through the arme, used by counterfeit Souldiers: / The making of the great Soare, (commonly called The Great Cleyme:) The / Mad-mens markes: Their phrase of Begging: The Articles and / Oathes given to the Fraternitie of Roagues, Vagabonds, and / sturdy Beggers at their Meetings. / And Last of all, / A New Canting-Song.* / [Cut of Bellman] / *Printed at London for Iohn Busbie, and are to be sould at his shop / in S. Dunstans Churchyard in Fleete-street. 1612.*[23] The title is explained by the author as referring to the title and refrain of a ballad, which he quotes (see p. 154 of this book). Frank Chandler (*Literature of Roguery,* I, 109) suggests that the phrase may allude to a passage in *Greenes News both from Heaven and Hell* (1593) beginning "It is I, *I per se I,* Robert Greene . . ." (A4).

24. Judges (p. 514), though granting the freshness of the added material, finds this work inferior to most of Dekker's prose work and thinks it may have been written by a hack-writing contemporary. But it is distinctly more vivid than any other part of Dekker's rogue pamphlets except the description of the Moon men (*Lanthorne,* Chapter VIII). It is interesting that just as Greene is

from observation rather than from report. The notes which his blackbirds sing, he says, are of his own setting, "not eyther borrowed or stolne from any other." His information here is based on his notes from his own experience in Queen Elizabeth's time when he served as a high constable in his own county (one is reminded of Greene's deriving information from a justice of peace). Some of his knowledge was learned from a clapperdudgeon (a born beggar) in his own employ, who revealed to him new phrases of canting, and whom he calls by the name of *O per se O*. In this work the author is at pains to display the canting language as often as occasion invites; and his discussion is more saturated with the terms than that of any other writer yet considered.

Despite his claims to originality, however, one finds hints of Harman and others as when he inveighs against bousing kens and stalling kens (ale houses and houses receiving stolen goods) as the chief supporters of roguery in the land. In a way that could have inspired Hogarth he pictures fairs also as breeders of the evil, and cites as the most famous example Durrest Fair near Tewkesbury in Gloucestershire (L3^{v}). Here, he says, gather more rogues than were ever whipped at cart-tail throughout London or beggars trooping out of Ireland. These locust swarms come from all parts. Buyers and sellers are alike, tawny sunburnt rascals. "The Shoppe-keepers are Theeves, and the Chap-men Roagues, Beggers and Whores." This fair begins before day and ends before nine the same morning, after which, led by the Lord of the Fair, they visit the ale house, and presently drunk, "up fling they the Cannes, downe goe the Boothes, about flye broken Iugges: here lyes a Roague bleeding, there is a Mort cursing, here a Doxie stabbing with her knife: and thus this Fayre which beginnes merrily, ends madly: for Knaves set it up, and Queanes pull it downe" (L4).

attacked by the author of the *Defence of Cony-catching,* so Dekker is reproached here by the author of *O per se O*.

The writer next explains the term *O per se O* as derived from a current ballad, of which he gives the chorus as sung by these knaves:

> Wilt thou a begging goe,
> *O per se, O. O per se, O.*
> Wilt thou a begging goe?
> Yes verily, yea.
> Then thou must God forsake,
> and to stealing thee betake.
> *O per se, O. O per se, O.*
> Yes verily yea, &c.

In the ensuing description of rogues, he limits himself to Abraham men, counterfeit soldiers, dummerers, and clapper-dudgeons,[25] for each of whom he gives somewhat more picturesque descriptions than may be found in earlier works, first describing the type generally, then giving special identifying marks and their manner of begging. His methodical procedure here for each seems to reflect Greene's compulsive care in establishing "laws" for each of his various forms of cozening. The rogues themselves seem drawn from life as may be seen from the description of the Abraham man (M2):

> The *Abram Cove,* is a lustie strong Roague, who walketh with a *Slade* about his *Quarrons* (a sheete about his body) *Trining,* hanging to his hammes, bandeliere-wise, for all the world as cut-purses and Theeves weare their sheetes to the Gallowes, in which their Truls are to bury them: oftentimes (because hee scornes to follow any fashions of Hose,) hee goes without breeches, a cut Ierkin with hanging sleeves (in imitation of our Gallants,) but no Sattin or Chamblet elbowes, for both his legges and armes are bare, having no *Commission* to cover his body, that is to say, no shirt: A face staring like a *Sarasin,* his hayre long and filthily knotted, for hee keepes no Barber: a good *Filch* (or Staffe) of growne Ash, or else Hazell, in his *Famble* (in his Hand) and somctimes a sharpe

25. In thus limiting his descriptions the author is probably governed by the same reasons that caused Harman to limit his list of rogues with actual names to four types: these descriptions largely cover the outstanding kinds; the other types do not exist separately save as fictions or guises assumed by these basic rogues.

> sticke, on which hee hangeth *Ruff-pecke* (Bacon.) These, walking up and downe the Countrey, are more terribly [*sic*] to women and Children, then the name of Raw-head and Bloody-bones, Robbin Good-fellow, or any other Hobgobling. *Crackers* tyed to a Dogges tayle, make not the poore Curre runne faster, then these Abram Ninnies doe the silly Villages of the Countrey, so that when they come to any doore a begging, nothing is denyed them.

Next *O per se O* gives a vivid account of their special marks:

> Some of these Abrams have the Letters E. and R. upon their armes: some have Crosses, and some other marke, all of them carrying a blew colour: some weare an iron ring, &c. which markes are printed upon their flesh, by tying their arme harde with two strings three or foure inches asunder, and then with a sharp Awle pricking or raizing the skinne, to such a figure or print as they best fancy, they rub that place with burnt paper, pisse and Gun powder, which being hard rubd in, and suffered to dry, stickes in the flesh a long time after, when these markes faile, they renew them at pleasure. If you examine them how these Letters or Figures are printed upon their armes, they will tell you it is the Marke of Bedlam, but the truth is, they are made as I have reported.

In these particular details the writer is much more specific than Harman, or for that matter, Dekker as well in his earlier accounts; but *O per se O* goes yet further in a dramatic and unforgettable picture of their behavior as beggars:

> And to colour their villanie the better, every one of these Abrams hath a severall gesture in playing his part: some make an horrid noyse, hollowly sounding: some whoope, some hollow, some shew onely a kinde of wilde distracted ugly looke, uttering a simple kinde of Mawnding, with these addition of words (*Well and wisely.*) Some daunce, (but keepe no measure) others leape up and downe, and fetch Gambals, all their actions shew them to be as drunke as Beggers: for not to belye them, what are they but drunken Beggers? All that they begge being eyther *Loure* or *Bouse,* (money or drinke.)
>
> *Their Mawnd, or Begging*
>
> *The first beginnes* Good Urship. Maister, or good Urships Rulers of this place, bestow your reward on a poore man that hath lyen in Bedlam without Bishopsgate three yeeres, foure moneths,

and nine dayes. And bestow one piece of your small silver towards his fees, which he is indebted there, the summe of three pounds, thirteene shillings, seaven pence, halfe-penny, (or to such effect,) and hath not wherewith to pay the same, but by the good help of Urshipfull and well-disposed people, and God to reward them for it.

The second beginnes: Now Dame, well and wisely: what will you give poore Tom now? one pound of your sheepes feathers to make poore Tom a blanket: or one cutting of your Sow side, no bigger then my arme, or one piece of your Salt meate to make poor Tom a sharing horne: or one crosse of your small silver towards the buying a paire of Shoes, (well and wisely:) Ah, God blesse my good Dame, (well and wisely) give poor Tom an old sheete to keep him from the cold, or an old dublet, or Ierkin of my Maisters, God save his life.

Then will he dance and sing, or use some other Anticke, and ridiculous gesture, shutting up his counterfeite Puppet-play with this Epilogue or Conclusion, Good Dame give poore Tom one cup of the best drink, (well and wisely,) God save the King and his Counsell, and the Governour of this place, &c.

The palliards or clapperdudgeons with their great cleyms (sores) are equally impressive with their pleas. They lie on the ground and with horrid noises cry out piteously (N2):

Ah the urship of God looke out with your mercifull eyne, one pittiful looke upon sore, lame, grieved and impudent (*for impotent*) people, sore troubled with the grievous disease, and have no rest day nor night by the Canker and Worme, that continually eateth the flesh from the bone: for the Urship of God bestow one cross of your small silver, to buy him salve and oyntment, to ease the poore wretched body, that never taketh rest: and Go-ad to reward you for it in Heaven. These Pallyards walk two or three together, and as one gives over this note, the second catcheth it at the rebound, using the self-same howling and grunting, which ended, they say the Lords Prayer and in many places the *Ave,* never ceasing till something be given them.

In addition, the author describes how the clapperdudgeons make their great *cleym,* and after this convincing realism, spoils the picture by inventing the articles of their fraternity. Somewhat more credible is the account of their nicknames (such as *Hurly Burly,* the *High Constable,* the *Great Bull*), though one wonders about the reality of the places listed as their lodgings (*Stophole Abbey, Blue Bull, Cow's Udder, Green Arbor,* and the like). At the end the author appends a canting song, a masterpiece in its sort, with a clever translation; and the question arises, who could have written it other than Dekker?

In 1616 Dekker published under a new title yet another revision of his *Lanthorne and Candlelight* which in turn proved so successful that it underwent seven reprintings during his lifetime. For brevity and for its completeness, we shall consider only the seventh of these, issued in 1632 under the title, *English Villanies.*[26]

This edition appears to have been supervised by Dekker, since at the end of the dedication he speaks of his age as "threescore yeares." The work recapitulates, as it promises on the title-page, all the discoveries of *Lanthorne and Candlelight* and *O per se O;* it is principally interesting for the light it throws on prison life of the time, the best picture written in this period of that misery, done by an author who wrote from close observation. Dekker's fellow prisoners were not ordinary rogues but an assortment of unthrifts imprisoned chiefly for debt, doubtless including many cozening rascals,

26. Dyce Library (STC 6491): *English Villanies / Six Several Times / Prest to Death by the Printers, But / (still reviving againe) are now the seventh / time (as at first) discovered by Lanthorne and Candle-light, And / The Helpe of a New Cryer, called / O per se. O: / Whose lowd voyce proclaimes to all / that will heare him, Another Conspiracie of / Abuses lately plotting together, to hurt the peace / of this Kingdome; which the Bell-man (because / hee then went stumbling i'the darke) could / Never see, till Now. / And because a Company of Rogues, cunning / Canting Gypsies, and all the scumme of our / Nation fight heere under their owne / Tottered Colours: / At the end is a Canting Dictionary, to teach their / Language: with Canting Songs. / A Booke to make Gentlemen Merry. / Citizens Warie. / Countreymen Carefull. / Fit for all Iustices to Reade over, because it is a Pilot, / by whom they may make Strange Discoveries. / London, / Printed by Augustine Matthews, and are to bee sold / by Iohn Grismond, at the Signe of the Gunne / in Ivie Lane. 1632.* The 1616 edition was the first to use the title of *Villanies:* Bodl., Douce D.204 (STC 5468): *Villanies discovered by Lanthorne and Candle-light. . . .*

but more commonly, it must be supposed, the "conies" or "cousins" of these rascals. But the picture is so evocative of the conditions faced by most of the rogues at one time or another that it is worth repeating in brief part here (I2–I2^{v}):

> . . . . Into a Iayle our infernall *Catchpoll,* the next morning convaid himselfe. And looking to heare there nothing, but sighing, lamenting, praying, and cryings out of afflicted and forloyne creatures, there was no such matter. But onely a clamorous noyse of cursing Creditors, drinking healths to their confusion, swaggering, roaring, striking, stabbing one another: as if that all *Desper-viewes* of sixeteene Armies had bin swearing together. Considering the desperate resolutions of some, hee wished himselfe in his owne *Territories,* knowing more safety there, then in this *Hospitall* of incurable mad-men, and could not till about dinner time be perswaded, but that the Iayle was Hell, every roome was so smoakie with Tobacco, and oathes flying faster about, then Tapsters could score up their frothy reckonings. But the time of munching being come, all the sport was to see, / how the Prisoners (like starking Souldiers at the rifling of a towne), ranne up and downe to arme themselves against that battaile of hunger. Some whetting knives that had meate, others scraping Trenchers aloud, that had no meate: Some ambling downe staires for Bread and Beere, meeting another comming up staires, carrying a platter more proudly aloft full of Powder Beefe and Brewis, then an Irish man does his enemies head, on the top of his sword. Every chamber shewing like a Cookes shop, where provant was stirring. And those that had no provander in the manger nor hay in the racke, walking up and downe like starv'd Iades, new overridden in Smithfield.

The cry that these prisoners make pierces the clouds (I3–I3^{v}):

> The Cry of these men is loud, it is heard above the starres; the cry is great, it incompasseth in, two *Cities;* it is the cry of Sicknesse, of Melancholy, Madnesse, Hunger, Cold, Thirst, Nakednesse, penury, beggery, misery.
>
> It is the cry of Church-men, Tradesmen, Husbandmen, Men undone: of Schollers, Souldiers, all Pennylesse, all Prisoners.
>
> And how far reacheth the ground thinke you, in which these cryes eccho one to another? let your eyes walke but over this paper, and here survay is drawne.

> Upon one side of the Thamis stand, the White Lyon, the Kings Bench, the Marshal-sea, the Clinke, the Counter in Southwarke. On the other side, the Gate-house, Ludgate, Newgate, Wood-streete Counter, Poultry Counter, Finsbury, New-prison, Lobs pound, and the hole at Saint Katherines. Fourteen Golgothas invironing one City! fourteene Charnell-houses where men are buried alive! . . .

One other feature of *English Villanies* deserves attention, namely Dekker's ambitious attempt to provide his readers with a collection of verses supposedly written by unknown bards among his knaves. Dekker provides no details regarding these, and one may assume that he had no information about them, and that indeed they did not exist. Who wrote the verses then? The ablest candidate is obviously Dekker himself. There are three new songs added to those in *Lanthorne and Candlelight,* the first of which had already appeared in *O per se O.* This song, which Dekker cites as "Another song by the Canters at their meeting" is almost a history of rogue experience. The two other songs, pretty and wanton, are less expository and more lyrical. All the words used in these songs are provided for in Dekker's dictionary following the songs, in which Dekker recapitulates Harman again without one added phrase or word.[27]

The center of much of the knavish activity described in these pamphlets was St. Paul's, as Greene earlier remarks, and as Dekker shows us in *The Dead Tearme* (1609) in which St. Paul's steeple laments the abuses going on beneath it (D4ᵛ–E):

> What whispering is there in Terme times, how by some slight to cheat the poore country Clients of his full purse that is stucke

27. The list in *English Villanies* omits (to avoid repetition, since the phrases are defined in the illustrations of the jargon) a handful of phrases found in Harman's list. Otherwise, *English Villanies* omits only Harman's phrase *the hygh pad* (the high way) and misdefines *quacking chete* as a *calf* or *sheep.* This error was caused by the printer's omission of the phrase "a duck or a drake" followed in the original by "a Bleting cheate; a Calfe or Sheepe" (N2ᵛ).

> under his girdle? What plots are layde to punish young gallants with readie money (which is shared afterwards at a Tavern) therby to distinguish [disfurnish?] him of his patrimony? What buying up of oaths, out of the hands of knightes of the Post, who for a few shillings doe daily sell their soules . . . What swearing is there: yea, what swaggering, what facing and out-facing? What shuffling, what shouldering, what Iustling, what ieering, what byting of Thumbs to beget quarels, what holding uppe of fingers to remember drunken meetings, what braving with Feathers, what bearding with Mustachoes . . .
>
> For at one time, in one and the same ranke, yea, foote by foote, and elbow by elbow, shall you see walking the Knight, the Gull, the Gallant, the upstart, the Gentleman, the Clowne, the Captain, the Appel-squire, the Lawyer, the Usurer, the Cittizen, the Bankerout, the Scholler, the Begger, the Doctor, the Ideot, the Ruffian, the Cheater, the Puritan, the Cut-throat, the Hye-men, the Low-men, the True-man, and the Thiefe: of all trades & professions some, of all Countryes some; And thus dooth my middle Isle shew like the *Mediterranean Sea,* in which as well the Merchant hoysts up sayles to purchace wealth honestly, as the Rover to light upon prize uniustly.[28]

On the whole, Dekker's contribution to the literature of roguery is seen to be large and full of color. It is true that, in his capacity as a reformer of social abuses, he seems harsh and uncompromising in his attacks on knaves and rogues as enemies of the commonwealth; but his humanity appears again and again in little touches that mitigate the severity of his attacks, as in his attempt to exonerate roaring Moll and in his sentiment for Bellafront, his sinner turned saint. When he is not pursuing his theme of the evils of knavery, even anonymous rogues elicit his pity, as when in his *Worke for Armorours* he expresses his distress at the cruelty of bear-baiting and remarks (B2): "methought this whipping of the blinde *Beare,*

28. B.M., C.39.c.4 (STC 6496): *The / Dead Tearme. / or, / Westminsters Complaint for Long Va- / cations and short Termes. / Written in a manner of a Dialogue betweene / the two Cityes London and Westminster. / The contentes of this discourse is in the / Page following. By T. Dekker. /* [Ornament] */London, / Printed and are to be sold by Iohn Hodgets at his house in / Pauls Churchyard. 1608.*

moved as much pittie in my breast towards him as ye leading of poore starved wretches to the whipping posts in *London* (when they had more need to be releeved with foode) ought to move the hearts of Cittizens, though it be the fashion nowe to laugh at the punishment."[29]

III
The Tradition of Dekker

Other dramatists were quick to appreciate the possibilities offered by the lore in Dekker's pamphlets and his own use of such material in his plays. Though Jonson's use of such subjects was also influential, the field is preeminently Dekker's and his were the pamphlets that were most available as source material. Out of several plays that employ this subject matter in various ways, two in particular deserve attention in that they represent a popular view of beggar life, the tradition of the happy beggar.

The first of these, *The Beggars Bush* (1623?) by John Fletcher and Philip Massinger, one of the most complete dramatizations of the vagabond life, following the bent of Jonson in romanticizing Gypsies into noblemen in *The Metamorphosed Gypsies,* turns some of its wandering beggars into earls and courtiers. The second, Richard Brome's *Jovial Crew or The Merry Beggars,* gently satirizes the tendency of glorifying the freedom of vagabondage, its release from care and anxiety.

The best play of the Fletcher-Massinger collaboration, *The Beggars Bush*[30] ingeniously weaves together the basic

29. B.M., C.39.c.57 (STC 6536): *Worke for / Armorours: / or / The Peace is Broken. / Open Wars likely to happin / this yeare 1609: / God help the Poore, The rich / can shift. / Saevit toto Mars impius Orbe. / Written by Thomas Dekker. /* [Device] */ London, / Printed for Nathaniel Butter dwelling in Poules / Church-yard at the signe of the Pide bull, / neere S. Austins gate. 1609.*

30. B.M., 1346.b.8: *The / Beggars / Bush. / Written by / Francis Beaumont, / And / John Fletcher, / Gentleman. /* [Ornament] */ London, / Printed for Humphrey Robinson, and Anne Mosely, / at the three Pigeons, and at the Princes Arms / in Saint Pauls Church-yard. 1661.*

Shylock-Antonio plot and a story of usurpation, using a band of beggars as the means to resolve the difficulties of the complex plot. At the outset, Wolfort, the usurper of the Earldom of Flanders, pretending to remorse, sends out honest Lord Hubert to search for the rightful heir, Florez, and his father, Gerrard, and other proscribed persons. At the same time he sends Hemskirk, his spy, along with Hubert. In another thrust of nefarious activity, Wolfort has stolen Gertrude, daughter of the Duke of Brabant, and lodged her in Bruges with the intent of wedding her and uniting Flanders and Brabant. Meanwhile Goswin, a young merchant of Bruges, bargains with four merchants for their commodities on time, pledging as security the return of his own ships. Goswin is then importuned by Gerrard, known to him as Clause, to come to Beggars' Bush (the beggars' rendezvous) to choose him as king. Clause tells him that the beggars have a king and commonwealth and that many great ones would part with half their wealth to be privileged to beg in the first rank.

At the Beggars' Bush, Ferret, Prig, Clause, Jaculine, Snap, Gynkes, and other beggars are listening to Higgen, their orator, professionally a dummerer, who asks all candidates for king to state their claims and then to stand in rank so that the first stranger to come may make his choice of the worthiest. Ferret promises if chosen to be a mild prince, but Prig promises tyranny (A3^{v}):

I must have my Capons
And Turkeys brought me in, with my green Geese,
And ducklings i'th'season: fine fat chickens;
Or if you chance where an eye of tame Phesants
Or Partridges are kept, see they be mine,
Or straight I seize on all your priviledge,
Places, revenues, offices, as forfeit,
Call in your crutches, wooden legs, false bellyes,
Forc'd eyes and teeth, with your dead arms; not leave you
A durty clout to beg with o' your heads,
Or an old rag with Butter, Frankinsence,
Brimstone and Rozen, birdlime, blood, and cream,

To make you an old sore; not as much sope
As you may fome with i'th' Falling-sickness;
The very bag you bear, and the brown dish
Shall be escheated. All your daintiest Dolls too
I will deflower, and take your dearest Doxyes
From your warm sides; and then some one cold night
I'le watch you what old barn you go to roost in,
And there I'le smother you all i'th'musty hay.

But thanks to Clause's foresight, Goswin names him as the most honest and upright, and the danger of tyranny is averted. Under Clause, Higgen says (A4[v]),

Each man shall eat his own stoln eggs, and butter,
In his own shade, or sun-shine, and enjoy
His own dear Doll, Doxy, or Mort at night,
In his own straw, with his own shirt, or sheet,
That he hath filch'd that day . . .

In the coronation song for Clause they hymn the good life (A4[v]):

Cast our Caps and cares away: this is beggars Holy-day.
At the Crowning of our King, thus we ever dance and sing:
In the world look out and see, where so happy a Prince as he?
Where the Nation live so free, and so merry as do we?
Be it peace, or be it war, here at liberty we are,
And enjoy our ease and rest; to the field we are not prest;
Nor are call'd into the Town, to be troubled with the Gown.
Hang all Officers we cry, and the Magistrate, too, by;
When the Subsidie's increast, we are not a penny ceast.
Nor will any go to Law, with the Beggar for a straw.
All which happiness he brags, he doth owe unto his rags.

To add realism to the romantic band, the authors present Higgen as a sow-gelder, singing three coarse songs in opening the third act; and in the same scene, Prig and Ferret cozen a group of boors by entertaining them with juggling while picking their pockets, a feat tracing back to Greene through similar scenes in Shakespeare and Jonson, though, as Gerrard now enters singing a cony-skin song reminiscent of

Autolycus's "Lawns as white as driven snow," we may assume that the authors primarily recalled Shakespeare here.

Gerrard and his crew rescue Goswin from an ambush prepared by Hemskirk and, in forcing Hemskirk's confession of his knavery, resort to the knavish torment of inserting a rush in his nose, a trick vainly used by Falstaff to cozen Hal. Admiring Hubert, the beggars install him as one of their band with the ritual first given by Harman, though familiar in Dekker (C2[v]):

> *Hig.* I crown thy *nab* with a gag of ben-bouse,
> And stall thee by the *salmon* into the *clowes,*
> To maund on the pad, and strike all the cheats
> To *mill* from the *Ruffmans,* commission and slates,
> Twang dell's in the stiromel [strommel] and let the *Quire Cuffin,*
> And Hermon Beck strine, and trine to the *Ruffin.*
>
> *Ger.* Now interpret this unto him.
>
> *Hig.* I poure on thy pate a pot of good ale,
> And by the Rogues oath, a Rogue thee install,
> To beg on the way, to rob all thou meets;
> To steal from the hedge, both the shirt and the sheets:
> And lie with thy wench in the straw till she twang,
> Let the Constable, Justice, and Divell go hang.

Next Goswin is rescued by Clause and his beggars from his imminent failure to meet his payment to the merchants; the beggars bring him a mighty sum, and Clause rejects all security save one ring, for which, on demand, Goswin is to grant him one petition. Hubert finds presently that the winsome beggar wench of the crew is his lost Jaculine, daughter of Gerrard. Goswin's ships come in, and he plans marriage with Gertrude. The ceremony, however, is interrupted by Clause with his one petition: Goswin must not marry but go with him, for what cause he does not know. In the last act, Hubert, who has lured Wolfort into supposing that he is betraying his wronged opponents into his hands, with the puissant aid of Gerard and his beggars, captures the usurper, who is at once banished from the realm. The beggar band is thinned: Clause (Gerrard), Gynkes, and Jaculine were nobles in disguise. Gerrard commands the rest to follow him to Bruges where he will give them manly and profitable work for the Republic. But Higgen and his friends left behind are skeptical about working for the state (E2):

> *Hig.* Yes, to beat hemp, and be whipt twice a week,
> Or turn the wheel for Crab the Rope-maker:
> Or learn to go along with him, his course;
> That's a fine course now, i'the Commonwealth, *Prig*,
> What say you to it?
> *Prig.* It is the backwardst course, I know i'the world.

They will seek another climate with their tattered group. Shall it be England? All assent. Here, as is probably manifest, rogue and Gypsy ways fuse.

Richard Brome's last and best work, *The Jovial Crew or The Merry Beggars* (1641),[31] a comedy of lively color and inspiration which Pepys liked well enough to see it three times,[32] also exploits the carefree beggar life, but does so with a gentle mockery, leaning on Dekker for the substance of its beggar lore but ignoring his harsher views (see Plate 15). The "jovial crew" of the play are technically not Gypsies;[33] this is clear from the fact that they sometimes refer to Gypsy associations. Though they bear the type names of the rogues of Harman and Dekker, they and their life are so idealized that they seem blood brothers of the Gypsies, however, and may be considered, along with Clause and his friends in *Beggars*

31. B.M., 644.d.33: *A / Joviall Crew: / or, / The Merry Beggars. / Presented in a / Comedie, / At / The Cock-pit, in Drury Lane, / in the year 1641. / Written by / Richard Brome. Mart. Hic totus volo rideat Libellus.* / [Device] /*London: / Printed by F.T. for E.D. and N.E. and are to be / sold at the Gun in Ivy-Lane. 1652.*

32. Thomas M. Parrott and Robert H. Ball, *A Short View of Elizabethan Drama* (New York, 1942), p. 174. Pepys speaks of it as "merry and the most innocent play that ever I saw" (*The Diary of Samuel Pepys,* ed. H. B. Wheatley [London, 1903], I, 70).

33. Parrott and Ball (p. 178) speak of them as Gypsies.

The Beggars CHORUS

In the Jovial Crew.

To an excellent New Tune.

There was a Jovial Beggar,
he had a wooden Leg;
Lame from his Cradle,
and forced for to Beg:
And a Begging we will go, we'll go, we'll go,
And a Begging we will go.

A Bag for my Oat-meal,
another for my Salt,
A little pair of Crutches,
to see how I can Halt:
And a Begging, &c.

A Bag for my Bread,
another for my Cheese,
A little Dog to follow me
to gather what I leese:
And a Begging, &c.

A Bag for my Wheat,
another for my Rye,
A little Bottle by my side,
to drink when I'm a dry:
And a Begging we will go, we'll go, we'll go,
And a Begging we will go.

PLATE 15. "The Beggar's Chorus." Pepys IV, 251, Magdalene College, Cambridge. Copyright, British Museum.

Bush, as representing another fusion of the ideas entertained by authors about rogues and Gypsies. With these creatures we have obviously come a long way from the realistic rogues of Harman.

At the opening of the play, Squire Oldrents, an ideal landlord loved by his tenants, is shown as distressed by a fortune-teller's prediction that his daughters Rachel and Meriel will live to be beggars (a fear so common as to be almost archetypal). His friend Hearty tries to relieve his gloom, pointing out that the prediction may turn out to be a "whim," true in a superficial sense, but not in reality; he cites many roguish examples, as, for instance, the prediction about the shepherd boy who was to become a drunkard and get his living from bands of thieves, and who in actuality became a suburb justice (thus whimsically fulfilling the prediction). The solution of Oldrents' problem is thus suggested.

Presently his steward, Springlove, whose name implies his wanderlust, enters, and giving over his accounts, craves to be freed to return to his life as a wanderer. May and the nightingale call him. Oldrents expostulates (B4ᵛ):

> Can there no means be found to preserve life
> In thee, but wandring, like a Vagabond?
> Does not the Sun as comfortably shine
> Upon my Gardens, as the opener Fields?
> Or on my Fields, as others far remote?
>
> . . .
>
> Do not the Birds sing here as sweet and lively,
> As any other where? is not thy bed more soft,
> And rest more safe, then in a Field or Barn?
> Is a full Table, which is call'd thine own,
> Less curious or wholsom, then the scraps
> From others trenchers, twice or thrice translated?

But Springlove, who finds the sufferings of vagabondage sweetened by delights, is obdurate, and Oldrents exclaims: "I will no longer strive to wash this Moor"—that is, he will no longer try to transform a Gypsy.

Oldrents is not only a good landlord but a good host to the wandering crews of vagabonds whom he welcomes in his barn with a kettle of beef, a basket of bread, and jugs of beer (we are reminded how Harman, Dekker, and others protested the hospitality of the inns that helped beggars to flourish). For years the beggars have come to receive his bounty, administered freely by Springlove and Oldrents' groom, Randall. As Springlove approaches the barn to join the jovial crew, he hears their chorus of the free life (C3):

> From hunger and cold who lives more free,
>   Or who more richly clad than wee?
> Our bellies are full; our flesh is warm;
>   And against pride, our rags are a charm.
> Enough is our Feast, and for tomorrow
>   Let rich men care, we feel no sorrow.
>   No sorrow, no sorrow, no sorrow, no sorrow,
>   Let rich men care, we feel no sorrow.

Springlove is warmly received by the crew, who hail him as master. These beggars are not palliards with great sores or wild rogues, but a decayed poet, a degraded lawyer, and a court beggar—though the soldier seems a true whipjack, and the Patrico, we are told, has lived with Gypsies.

In the second act, Rachel and Meriel trick their lovers, Vincent and Hilliard, into turning beggars for the fun of adventure (E):

Ra. I mean stark, errant downright *Beggars,* I,
Without equivocation, Statute *Beggars.*

Mer. Couchant and Passant, guardant, Rampant *Beggars.*

Vin. Current and Vagrant—

Hil. Stockant, whippant *Beggars!*

Vin. Must you and we be such? would you so have it?

Ra. Such as we saw so merry; and you concluded
Were the onely happy People in a Nation.

Mer. The onely Freemen of a Common-wealth;
Free above *Scot-free;* that observe no Law,
Obey no Governour, use no Religion,
But what they draw from their own ancient custom,
Or constitute themselves, yet are no Rebels.

Since by their assuming beggary in jest, they will fulfill the prediction harmlessly, Springlove gladly instructs them in the arts of begging, a craft in which he has been adept from childhood. He tells them how for seven summers he had returned to beggary, always coming back to his master when forced to do so by winter. Two years earlier Oldrents had identified him in his disguise, which reminds one of that assumed by Harman's Nicholas Jennings (see Plate 4):

My head was dirty clouted, and this leg
Swaddled with rags, the other naked, and
My body clad, like his upon the Gibbet. (E3)

For two seasons he has been true to his master, but has now yielded again to his wanderlust.

Meanwhile, Oldrents and Hearty overhear the beggars making merry to drown the cries of a doxy in labor, and presently Randall opens the curtain to let them witness the beggars at their feast, singing a lively pedlar's French song composed for the event, of which the first stanza runs (F3):

Here, safe in our *Skipper*, let's cly off our *Peck*,
And bouse in defiance of th' *Harman-beck*.
Here's *Pannum* and *Lap*, and good *Poplars* of *Yarrum*,
To fill up the crib, and to comfort the *Quarron*,
Now bowse a round health to the Go well and Com well
Of Cisley Bumtrincket that lies in the *Strummel*.

And there is much else in this act to show that Brome had studied his pedlar's French with care.

The third act is given over to the amusing attempts of the lovers at begging, which come to a climax with the group, too well instructed, getting out of hand, to Springlove's distress, as they chorus together:

All together

Spr.	No House nor home; nor covering from the cold, no health, no help but your sweet charity.
Mer.	No Bands or Shirts but Lowsie on our backs.
Hil.	No smocks or Petticoats to hide our Scratches.
Ra.	No Shoes to our Legs, or Hose to our Feet.
Vin.	No Skin to our Flesh, nor Flesh to our Bones shortly.
Hil.	If we follow the Devil that taught us to beg.
All.	*Duly and truly pray for you.*
Spr.	I'll run away from you if you beg a stroak more.

On this occasion they are begging for alms from yet another pair of eloped (supposed) lovers, Martin, the clerk of Justice Clack, and Annie, the Justice's niece. But in Act IV, partly through the devices of Rachel and Meriel, Annie discards her clerk for Springlove, who as upright man has already angered Martin by claiming proxy-wedding rights (Brome pictures the wedding of two elderly beggars at this point to compensate for the lack of such a ceremony for the lovers). Next follows the beggars' poet's proposal of a play on Utopia in which a beggar overcomes all other citizens and brings them all to Beggars Hall. But before the play can be acted, all are arrested and brought before Justice Clack. In the final act, a play is presented recapitulating the whole story and revealing that Springlove is Oldrents' son, his mother being the sister of the Patrico. The beggars are all pardoned, Springlove marries Annie, and with his uncle Patrico surprisingly gives over the begging life.

V

Sir John Rogue and his Moon-Men

JACK FALSTAFF is Sir John to all Europe and the wide world as well: he has given most of us medicines to make us almost forget that he is basically a rogue leading, from a detached view, an even more picturesque group of knaves than that of Cocke Lorell, but regarded more closely, deserving the estimate of Greene on creatures of their sort, a "cursed crue, these Machiavilians, that neither care for God nor devill, but set with the Epicures gaine, and ease, their *summum bonum* [and] cannot be called to anie honest course of living . . ."[1] Outwardly a soldier and a captain,[2] Falstaff is essentially a two-fold figure, metaphorically a Vice contending for the control of Prince Hal's fortunes, and secondly in metaphor and in reality, a master rogue and knave with the rogue's outlook on life. His nature as a Vice has been explored fully by various scholars;[3] and surely enough has been

1. *The Second and last part of Conny-catching*, A2v.
2. This aspect of his nature has been adequately studied by Professors Draper, Harrison, Jorgensen, and others; see the review of their studies by Professor J. Blakemore Evans, *Supplement to Henry IV, Part I, A New Variorum Edition of Shakespeare, Shakespeare Quarterly,* VII (Summer, 1956), pp. 87–88.
3. See in particular J. W. McCutchan, "Similarities between Falstaff and Gluttony in Medwall's *Nature,*" *SAB,* XXIV (1949), 214–219; Willard Farnham, "Medieval Comic Spirit in the English Renaissance," *Adams Memorial Studies* (Washington, 1948), pp. 436–437. These articles are reviewed by Evans, pp. 85–86; see in addition his review of the studies of other aspects of Sir John's character, such as that of the parasite, *miles gloriosus,* and professional fool, pp. 84–86. See also Professor Bernard Spivack's full analysis of the Vice relationship in *Shakespeare and the Allegory of Evil* (New York: Columbia Univ. Press, 1958), pp. 87–91, 203–205.

said about him as a Lord of Misrule who must be repudiated by a Prodigal Prince, as a scapegoat whose death is necessary for a mythic regeneration.[4] Our concern here is with the guise that the Vice-figure assumes (since he cannot appear on the stage as a Morality-play figure), that of the gentleman rogue. From first to last Falstaff's record is that of a knavery so palpable that it hardly needs review save for the purpose of emphasizing its meaning to the Henriad. The record considered in full is impressive; indeed it was so impressive to Alexander Smith, author of *A Complete History of the Lives and Robberies of the Most Notorious Highwaymen* (1714), that he included Falstaff (along with Robin Hood) in what appears to be otherwise an authentic history of rogues and villains.[5]

The first hint of Sir John's vocation, as he himself calls it, is given us when in *Richard II* Henry IV laments the waywardness of his unthrift son, who is frequenting taverns with a dissolute crew, cousins of the masterless men of the *Hye Way to the Spyttell hous,* "Even such, they say, as stand in narrow lanes / And beat our watch and rob our passengers" (V.iii.8–9). And from this point on, we rarely lose sight of the rogue-aspect of Sir John's character. When we meet him first he brazenly acknowledges his identity as a rogue: "Indeed you come near me now, Hal; for we that take purses go by the moon and the seven stars, and not by Phoebus, he, that wand'ring knight so fair" (*I Henry IV,* I.ii.14–17). When Hal is king, Falstaff hopes that rogues will be called "Diana's Foresters, Gentlemen of the Shade, Minions of the Moon,"

4. See particularly the studies of J. Dover Wilson, *The Fortunes of Falstaff* (New York, 1944); C. L. Barber, "From Ritual to Comedy: An Examination of *Henry IV,*" *English Stage Comedy: English Institute Essays,* 1954, pp. 22–51; and J. I. M. Stewart, "The Birth and Death of Falstaff," *Character and Motive in Shakespeare* (London, 1949), pp. 111–114.

5. *A Complete History of the Lives and Robberies of the Most Notorious Highwaymen, Footpads, Shoplifts, & Cheats of Both Sexes . . . by Captain Alexander Smith,* ed. Arthur L. Hayward (New York, 1920, reprinted from the fifth ed., 1719).

and that men will call them men of good government, governed as they are by that mistress. Hal approves the aptness of the designation: "Thou sayest well, and it holds well too; for the fortune of us that are the moon's men doth ebb and flow like the sea, being governed, as the sea is, by the moon. As for proof now: a purse of gold most resolutely snatch'd on Monday night and most dissolutely spent on Tuesday morning; got with swearing 'Lay by,' and spent with crying 'Bring in'; now in as low an ebb as the foot of the ladder, and by-and-by in as high a flow as the ridge of the gallows." This naming of rogues as "moon's men," small as its influence is, appears to be another Shakespeare "first." The term is used in 1608 by Dekker to describe the Gypsies, though he admits that English rogues are of the same nature, and Jonson adopts it in 1621.[6]

Early and late Falstaff is concerned for the fortunes of thieves: there should be no gallows when Hal is king, and resolution should not be curbed by "old father antic the law." More subtly than his grandsire Vice of the morality plays but none the less surely, he aims to corrupt the prince, mislead his youth, as Hal recognizes, and institute a reign of license; this is the sinister rogue hardly below the surface of sweet, kind, true, and valiant old Jack Falstaff. Shakespeare's depiction of so realistic and yet so generalized a character, so true to the dual, or better, manifold natures of rogues of high and low station of any time and place apotheosizes the rogue, gives him a niche of bibulous grandeur. He is not merely a "great fool" as the Lord Chief Justice calls him, but the very King of Knaves.

At the Boar's Head Tavern, an inn like those inveighed

6. *OED* lists this as the first known usage and cites also Dekker's *Lanthorne* (see p. 267 of this study) and Jonson's *Gipsies Metamorphosed, Works* (1641), 65: "They are Gypsies of this yeare, o' this Moone . . . *C1*. Oh they are called the Moone men I remember now." Dekker's specification of the moon-men as Gypsies appears to have been accepted. In 1699, B.E., Gent. lists moon-men as Gypsies in *A New Dictionary of the Terms Ancient and Modern of the Canting Crew.*

against by Copland, Harman, and Harrison, Falstaff holds revelry with his band of knaves and two daughters of the game, all of whom have taken the primrose path. The most respectable, Poins, a "second brother" of a good family, is clearly a wastrel and a thief (indeed "a proper fellow of [his] hands"). Gadshill, a clerk of St. Nicholas,[7] is a recognized knave type, the setter, who, in collusion with the chamberlain, arranges the scheme of the robbery, lays the plot how. The term *setter* is borrowed from the literature on cozening in which the setter is represented as the conycatcher who decoys the cony into the hands of the verser and barnacle (barnard).[8] Bardolph, though bearing a name of a noble family, is an equally characteristic rogue. Like many of Harman's knaves, he has a distinguishing physical mark (his salamander nose), he was bought in Paul's (hence a "knave" as a serving man), and he dies by hanging, like Greene's notorious thief Ned Brown, for stealing from a church in France. Bardolph could have qualified as a whipjack had he evaded his rogue destiny in France; Shakespeare is kind to him in recreating him as a tapster in *Merry Wives*. Peto has a name that may trace like that of Bardolph to an old family; but it also suggests a beggar though Shakespeare nowhere develops the idea. Peto seems to be one of the Prince's attendants, but he is one of the crew at Gadshill.

The Ancient Pistol, a manifest *miles gloriosus,* is also, along with Falstaff, one of the first literary examples of the "roaring boy," an acknowledged rogue type. Gower, who has recognized him as a counterfeit rascal, a bawd, and cutpurse, qualifies him as the most picturesque of all whipjacks:

> Why, 'tis a gull, a fool, a rogue, that now and then goes to the wars to grace himself, at his return into London, under the form of a soldier. And such fellows are perfect in the great commanders' names, and they will learn you by rote where services were done:

7. G. S. Haight interprets this term as indicating highwaymen (see "St. Nicholas's Clerks," *TLS,* Sept. 16, 1955, p. 451); see also Evans, p. 14.
8. See Greene, *Notable Discovery,* B–C2; Harrison, pp. 18–30.

> —at such and such a sconce, at such a breach, at such a convoy; who came off bravely, who was shot, who disgrac'd, what terms the enemy stood on; and this they con perfectly in the phrase of war, which they trick up with new-tuned oaths; and what a beard of the General's cut and a horrid suit of the camp will do among foaming bottles and ale-wash'd wits is wonderful to be thought on. But you must learn to know such slanders of the age, or else you may be marvellously mistook. —*Henry V,* III.vi.70–85.

In his farewell speech Pistol openly plans to embrace a life of knavery in the guise of a whipjack (V.i.85–94):

> Doth Fortune play the houswife with me now?
> News have I, that our Nell is dead i'th'spital
> Of malady of France;
> And there my rendezvous is quite cut off:
> Old do I wax, and from my weary limbs
> Honour is cudgell'd. Well, bawd will I turn,
> And something lean to cutpurse of quick hand.
> To England will I steal, and there I'll steal;
> And patches will I get unto these cudgell'd scars
> And swear I got them in the Gallia wars.

Pistol had won his Nell from yet another rogue, Corporal Nym (Thief). Their quarrel over her, also characteristic of rogue ways, is forcibly reconciled by Bardolph. All three will be sworn brothers in France, and Pistol plays on the significance of Nym's name: "I'll live by Nym, and Nym shall live by me." And they keep their pledge; the Boy tells us that Nym and Bardolph are sworn brothers in thieving. They have even tried to make him a pickpurse, after the fashion of other rogues who, as Harman tells us, thus employed young boys.

Just as the rogues have their doxies and morts, so this crew has its Dame Quickly, masquerading as a hostess (warned by Master Tisick the Deputy) and Doll Tearsheet, who are eventually dragged off to prison by the beadles, and who both finally die of the French malady in the hospital, fulfilling the sad conventional end of their sort.

To the Elizabethan audience all these were familiar

rogue-knave types that they encountered every day, ingenious, clever, and, when their own preserves were not in danger, amusing creatures, but manifestly rascals and wantons. That a prince should consort with such rabble was as shocking as it was amusing. The audience would laugh at and enjoy the youthful escapade of Hal's descent to the underworld, knowing that Hal must in time repudiate such company entirely, and while some would be unhappy at having Falstaff disappear from the scene, all would respect the necessity of his doing so, and would see the repudiation as requisite and just. As has often been pointed out, Shakespeare carefully prepares us for the rejection in a series of events, beginning with the Prince's first chorus-like soliloquy and continuing with the mock banishment and the reappearing symbolism of the applejohns down to the actual banishing itself.

The story itself of Sir John and his crew, reduced to its basic outlines, a story which reads almost like pages out of Harman and Greene, may be summarized in this light: Sir John is a gentleman-thief or a thieving gentleman, depending on the focus, and an unthrift, a ne'er-do-well who is (abhorrent to Elizabethan rectitude) a time-waster, one who would measure time (if he measured it at all) by cups of sack and the tongues of bawds. However respectable his connections, robbery is genuinely his vocation. How far Hal is involved in these robberies is not clear, as Empson indicates.[9] Though he speaks as one of the moon's men, apparently committed to their practices of robbery and revelry, he agrees to go along at Gadshill for once in his days, to become a false thief (a thief only in appearance) for recreation's sake.

The preparations for the robbery follow the usual procedure among thieves on such occasions. The chamberlain informs Gadshill about the party of travellers with fat purses, and Gadshill as setter supposedly makes the general arrange-

9. William Empson, "Falstaff and Mr. Dover Wilson," *Kenyon Review,* XV (1953), 225.

ments for the robbery. Harrison in his *Description of England* tells of the association of the chamberlain and other servants of inns with professional thieves:

> Seldome also are they or anie other waifaring men robbed without the consent of the chamberleine, tapster, or ostler where they bait & lie, who feeling at their alighting whether their capcases or budgets be of anie weight or not, by taking them down from their sadles, or otherwise see their store in drawing of their purses, do by and by give intimation to some one or other attendant dailie in the yard or house, or dwelling hard by, upon such matches whether the preie be worth following or no. If it be for their turne, then the gentleman peradventure is asked which waie he travelleth, and whether it please him to have another ghest to beare him companie at supper, who rideth the same waie in the morning that he doth, or not.[10]

In like manner the chamberlain informs Gadshill that a wealthy franklin with three hundred gold marks and an auditor with moneys for the Exchequer and other company have spent the night at the inn and are about to ride on their way to London, and thus the match is set. The affair at Gadshill itself we expect to assume the marks of a true highway robbery, as it does. Even the device of Poins for robbing the robbers savors of the trick practiced by the barnard and the rutter in Greene's *Notable Discovery*. Gulled and robbed of his money by the devices of the setter, the verser, and the barnard, the cony, becoming aware of the fraud, demands his money; at this point the rutter picks a quarrel with a tapster and in the diversion the barnard runs off with the money, which is later divided among the thieves at their tavern.[11]

After the hurly-burly of the robbery, true and false thieves alike steal away to their appointed place, the Boar's Head Tavern, for division of the spoils and a season of revelry. The spoils, however, have to be returned to their proper owners, to Falstaff's distaste; but though, secure in the

10. *Description of England,* ed. F. J. Furnivall (London, 1877), Book II, Ch. xvi, p. 283.
11. *Notable Discovery,* A4; Harrison, p. 13.

Prince's favor, he does not appreciate it, the audience understands that he has been saved from Tyburn. The revelry of this first Boar's Head Tavern scene is pale compared to that of the second one in Part II; Shakespeare has other themes in mind. Yet we are aware that a group of thieves, including the Prince as "false thief," has gathered at the inn, that the robbery in its double nature is a subject for merry-making, and that the true nature of Sir John as a rogue as lawless as he is witty is being exposed. This rogue is seriously playing for large stakes. This reverend vice, gray iniquity, father ruffian, as the Prince describes him, is sweet, kind, true, and valiant in his own version of his nature and a proper substitute father for the erring prince. And though he almost always seems to be jesting, we know that he means it when he urges the Prince to rob the King's exchequer with unwashed hands. It is fitting that the soldiers he impresses (*I Henry IV,* IV.ii.12–52) should remind us of Copland's rout of knaves and unthrifts.

Two other actions may be briefly noted, that of the exposure of Falstaff's real attitude towards Hal in the second Boar's Head Tavern scene and the fleecing of Justice Shallow. The first presents Falstaff as a king of rogues surrounded by his court, but a king who is to be unmasked, as indicated by the little stage business of the applejohns. It is ironically fitting that Falstaff should enter singing the first lines of a ballad relating to an ideal king. The courtiers of this king of knaves are unexampled in the realm of knavery. Both Doll and the Hostess have been drinking heavily, Pistol the Swaggerer and not-so-tame cheater is roaring drunk, and Bardolph needs no liquor to qualify: "The fiend hath prick'd down Bardolph irrecoverable." With Doll's help,[12] Falstaff's pretensions of devotion to Hal are unmasked, and Hal's last words to Falstaff are more than casual: there will be no good morning after this good night.

12. Spielmann's interpretation of "some road" (II.ii.161) as indicating that Doll was to be used as an instrument to unveil Falstaff is doubtless right (*Variorum* ed., p. 152).

The fleecing of Justice Shallow literally exhibits our rogue in the guise of a common cozener or cheater winning money through promises of good fortune that never mature; but metaphorically dishonest justice is seen the victim of the knavery it has countenanced (as in the affair of William Visor): set a thief to catch a thief. And as the play draws to a close, with the recognition of true justice, the rogues are at last subdued by the law which they have flouted. Even as the new king takes the Lord Chief Justice as his new father, the inexorable vengeance of the law has begun. The Hostess and Doll are dragged off by the beadles; they are still superficially funny, but the man they and Pistol beat is dead (by some chance they will escape death by means of human law, but their being carried off to prison is sufficient for the design of this play). And when, stained in apparel as they are in their lives, Falstaff and his fellow rogues, with false justice by their side, stand before the King like a grimy tableau of his former life, the King makes his necessary public repudiation, and only those who have forgotten the significance of Falstaff's basic nature as a rogue can be sentimental about the King's harshness.[13] Sir John goes to the Fleet and with him his company, including Master Robert Shallow (Silent Justice has already been put to bed [V.iii.125]): rogue and dishonest justice alike feel the force of the new order.

Is there possibly a larger meaning to Shakespeare's special development of the tradition of Hal's youthful misdemeanors? Are the scenes of roguery, as Eliot intimates,[14] an ironic counterpoint to the political scenes? Probably Shakespeare had this intention. It is obvious at the start that Hotspur is using his time in pursuit of honor while Hal is wasting his time in vanity and disorder; but Hotspur's conception of honor is false, a self-centered aim that is vanity itself as is

13. See H. M. McLuhan's effective defense of Shakespeare's soundness here ("*Henry IV,* A Mirror for Magistrates," *Univ. of Toronto Quarterly,* XVII [1948], 152–160).

14. T. S. Eliot, "Poetry and Drama," *Atlantic* (Feb. 1951), p. 32.

finally demonstrated when Falstaff (Vanity and Idleness) carries Hotspur (selfish honor) off the field at Shrewsbury. Hal's sharing of honor on this occasion and elsewhere represents an ideal. Falstaff and his crew rob men bearing the revenues of the King at Gadshill and then are robbed themselves, but the moneys are returned. Hotspur has taken prisoners in Scotland but has withheld them from the King who is demanding their return. Are Hotspur's grievances valid or is he being cozened to rebellion by Worcester and by his own vain pursuit of honor? Hal rehearses with Falstaff the robber as his substitute father for his meeting with his father the usurper. Falstaff, an unblushing rogue and a Machiavellian for his own cause, would make license the law of the realm, and hopes to use Hal to this end. The King, who has achieved his crown by "indirect crook'd ways," commends a policy of craft to his son as the means of retaining the crown. The rebels are disposed of at Shrewsbury and at Gaultree Forest; with the conclusion of the Henriad, the rogues are all eliminated or discredited. And with Hal's assumption of the kingship, the mode is changed (IV.v.200): craft and usurpation give way to lineal rights, to a king, whatever may be his conduct later, "full of grace and fair regard." Falstaff has no place in the new order, and Shakespeare's new comic hero (Fluellen), a comedy-of-humors figure, is as respectable and unfunny as the King himself (the King can no longer have knave associates).

When Shakespeare, for whatever reason, found it desirable to exhume Sir John, he could not rehabilitate him in the flesh of the cunning-sinister Morality rogue contending for the soul of Hal. In the new Sir John we have only one basic substance of the old, the gentleman-rogue stripped of all pretensions except his vanity, the would-be cozener cozened not only by the merry wives of Windsor but even by his own knaves. *The Merry Wives of Windsor* itself is a tissue of cozenry. In the first sub-plot, Doctor Caius and Abraham Slender are cozened of their hopes in Anne Page who marries Master Fenton. The second sub-plot, involving the Host, Sir

Hugh Evans, Doctor Caius, Bardolph, and several other curiously interesting persons, is fragmentary, perhaps witnessing in its incompleteness to the haste in which the play was composed, but sufficient details exist, as we shall see, to deserve a special page in the record of Elizabethan conycatching.

The play is primarily interesting to us, however, as it illustrates precisely the foundation on which the superstructure of the rogue-gentleman Sir John of the Boar's Head Tavern was built. Sir John of the Garter Inn is the gentleman-rogue in decline; he is obliged to turn away his followers (and we are reminded that such action was one of the causes for the notable increase in vagabondage in the Renaissance). The withered serving-man Bardolph will be accepted by the Host as a tapster. Falstaff is glad to see him go: "His thefts were too open. His filching was like an unskilled singer; he kept not time" (I.iii.28–29). Falstaff plans to retain Nym, who can convey (steal) like a flash, and Pistol provided they help him conycatch Mistresses Ford and Page. When these rascals develop a sudden squeamishness at becoming panderers, Sir John employs his page Robin on the mission and dismisses Nym and Pistol: "Rogues, hence, avaunt! Vanish like hailstones, go! Trudge, plod away o' th' hoof! seek shelter, pack!" Pistol retorts to the disappearing Falstaff with heat, but is sure of his own future with cards and dice: "Let vultures gripe thy guts! for gourd and fullam holds, / And high and low beguiles the rich and poor."[15] Nym proposes revenge, and the two agree to reveal Falstaff's mischief to Masters Page

15. *Gourd* and *fullam, high* and *low:* Shakespeare here shows that he has been reading either *A manifest detection* or the plagiarized version of the same work, *Mihil Mumchance* or that this information on false dice had become current. *Mihil Mumchance* (C2): "Provide also a bale or two of Fullams, for they have great use at the *Hazard,* and though they be square outward, yet being stopt within at the corner with white lead and other ponderous matter, minister as great an advantage as any of the rest. Ye must be also furnished with *High men* and *Low men* for a passage, yee and a long Dye for even and odde, is good to strike a stroake withall for a Crowne or Two, or the price of a Dinner. As for *Goards* and *Bristell* Dyce, be now too grosse a practice to bee put in use . . ." (Pistol's knowledge of dice comes under criticism here.) See

and Ford. As Page points out to Ford, Nym and Pistol are not reliable informers since they are "discarded men, very rogues, now they be out of service" (II.ii.181–182), but Ford is eager to believe their news.

Meanwhile, Pistol, not accepting his discharge, once more appeals to Falstaff for support, and when Falstaff refuses him a loan, he threatens to turn highwayman and win his living by violence. Falstaff is not moved (II.ii.5–12):

> Not a penny. I have been content, sir, you should lay my countenance to pawn. I have grated upon my good friends for three reprieves for you and your coach-fellow Nym; or else you had look'd through the grate, like a geminy of baboons. I am damn'd in hell for swearing to gentlemen my friends you were good soldiers and tall fellows; and when Mistress Bridget lost the handle of her fan, I took't upon mine honour thou hadst it not.

Pistol reminds him that he had fifteen pence from that theft; and Falstaff's response is a compact of many themes of roguery (II.ii.15–29):

> Reason, you rogue, reason! Think'st thou I'll endanger my soul gratis? At a word, hang no more about me. I am no gibbet for you. Go! a short knife and a throng! To your manor of Pickt-hatch![16] Go. You'll not bear a letter for me, you rogue? You

---

also *The Letting of Humours Blood in the Head-Vaine, Complete Works of Samuel Rowlands,* Hunterian Club, I, 58–59, Satire 3:

> His witt's his lyving: one of quaynt device,
> For Bowling-allies, Cockpits, Cardes, or Dice,
> To whose exployts he ever standes prepar'd:
>
> . . .
>
> But come to Dice, why that's his onely trade,
> *Michell Mum-chaunce,* his owne Invention made.
> He hath a stocke, whereon his lyving stayes,
> And they are *Fullams,* and *Bard quarter-trayes:*
> His *Langrets,* with his *Hie men* and his *low,*
> Are ready what his pleasure is to throw.

16. A low quarter of London, famous for harlots and pickpockets. Wheatley and Cunningham observe that it has been generally considered a part of Turnmill Street near Clerkenwell Green, but that in Elizabethan times it was a street at the back of Middle Row (formerly Rotten Row), opposite to Charter House in Goswell Road. Allusions to this district are frequent in rogue literature.

> stand upon your honour! Why thou unconfinable baseness, it is as much as I can do to keep the terms of my honour precise. I, I, I myself sometimes, leaving the fear of God on the left hand and hiding my honour in my necessity, am fain to shuffle, to hedge, and to lurch;[17] and yet you, rogue, will ensconce your rags, your cat-a-mountain looks, your red-lattice phrases, and your bold-beating oaths under the shelter of your honour?

Pistol has relented, but page Robin already has his post; revenge is his only satisfaction. He will have part in Falstaff's final discomfiture at Herne's Oak.

Bardolph even as a tapster has his troubles; the three Germans whom he was escorting to court for the Host turn out to be cozener-germans that have cozened all the hosts of Reading, Maidenhead, and Colebrook, and have ditched Bardolph in the mire and run away with the horses, a typical horse-courser feat, as will be shown.

And Falstaff uses the event to sum up his own tribulation (IV.v.95–96): "I would all the world might be cozen'd, for I have been cozen'd and beaten too." Only his ability to counterfeit the carriage of an old woman has saved him from being set in the stocks as a witch. The scene of the last discomfiture of Falstaff at Herne's Oak makes it possible for Master Fenton to marry Anne Page through a neat cozening of her father and her mother.

Finally let us consider the story of the theft of the Host's horses. This episode as it stands seems an isolated bit of action, almost unrelated to the rest of the play, but the conjecture of H. C. Hart that it was meant to be part of the second subplot is probably true.[18] In the second subplot, Doctor Caius and Sir Hugh Evans, who consider themselves mocked

17. *shuffle, hedge, lurch:* these terms refer to rogue behavior. *OED* lists this use of *shuffle* in *Merry Wives* in the sense of acting in a shifting or evasive manner and a like usage in IV.vi.27–30 as its first examples (5b, 7). *Hedge* ("to shift, shuffle, dodge") is likewise recorded as the first example in OED. *Lurch* ("to remain in or about a place furtively or secretly, esp. with evil design") has a more ancient history, with a record beginning as early as c.1420.

18. *The Merry Wives of Windsor,* ed. H. C. Hart, Arden ed. (London, 1932), pp. lxxii–lxxiv.

by the Host (III.i.119–123), plan a revenge which seems somehow connected with the theft of the Host's horses. This we may assume from their complacent mocking of the Host as they warn him about the danger from the three "cozen-germans" immediately after he has been cozened by these knaves (IV.v.75–92). These knaves themselves require special attention, as their story relates to conycatching and to topical history.

The actual history, unusually well authenticated,[19] concerns a Count Mumpellgart (Duke of Wurtemberg in 1593) who, with a retinue in black velvet, spent a month in England in 1592. He visited the Queen at Reading August 17 to 19, afterwards going to Windsor for two days, and thence to Oxford and Cambridge, enjoying full hospitality at each place. He appears to have barely escaped a highway robbery at Gadshill (not related to the famous one, so far as is known). At Windsor he received a passport for his return home from the Lord High Admiral Howard, a document providing him with posthorses and shipping, all free of charge. While in England he seems to have won Elizabeth's promise to appoint him to the coveted Order of the Garter, a promise of which he kept reminding her to her apparent irritation. His election was finally permitted in 1597, but his installation was delayed until 1603 when the honor was conferred with full ceremonies at Stuttgart.

The Duke, then, was a living memory, and according to Hart, an unpopular one, in the region of the setting of the play at the time when it was written and performed. To Elizabeth he was Cousin Mumpellgart (by anagram, as Hart points out, "cozen garmombles" of the Quarto). He might even have been a guest at the Garter Inn, and an actual cozening horse-theft may have been performed in his name, as Hart tells us: "At present it is mainly guesswork, but the guess would be

19. Charles Knight first called attention to this story (Hart, p. xli), which is translated from the Journal of the Duke of Wurtemburg in William B. Rye's *England as Seen by Foreigners,* London, 1865.

that in 1592 during the Duke's visit, or immediately after it, certain rogues made use of the order he was known to possess, and as either his servants or pretending to be his servants, levied and stole horses in his name from innkeepers."[20]

Who were the three "cozen-germans" who ran away with the horses to newly honest Bardolph's and the Host's dismay? Hart, in reconstructing the second subplot, conjectures that they may well have been John Rugby, Doctor Caius's servant, and Nym and Pistol, very likely candidates, but their personal identity must remain unknown. We do, however, have some information about the rogue-types they represent. Two or three years after the composition of the play, Samuel Rowlands describes such knaves as "rank riders" in his *Greenes Ghost Haunting Conie-Catchers* (1602):

> There is a certain kind of cosonage called horsecoursing, which is when a man goes to the Cariers of Cambridge, Oxford, Burie or Norwich, or anie great towne of trade, and hires a horse to ride downe with them, as these odde companions will doe: and what doth me he, but as soone as he hath him, steps aside into some blind towne or other, and there lies till he have eaten him out lim by him in wine and capons, and then when he can get no more on him, he sends the Carier word where he is; who in the end is faine to pay some fiftie shillings or three pounds for his victuals that hired him ere he can have him. Rochester hackney men do knowe what belongs to this trade, for they have beene often times fleeced by these ranke riders, who coming to a towne with a cloke-bag of stones caried after them, as if they were men of some worth, hire a horse to Canterburie, and ride quite away with him.[21]

Rowlands's account of these cozeners is manifestly not based on the episode in *The Merry Wives,* and it would appear that both Rowlands and Shakespeare have recourse to an actual tradition of cozening of this sort. Since the known sources of either writer do not otherwise provide for this cozening

20. Hart, p. xlv.
21. *The Complete Works of Samuel Rowlands,* I, p. 14.

story,[22] their accounts seem the earliest records of this form of knavery. In due course, Dekker in *Lanthorne and Candle-light* formulates this brand of cozening in a chapter devoted to rank riders (F3^{v}–F4^{v}), with specific details of how these knaves practice their art on innkeepers and hackneymen.

22. Edward D. McDonald in his careful study of Rowlands's debt to various authors finds that this particular material seems original with him ("An Example of Plagiarism among Elizabethan Pamphleteers: Samuel Rowlands' *Greenes Ghost Haunting Conie-Catchers," Indiana Univ. Stud.,* IX (1911), 145–170).

VI

The "Theefe in Societie" and the Knave of Fashion

THOUGH FALSTAFF'S personality overshadows his symbolic meaning, there can be little doubt that the symbol becomes more emphasized in the rogues and knaves in the plays of Shakespeare and the other dramatists immediately following the Henriad, to the extent that the most notable of the knaves often impress us more with their symbolic value than with their qualifications as individuals. For creating such figures the dramatists had plenty of literary precedent as well as their own observation to draw upon. The satirists of the last decade of the century, inspired in part by the attacks on the evils of fashion by Barclay and Andrew Borde with their memorable woodcuts (see Plates Nos. 16, 17) and by Phillip Stubbes's elaborate polemic on the subject in his *Anatomie of Abuses in Ailgna* (Anglia), had been busy fashioning rogue and knave figures with symbolic meaning as the media for their attacks on social abuses. With them the rogue-knave becomes a metaphor for the deceptions and dissimulations they found practiced in society in general. Their creatures were not based merely on imagination: the last years of the century seem to have witnessed a remarkable proliferation of a relatively new set of knaves, who bore some faint resemblance to the earlier whipjacks of Harman and the cony-catchers of Greene, but who were more notable for their appearance. One might call them whip-jack cozeners newly

¶ Of newe fassions and disgised Garmentes.

¶ Who that newe garmentes loues/or deuyses.
Or werryth by his symple wyt/and vanyte
gyuyth by his foly and vnthryfty gyses
Moche yl example to yonge Comontye.
Suche one is a Fole and skant shal euer thee
And comonly it is sene that nowe a dayes
One Fole gladly folowes anothers wayes.

Virorum effe minatio.

Rasit Amō di midiā partem barbę eorum: & pręscibit ve stes eorū me= dias vsq; ad nates. Erant autē viri tur= piter confusi valde. Ve mū do a scandalo Vos eteni iu= uenes/aios ge ritis mulieri= bres Illaq; vir go viri. Ennius&Tul lius in offitijs

caillete

Drawe nere ye Courters and Galantz disgised
ye counterfayt Caytifs. that ar nat content
As god hath you made:his warke is despysed
ye thynke you more crafty than God onipotent.
Unstable is your mynde:that shewes by your garment.
A fole is knowen by his toyes and his Cote.
But by theyr clothinge nowe may we many note.

Math. xviii.

Aparayle is apayred. Al sadnes is decayde
The garmentes ar gone that longed to honestye.
And in newe sortes newe Foles ar arayede
Despisynge the costom of good antiquyte.
Mannys fourme is disfigured with euery degre
As Knyght Squyer yeman Jentilman and knaue
For al in theyr goynge vngoodely them behaue

ij. Regum. x
Nouitatib⁹ in dulgēduz nō ē. ri. dis C. fide cō sue. cū ꝯsuetu= dinibus.

PLATE 16. Fashion and Folly. Barclay, *Ship of Fools*, Fol. XVIII. British Museum, G.11593.

dressed up, but the emphasis is on the dress, the fashion, the pretense to gentility.

"Cuthbert Conny-catcher" describes these new knaves as "a crew of terryble Hacksters in the habite of Gentlemen, wel appareld, and yet some weare bootes for want of stockings, with a locke worne at theyr lefte eare for their mistrisse favour, his *Rapyer Alla revolto,* his Poynado pendent ready for the stab, and *cavilevarst* like a warlike *Magnifico*. Yet for all this outward shew of pride, inwardly they be humble of minde, and despise worldly welth, for you shal never take them with a penny in theyr purse" (C3ᵛ).[1] Ned Browne, we remember, was such a knave, "in outward shew a Gentleman-like companion attired very brave, and to shadowe his villany the more would nominate himself to be a Marshall man." Even the love-lock apparently is typical (Nash speaks of it as "a nittie love locke")[2]; Joseph Hall describes one such gallant as having "One locke *Amazon-like* disheveled: / As if he ment to weare a native cord / If chaunce his *Fates* should him that bane afford."[3]

Most of these are actual knaves, shifty cozeners, men who prey on society; but as Cuthbert Connycatcher asks, "what about the Fox-furd Gentlemen that hyde under their gownes faced with foynes, more falsehood then all the Conny-catchers in England" (A4ᵛ)? Are not these also knaves? The transfer of the image of the knave to the malefactors of trade and established position or the "theefe in societie," as Lodge calls him, is natural and inevitable and becomes one of the main weapons in the arsenal of the satirists attacking social abuses.

1. *Defence of Conny-catching* (1592), C3ᵛ; Harrison, p. 38. See also *Much Ado About Nothing, Variorum* ed., pp. 173–174, for the significance of this lock.

2. *Piers Penilesse,* B2, McKerrow, I.170. This portrait of a malcontent knave of fashions is one of the best.

3. B.M., C.39.a.3 (STC 12716): *Virgidemiarum, / Sixe Bookes. / First three Bookes, / Of Toothlesse Satyrs. / 1. Poeticall. / 2. Academicall. / 3. Morall. /* [Ornament] */ London / Printed by Thomas Creede, for Robert / Dexter. 1597,* Book III, Satire VII, F2 (p. 65).

¶The fyrst chapter treateth of the naturall dyspoſicion of an Englyſhman, and of the noble realme of England, & of the money that there is vſed.

¶I am an Engliſh man, and naked I ſtand here
Muſyng in my mynde, what rayment I ſhal were
For now I wyll were thys and now I wyl were that
Now I wyl were I cannot tel what
All new faſhyons, be pleſaunt to me
I wyl haue them, whether I thryue or thee
Now I am a fryſker, all men doth on me looke
What ſhould I do, but ſet cocke on the hoope
What do I care, yf all the worlde me fayle
I wyll get a garment, ſhal reche to my tayle
Than I am a minion, for I were the new gyſe

The

PLATE 17. The Englishman and Fashion. *The fyrst boke of the Introduction of knowledge*. British Museum, C.71.b.29.

Among these satirists none was more vehement than Lodge, who makes free use of the knave metaphor in *Wits Miserie and the Worlds Madnesse* (1596)[4] in describing these vices. Lodge visualizes these abuses as sons of the devils representing the seven deadly sins, but his devils quickly take on the shape of knaves and rogues in "clokes of the new fashion." Thus Vainglory (son of Leviathan or Pride) appears in various shapes to men of all nations and humors (Bii^{v}–Biii):

> In Powls hee walketh like a gallant Courtier, where, if he meet some rich chuffes worth the gulling, at every word he speaketh, hee makes a mouse of an elephant, he telleth them of wonders done in *Spaine* by his ancestors: where if the matter were well examined, his father was but a Swabber in the ship where Civill [Seville] Oranges were the best merchandize. . . . Sometime like a Merchant he haunteth the Exchange; there iets hee in the dispoils of a Brokers shop, grave in lookes, courtly in behaviour, magnificent to the simple sort, affable to the wiser . . . filling all mens ears with so great opinion of his wealth, that every one holdeth him happy that trust him, till in the end both hee and they, proove bankruptes.

Curiosity, yet another of Leviathan's sons, is a well-tanned knave who "promised to find any mans oxen where they were lost, restore any mans goods if they were stolne, and win any man love where, or howsoever he settled it: but his Iugling knackes were quickly discovered, and now men that in their opinions held him for a right coniurer, dare boldly sweare that he is a rancke cousener" (Ciii).

One of the most popular of Leviathan's sons and least suspected of evil is named "*Superfluous Inventions* or as some tearme him *Novelmonger* or *Fashions*." It will be observed that "Fashions" clearly signifies the deceptions of evil behavior as well as the vanities of attire (Ciii–Ciii^{v}):

> Sometimes he is a cooke, inventing new sauces and banquets, sometimes devising strange confections to besot an idolater of his

4. B.M., C.30.d.19 (STC 16677): *Wits Miserie, / and the Worlds / Madnesse: / Discovering the Devils Incarnat / of this Age. /* [Ornament] */ London, / Printed by Adam Islip, and are to be / sold by Cutbert Burby, at his shop by / the Roiall-Exchange. 1596.*

> bellie, sometimes for an irefull man he deviseth strange revenges. . . . *Cleopatra* in her time was his dear friend, and in our age he is sought too both in Towne and Countrie . . . the Elephant is admired for bearing a little castle on his back, but what say you to a tender, faire, young, nay a weakling of women-kind, to wear whole Lordships and manor houses on her backe without sweating . . . Is not *Fashions* a iolly fellow that worketh this?

Fashions has a brother named Scandal and Detraction who anticipates the popularity of the malcontent on the stage, and could have served as understudy for Don John who was to skulk in the Globe two years later: "This is a right malcontent Devill, You shall alwaies find him his hat without a band, his hose ungartered, his Rapier *punto r'enverso,* his lookes suspitious and heavie, his left hand continually on his dagger: if he walke Poules, he sculks in the backe Isles, and of all things loveth no societies: if at any time he put on the habit of gravitie, it is either to backbite his neighbor, or to work mischiefe" (D).

Not less knavish are such devils as Lying, the great traveller with his Spanish hat, Italian ruff, French doublet, Toledo rapier, German hose, English stockings, and Flemish shoes, with his many trophies (among them St. Peter's forefinger, St. Dunstan's walking staff, and a piece of the chair Caesar sat in when he was stabbed in the Senate); Malicious Hatred; Brawling Contention; and a score of other devils who constantly afflict mankind.

This device of assailing social vices by representing them as knaves of fashion and dissimulation thus established by Greene, Nashe, and Lodge proved enormously popular and all the writers of prose and verse satire of the time employ it, some happily improving on their models, but others lamely following the style. The satirists most devoted to the conception are Rowlands, Dekker, Marston, and Guilpin, though one can observe traces of it everywhere in the various works of satire.

Less happy than his master Lodge's inventions are the

multitudinous efforts of Samuel Rowlands on the same subject (at times almost in the same words), but they have a historical interest as they illustrate the popularity of the theme. In a series of pamphlets from 1600 to 1622, whose titles speak for the theme themselves (*The Letting of Humours Blood in the Head-Vaine, Looke to it: for Ile Stabbe ye, The Knave of Clubbes, The Knave of Harts, More Knaves Yet? The Knaves of Spades and Diamonds, The Night Raven,* and *A Paire of Spy-Knaves*), Rowlands gambles (and loses) his literary future principally on this theme. In these booklets, borrowing heavily from Lodge and Greene, he gives us verse sketches of Sir Lancelot, the blustering captain of the Queen's highway; Sir Revell, ape of the world's fashions; and a host of panderers, cozeners, night-swaggerers, roaring boys, and punks, all exhibiting the dissimulations practiced by rascals in all walks of life, and all representing the large symbolism of fashion:

> *Fashions* is still consort with new fond shapes,
> And feedeth dayly upon strange disguise:
> We shew our selves the imitating Apes
> Of all the toyes that Strangers heades devise.
> For ther's no habite of hell-hatched sinne,
> That we delight not to be clothed in.[5]

Rowlands very literally illustrates the transfer of the image of the thief to the established member of society in *Diogines Lanthorne* (1607) (see Plate 18):

> If a Theife should meete me going home, and take away my pursse, I would say I met with an honester man than hee that couson'd me in the buying of my Gowne, for the Theife would prove a man of his worde, and tell me what I should trust to in the peremptory tearmes of *Stand, deliver your Pursse.*
>
> But my Gowne-brother, he promist me good stuffe *truly,* a great penyworth *indeed,* and verily did gull me. But let him take

5. B.M., C.58.cc.31 (STC 21393): *The Letting / of Humours / Blood in the / Head-Vaine. / With a new Morisco daunced by / Seaven Satyres, upon the bottome / of Diogenes Tubbe /* [Ornament] */ At London, / Printed by W. White for W.F. / 1600,* sig. A2.

DIOGINES
LANTHORNE.

Athens I ſeeke for honeſt men;
But I ſhal finde thẽ God knows when.

Ile ſearch the Citie, where if I can ſee
One honeſt man; he ſhal goe with me.

LONDON
Printed for *Thomas Archer*, and are to be ſolde at his Shop
in Popes-head Pallace, neere the Royall-
Exchange. 1 6 0 7.

PLATE 18. *Diogenes Lanthorne*. Title page. Malone 660, Bodleian Library.

leave of my pursse, hee's a villain, an arrant villain, and I could finde in my harte to eat his Liver fry'd with Parsley to morowe morning for my breakfast (Bii).[6]

Dekker plays with the metaphor frequently, especially in a work whose title signifies its lineage in Nashe and Lodge, *The Seven Deadly Sinnes of London.*[7] The first of these sins, "Politick Bankruptisme" he denounces as (D) "a harpy that lookes smoothly, a hyena that enchants subtilly, a mermaid that sings sweetly, and a cameleon that can put himselfe into all colours"; but presently the knave of fashion emerges: "he jets up and downe in his silkes woven out of other mens purses, rides on his ten pound geldings in other mens saddles, and is a new man made out of wax; that's to say out of those bonds whose seales he most dishonestly hath canceld. O velvet garded theeves! O yea-and-by-nay cheaters! O grave and right worshipful cozeners!"

One finds the image no less often in Marston's *Satires* with their significant motto, *Quaedam videntur, et non sunt,* and it achieves characteristic expression in the *Scourge of Villainy* (1598):

> O spruce! How now, Piso, Aurelius's ape,
> What strange disguise, what new deformed shape,
> Doth hold thy thoughts in contemplation?
> Faith say, what fashions thou art thinking on?
> A stitch'd taffeta cloak, a pair of slops
> Of Spanish leather? O who heard his chops
> E'er show of ought but of some strange disguise?
> This fashion monger, each morn 'fore he rise,

6. Bodl., Malone 660 (STC 21368): *Diogines Lanthorne. . . . / London / Printed for Thomas Archer, and are to be solde at his shop / in Popes-head Pallace neere the Royall- / Exchange. 1607.* This work may have suggested to Dekker the image of the Bellman and his lantern.

7. B.M., 2326.C.b. (STC 6522): *The / Seven Deadly Sinnes of London: / Drawne in Seven Severall Coaches Through / the Seven Severall Gates of / the Cittie / Bringing the Plague with them. / Opus septem Dierum. / Tho. Dekker / At London / Printed by E.A. for Nathaniel Butter and are / to be sold at his shop neere Saint Austens gate. / 1606.* Reprinted in *Illustrations of Old English Literature,* ed. J. P. Collier, II (1866).

Contemplates suit-shapes, and once from his bed,
He hath them straight fully lively portrayed.[8]

But the sprightliest and most challenging of all these volumes of satire, though neglected and forgotten until Professor G. B. Harrison called attention to it, is Edward Guilpin's *Skialetheia or A shadowe of Truth in certaine Epigrams and Satyres* (1598).[9] Guilpin knew and appreciated the satires of Greene and Lodge, but he also knew his London, its fashions and behaviors, and the London of rogue life (Satyre V):

What more variety of pleasures can
An idle Citty-walke affoord a man?
More troublesome and tedious well I know
T'will be, into the peopled streets to goe:
Witness that hotch-potch of so many noyses,
Black-saunts of so many severall voyces,
That chaous of rude sounds, that harmony
And *Dyapason* of harsh *Barbary,*
Compos'd of severall mouthes, and severall cries,
Which to mens eares turne both their tongs and eies,
There squeaks a cart-wheel, here a tumbrel rumbles,
Heere scolds an old Bawd, there a Porter grumbles,
Heere two tough Car-men combat for the way.
There two for lookes begin a coward fray.
Two swaggering Knaves here brable for a whore:
There brawls an Ale-Knight for his fat grown score.
But oh purgation! You rotten-throated slaves
Engarlanded with coney-catching knaves,
Whores, Bedles, Bawdes, and Sergents filthily,

8. *The Works of John Marston,* ed. A. H. Bullen (London, 1887), III, 377, Satire XI, ll. 156–160. Cf. Claudio (*Much Ado,* II.iii.13–15), who lies awake nights carving the fashion of a new doublet.
9. B.M., C.32.b.9 (STC 12504): *Skialetheia / or, / A shadowe of Truth, in cer- / taine Epigrams and / Satyres. /* [Ornament] */ At London: / Printed by J.R. for Nicholas Ling, and are / to bee solde at the little Westdoore of / Poules. 1598.* This book was entered in the Stationers' Register on September 15, 1598. It was one of seven books burnt in the following year, June 4, 1599, at Stationers' Hall as a result of an edict banning such books (see note 23). It was edited by Professor G. B. Harrison (Shakespeare Assoc. Facs., No. 2, 1931), who discusses Guilpin's probable allusions to various plays of Shakespeare which he appears to have witnessed.

Chaunt Kemps Iigge, or the Burgonians tragedy,
But in good time, there's one hath nipt a bong,
Farewell my harts, for he hath marrd the song.

In this atmosphere his knaves of fashion strut and jet. Among these is the great *Faelix* (in Satyre I), who seems modelled, as Professor Harrison suggests, on no less a Machiavellian than the great Bolingbroke (Guilpin also knows his theatre):

For when great *Faelix* passing through the street,
Vayleth his cap to each one he doth meet,
And when no broome-man that will pray for him,
Shall have less truage than his bonnets brim,
Who would not thinke him perfect curtesie?
Or the honey-suckle of humilitie?
The devill he is as soone: he is the devill,
Brightly accoustred [accoutred] to bemist his evill:
Like a Swartrutters hose his puffe thoughts swell
With yeastie ambition: *Signior Machiavell*
Taught him this mumming trick, with curtesie
T'entrench himselfe in popularitie,
And for a writhen face and bodies move,
Be Barricadode in the peoples love.[10]

At the court Balthazar pours his fountain of holy and rose-water words, but is blind when one needs him. Still another knave is Don Fashion, "Neate as a Merchants ruffe" (Satyre V), a dancer with a feather in his hat. Yet more striking for his being out of step with fashion is the dark malcontent, suggestive of Lodge's creature Scandal, and very possibly reminiscent of Don John himself (Satyre V):

But see yonder
One like the unfrequented Theater
Walkes in darke silence and vast solitude,
Suited to those blacke fancies which intrude
Upon possession of his troubled breast:
But for blacks sake he would looke like a ieast,
For hee's cleane out of fashion: what he?
I thinke the *Genius* of antiquitie

10. Cf. *Richard II,* I.iv.23–36.

Come to complaine of our varietie,
Of fickle fashions: then you iest I see.
Would you needs know? he is a malcontent.

All are victims of dissembling fashion, which becomes a large symbol, as we have seen elsewhere, of dissimulation and knavery in general (Satyre I):

Thus all our actions in a simpathy,
Doe daunce an anticke with hypocrisie,
And motley fac'd Dissimulation
Is crept into our every fashion
Whose very titles to are dissembled:
The now all-buttockt and no bellied
Doublet and Hose which I doe revell in,
Was my great grandsires when he did begin
To wooe my Grandame, when he first bespake her,
And witnesse to the joynture he did make her:
(Witness some antient painted history
Of *Assuerus, Haman, Mardoche*
For though some gulls me to beleeve are loth,
I know thei'le credite print, and painted cloth)
Yet like th' olde Ballad of the Lord of *Lorne*
Whose last line in King *Harries* dayes was borne,
It still retains the title of as new,
And proper a fashion, as you ever knew.
All things are different from their outward show . . .[11]

I
The "Thief Deformed" and Much Ado about "Noting"

Doubtless the theme and image could be traced in numerous dramas, but at least three plays, *Much Ado about*

11. Other possible allusions or resemblances to *Much Ado* occur in various places. Thus in Satire III, Jealousy has a windmill head in which ten thousand thoughts run whirligig (one is fleetingly reminded of the submerged image of the weathervane of Borachio's thief of fashion giddily turning about all the hot-bloods). Guilpin's reference to verjuice (spelled *Varges* as Goodman Verges's name was pronounced) associated with the theme of dialect and two-necked falsehood seems to parallel the veiling of truth in the double-meaning dialect of Dogberry and Verges. One allusion to a theater scene of a Mistress Minx (Satire V) at a window beckoning to a "copesmate" may be a reminiscence of Margaret's described behavior with Borachio.

Nothing, Cynthia's Revels, and *Othello* seem specifically composed in this period to dramatize the concept, their composition, to some degree, growing out of its currency as a favorite literary theme among the satirists. In *Much Ado About Nothing* with its punning and thematic title, the relationship to the metaphor turns on the identification of the curious "thief Deformed," who provides what has been considered a puzzling passage of wit at the very climax of the play.[12] The puzzle, seen from the vantage of the knave literature, is not difficult. In actuality, it appears that Borachio explains in the simplest possible way that he is talking about our knave of fashion, one who deforms[13] his appearance with the latest fads and who is symbolic of the deceptions one encounters everywhere and hence of the manifold deceptions in the plot.

12. For my discussion of *Much Ado* and *Cynthia's Revels* I am freely drawing upon my article "The Thief 'Deformed' and Much Ado About 'Noting,'" *Boston Univ. Stud. in English,* IV (1960), 65–84. See also Shakespeare's like use of the symbolic figure of Rumor, presented in the Prologue to *Henry IV, Part II* as a motivating force in the opening scene of the drama.

13. The term "thief Deformed" associates the thief or knave of fashion with the idea that the various fashions of the age "deform" the person, which should be clothed decorously but not extravagantly. The idea, encountered frequently, has an early expression in Barclay's version of *The Ship of Fools* (Fol. XIX):

> Some theyr neckes charged with colers and chaynes
> As golden withtthes: theyr fyngers ful of rynges:
> Theyr neckes naked: almoste onto the raynes
> Theyr sleves blasinge lyke to a cranys wynges
> Thus by this devysinge such counterfayted thinges
> They dyffourme that figure that god himselfe hath made
> On pryde and abusion thus ar theyr myndes layde.

Phillip Stubbes, in his *Anatomie of Abuses in Ailgna* (Anglia) (London, 1583), stresses the theological argument that attire originated to hide men's nature deformed by sin (p. 10): "[Adam and Eve] being both naked, were not ashamed; but sinne once committed, thei became uncleane, filthie, lothsome, and deformed, and sewed them garmentes of *Figge leaves* together, to cover their shame withall. Then the Lord pitying their miserie, and loathing their deformitie, gave them peltes, felles & skins of beastes to make them garments withall." In his satire Stubbes particularly attacks the vice of pride in apparel as the besetting sin of the land. His book was a source of inspiration for many if not all the satirists dwelling on this and other abuses.

Standing under a penthouse out of the rain, Borachio, like a true drunken knave,[14] tells his story to Conrade. He has earned a thousand ducats from Don John, and he proceeds very logically to explain how he won it. Fashion, he reminds Conrade, is nothing to a man, that is, one should always look below the surface to discover reality (III.iii.125–126). This fashion, his argument continues, is a deformed thief: "But seest thou not what a deformed thief this fashion is?" The eavesdropping watchman agrees: "I know that Deformed. 'A has been a vile thief this seven year; 'a goes up and down like a gentleman. I remember his name."

The superficial implication here is that the watchman has mistaken Borachio's term "deformed" for the name of some actual rogue of the time.[15] But the watchman does not alter the form of the name. Shakespeare seems to be con-

14. Professor Harrison appears to regard Borachio's name (*Drunkard*) as significant of his condition in this incident (*Shakespeare: 23 Plays and the Sonnets,* p. 436). Furness says that nothing in the passage suggests that Borachio is drunk; his conjecture that the phrase "true drunkard" alludes to the maxim *in vino veritas* is finely pertinent (*Variorum* ed., p. 168). Kittredge observes that Borachio has been drinking but "is by no means drunk" (*Sixteen Plays,* p. 128). He is possibly in that state in which his released inhibitions permit him to speak freely. Did the actor performing the part actually stagger and reel as he spoke of how the thief of fashion turned his devotees about? There is perhaps reason to believe that he did, as we shall see later. In any event, it is arch wit on Shakespeare's part thus to have a drunkard and fools reveal the truth of the situation.

15. This problem has doubtless puzzled many readers of the play. Fleay tried to explain it by identifying Deformed as Shakespeare (*Introduction to Shakespearian Study,* London and Glasgow, 1877, pp. 23, 116) on very slight grounds, as Furness points out (*Variorum* ed., p. 169); see also Furness's more reasonable view (p. xxxii). Later Fleay, with no explanation of his change of thinking, identified Deformed as Nashe (*A Biographical Chronicle of the English Drama,* London, 1891, II, 144) on the basis of the description of Nashe in *The Trimming of Thomas Nash* (1597). Nashe qualifies as a good example of a "deformed" character; but there is no evidence in the text that Shakespeare knew this piece of satire, and though he doubtless knew of Nashe's reputation, there is no way of showing that Shakespeare alludes to any person here. The attempt to explain the allusion as possibly referring to some lost topical incident and personage is made improbable by the phrase "this seven year" which suggests an indefinite and long time rather than any recent occurrence or situation.

cerned here not in making merely a topical allusion, but rather in heightening, through a device of seeming misconception, the meaning of Borachio's metaphor. As we shall see, the characteristics of Deformed as known by the Watchman are very like those of our knave of fashion. "Deformed" goes up and down like a gentleman—and the audience would surely understand that he wore the attire assembled from many nations described in many satires and mocked by Shakespeare himself in his description of Benedick's new devotion to fashion (III.ii.31–39). He has been carrying on his dark practices for "this seven year," an indefinitely long time, as the words imply.

At this point Borachio thinks that he hears some one, but Conrade tells him it was only the weathervane (another double entendre), and he resumes his allegory, fusing the image of the weathervane with it (III.iii.139–142):

> Seest thou not, I say, what a deformed thief this fashion is? how giddily 'a turns about all the hot-bloods between fourteen and five-and-thirty? sometimes fashioning them like Pharaoh's soldiers in the reechy painting, sometime like god Bel's priests in the old church window, sometime like the shaven Hercules in the smirch'd worm-eaten tapestry, where his codpiece seems as massy as his club?

In like vein, as observed earlier, Lodge describes Cleopatra as being the dear friend of fashion in her time. Shakespeare gives the idea a relatively new twist by illustrating it through a painting, a church window, and a tapestry, a device used also by Guilpin, as we have seen, perhaps under the inspiration of Shakespeare. Conrade understands the literal level of Borachio's statement, but cannot divine its application: "All this I see; and I see also that the fashion wears out more apparel than the man. But art thou not thyself giddy with the fashion too, that thou hast shifted out of thy tale into telling me of the fashion?" And Borachio's answer completes his allegory: "Not so neither. But know that I have tonight wooed Margaret, the Lady Hero's gentlewoman by the name of Hero . . ." (III.iii.148–155). Borachio insists that he has not shifted out of his tale: the deformed thief of fashion, this contriver of appearances, has been busy this very evening. Claudio and Don Pedro have been completely cozened by him into thinking that Margaret was Hero; but, says Borachio, "the devil my master knew she was Margaret."

Though the watchmen are very simple folk, they surmise that villainy is afoot, make their arrest at once, and call for the Constable. Not only have they "recovered the most dangerous piece of lechery that ever was known in the commonwealth," but they also somehow dimly perceive that Deformed is part of the conspiracy. The second watchman has seen him: he wears a lock—and scholars appear to agree that the reference is to the locks worn by our gentlemen-knaves. The First Watchman promises that Borachio and Conrade will be forced to reveal the whereabouts of Deformed: "You'll be made to bring Deformed forth, I warrant you."

Later, after the prisoners have been remanded to Leonato's custody, Dogberry tells us more about Deformed (V.i.316–322): "And also the watch heard them talk of one Deformed. They say he wears a key in his ear, and a lock hanging by it, and borrows money in God's name, the which he hath us'd so long and never paid that now men grow hard-hearted and will lend nothing for God's sake. Pray you examine him upon that point." Deformed wears a lock, apparently a love-lock; but Dogberry, with his two-headed jargon, interprets it otherwise: Deformed, he says, wears a key in his ear and a lock hanging by it. Capell felt rightly that the wit here lacks point to the modern audience unaware of Shakespeare's reference: "This humor about a 'lock' and a 'key,' of personizing 'Deform'd' and of making him the extraordinary borrower that follows after these words should (in likelihood) be founded upon something particular that was the public talk of the time; otherwise the wit is poor, and we to whom the knowledge of that particular has not descended, can scarce laugh at it."[16]

16. *Variorum* ed., p. 264, note 318.

But if it be granted that Deformed is a thief of fashion or appearances, as Borachio says he is, the key that Deformed wears in his ear—with the lock hanging by it (Dogberry's characteristic inversion of a lock with a key hanging by it) may be read as symbolic of the meaning of the play: *the key is in the ear*—our ear. Note well, Shakespeare appears to be saying, what is being said and done here. Deformed, the deformed thief of fashion, this gentleman thief who goes up and down abusing his credit this seven year (like Lodge's sinister knave Curiosity) is the key to the meaning of this drama. As a gentleman, Deformed has social license to continue his career of deception: appearance so often coincides with reality that people are habitually led into trusting appearances. Only those who *note* carefully, who weigh all evidence with care and are prepared to discount even the testimony of their own eyes and ears, only those who guard against the myriad guises of seeming are truly wise.

It seems fairly certain, then, that Borachio's "thief Deformed" is related to our knaves of fashion—that he is indeed the knave of fashion, a symbol of the difficulty people have in distinguishing the real from the apparent. It also seems plausible that the allegory was meant to apply to the play as a symbolic expression of its unifying theme of appearance and reality. That theme is manifest everywhere in the play, in plot, characterization, imagery, and the expression and thought of the play in general. For reasons of space, a full analysis is not possible here, but the application of the theme to the outstanding features may be briefly suggested. The main action is based on four situations, all involving manifest misconceptions, namely the proxy wooing of Hero by Don Pedro for Claudio,[17] the deception-conversion of Benedick

17. The resolution of this complication, which makes it necessary for the plot against Claudio and Hero to be started over again, has been regarded as a flaw in the plot; but what seems here like a tentative searching for a plot is, if the play is viewed thematically, part of a rich design. Surely now that the characters have been so soundly deceived they will be on guard against later deceptions. But people do not learn much from experience and they will almost

and Beatrice from their heresy against love, the defamation of Hero by Don John and Borachio, and the deception-conversion of Claudio and Don Pedro by Friar Francis. The characters illustrate the theme in a variety of ways: Claudio, who relies on others for his vision,[18] is the most deluded by appearances. Benedick and Beatrice, whose vision is much better (we like them most because of their inner vision) are apparently deceived into thinking each is in love with the other, though the audience surmises that they are tricked into realizing what was true from the start. Poor Hero is the victim of mistaken appearances: she is what she seems (IV.i.35–41); as Friar Francis observes (IV.i.156–165), appearances can be true and benign (this is what makes appearance so deceptive). All the imagery, both that of sporting (including images of netting, trapping, angling) and the much more striking fashion imagery (*Much Ado* has more than twice as many fashion images as any other play),[19] illustrates the theme vividly, as when Claudio and Benedick betray themselves as lovers through their sudden interest in fashions; and Benedick's new apparel in particular is like that of our knaves of fashion:

> *Pedro.* There is no appearance of fancy in him, unless it be a fancy that he hath to strange disguises; as to be a Dutchman today, a Frenchman tomorrow; or in the shape of two countries at

immediately be taken in by appearances again. A detailed analysis of these manifestations is given in my article (see Note 12).

18. Claudio uses both Benedick and Don Pedro as his spectacles in looking at Hero (I.i.163–235). This theme of borrowed vision is applied to Benedick and Beatrice also (V.iv.21–23).

19. Caroline Spurgeon (*Shakespeare's Imagery,* Boston: Beacon Press, 1961, p. 264) finds that images of sporting are more frequent in this play than in any other. But these images are not so numerous nor so fully developed as those of fashion. Bartlett records sixteen direct references to fashion and fashion-monging in *Much Ado,* over twice as many as in any other play. These references do not include several associated images dealing with clothing and appearance in general. Most, if not all, of the sporting images, notably those of netting, trapping, and angling, also illustrate the theme of appearance and reality.

> once, as a German from the waist downward, all slops, and a Spaniard from the hips upward, no doublet. Unless he have a fancy to this foolery, as it appears he hath, he is no fool for fancy, as you would have it appear he is. (III.ii.31–39).

Moreover, the word *fashion* itself is used in key incidents as a verb meaning to shape or contrive events.[20]

In short, all features of the play illustrate the great human problem in seeing things as they are. And as if to make sure that we do not miss the point, Shakespeare deftly introduces Deformed, the curious symbol of his meaning, and gives the whole an ambivalent name. What better title could have been devised to illustrate the theme itself? The common pronunciation of the two terms *noting* and *nothing*,[21] the early emphatic parrying on the likeness,[22] the significant use of the word *noting* as Friar Francis comes to the defense of Hero (IV.i.156–170) and the accepted fact that *nothing* to Shakespeare is often a loaded word, all these considerations suggest the double meaning of the title. To the audience we may assume that it was as if Shakespeare was saying, "This play might have been tragedy: hence this great ado about *noting;* but this time all ends well: much ado about nothing!"

20. *Much Ado,* II.i.384; II.ii.47; IV.i.236.
21. The meaning of this title has been much discussed. The view of White (*Variorum* ed., pp. 6, 113–114) that Shakespeare pronounced *nothing* like *noting* and that the pun is intentional, suiting the meaning of the play, seems to be winning general acceptance. White's argument is soundly based from a linguistic point of view (see Helge Kökeritz, *Shakespeare's Pronunciation,* New Haven, 1953, p. 132). Paul A. Jorgensen accepts White's interpretation but stresses the ambivalence of the title ("Much Ado About *Nothing,*" *SQ,* V(1954), 287–295.
22. The passage (II.iii.54–59) deserves quoting (italics mine):

> *Pedro.* Nay, pray thee come;
> Or if thou wilt hold longer argument,
> Do it in *notes.*
>
> *Balth.* *Note* this before my *notes:*
> There's not a *note* of mine that's worth the *noting.*
>
> *Pedro.* Why these are very crotchets that he speaks!
> *Note notes,* forsooth, and *nothing!*

II
The Knave of Fashion and *Cynthia's Revels*

The career in formal satire of these shape-changing Proteans underwent a brief partial eclipse on June 1, 1599, when the Archbishop of Canterbury and the Bishop of London issued an edict against the publication of satire, banning the further printing of such works and committing to the fire those already in print.[23] Professor Oscar James Campbell has shown how the dramatists responded to this challenge, with "comicall satyre"; Deformed and his brothers, already very much at home in drama, continue their activities without abatement. The next outstanding appearance of Deformed himself was to be in *Cynthia's Revels,* which seems to have been composed shortly after the edict and entered in the Stationers' Register on May 23, 1601.[24]

It has been remarked how Jonson sought to conceal the satiric structure of *Cynthia's Revels* by his use of classical myth and masques.[25] One must wonder whether the deft veiling of Shakespeare's theme in *Much Ado* might not have excited him to emulation, for *Cynthia's Revels* is also an elaborate, though much more obvious exposition of a like theme. The play is dedicated to fashion—to virtuous manners as opposed to deformed manners: "TO THE SPECIALL / FOUNTAINE

23. For a copy of this act, see Arber, Stationers' Registers, III, 316. On June 4, *Pygmalion, The Scourge of Villany, Skialetheia,* Davies's *Epigrams,* and three other books were burnt. See also Oscar James Campbell, *Comicall Satyre and Shakespeare's Troilus and Cressida* (San Marino, Calif., 1938), p. 1. The composition of *Much Ado* appears to have preceded this ban. Allison Gaw sums up briefly the evidence that dates *Much Ado* in the fall or winter of 1598–1599 in "Is Shakespeare's *Much Ado* a Revised Earlier Play?", *PMLA,* L (1935), 715–738. If, of course, Guilpin wrote *Skialetheia* after seeing *Much Ado,* as seems most likely, it would appear that *Much Ado* must have been first acted early in 1598.

24. *Ben Jonson,* ed. C. H. Herford, Percy and Evelyn Simpson (Oxford: Clarendon Press, 1932), IV, 3.

25. This represents, as Professor Campbell points out (p. 83), a distinct departure from his practice in *Every Man Out of His Humour* in which he emphasizes the "satiric scaffolding."

OF / MANNERS: / The Court." And the theme of the dedication is the theme of the play:

> Thou art a bountifull, and brave spring: and waterest all the noble plants of this Iland. In thee, the whole Kingdome dresseth it selfe, and is ambitious to use thee as her glasse. Beware, then, thou render mens figures truly, and teach them no lesse to hate their deformities, then to love their formes: For, to grace, there should come reverence; and no man can call that lovely, which is not also venerable. It is not pould'ring, perfuming, and every day smelling of the taylor, that converteth to a beautiful obiect: but a mind, shining through any sute which needes no false light either of riches, or honors to help it . . .[26]

Opposed to the ideal fountain of the court is the spring of self-love, whose waters are further to deform the deformed courtiers who are misshaping the manners of the court. All the characters except Arete, Crites, and Cynthia, are deformed, or impostors in disguise, as Jonson makes abundantly clear. In the Induction (lines 55–74), he begins the analysis of the nature of the deformed characters by pairing the gallants and their ladies. Philautia (self-love) is mistress to Hedon (the voluptuous); Phantaste ("a light wittinesse"), to Anaides (the impudent); Argurion (money) to Asotus (the prodigal). The ladies have a *Guardian,* Moria ("Mistress Folly") whom Jonson probably expected us to associate with the most important of the courtiers, named explicitly "AMORPHUS, or the *deformed.*"[27]

It is possible, in view of the emphasis on deformity in fashion and manners in the satires, that it might have occurred independently to Jonson to call his principal knave of fashion "the deformed," but there are many resemblances between *Cynthia's Revels* and *Much Ado* which suggest that Jonson knew the latter play and probably understood it

26. *Ben Jonson,* IV, 33.

27. Richard Simpson ("The Political Use of the Stage," *Transactions of the New Shakespeare Society,* II, 1874, 391) appears to have been one of the first to remark this relationship. See also Josiah H. Penniman, *The War of the Theatres* (Boston, 1897), p. 94.

much as it has been interpreted here. In any event, the presence in *Cynthia's Revels* of another Deformed, a leader in misshaping the manners of court, affords a remarkable parallel to the nature and activities of our famous thief.

Like Deformed, Amorphus is all appearance. He appears to be a great traveler, like his cousins in the satires; though Shakespeare neglects this characteristic in the quick sketch of Deformed, Beatrice does suggest that Benedick is such a voyager, and Jaques is later to illustrate the type under the scorn of Rosalind.[28] Amorphus is "one so made out of the mixture and shreds of formes, that himselfe is truly deform'd" (II.iii. 86–87).[29]

Amorphus is also a thief. He advises his pupil Asotus on how to "lift" phrases from the wit of other men by means of a "quick nimble memory" (III.i.41–45); and along with the other false courtiers, he is guilty of the "theft" as Cynthia calls it (V.xi.62) of appearing as other than he is in the final masque—which is, of course, the specialty of Deformed.

28. *Much Ado,* I.i.82–83 (see also Benedick's momentary assumption of the role, II.i.271–280); *As You Like It,* IV.i.21–37. See also Rosalind's condemnation of the deformity of Jaques's pose in general (*As You Like It,* IV.i.9–36).

29. There are numerous other resemblances to *Much Ado.* Thus Amorphus usurps the talk wherever he goes: "ten constables are not so tedious"; this is a probable allusion to Dogberry, as Herford and Simpson suggest (X, 174). Amorphus has a remarkable hat which he calls the "*hieroglyphicke* of my affection" and which will take any block (I.iv.184–186), a possible echo of Beatrice's swift jest about Benedick (I.i.75–77). Crites condemns the courtiers for aping fashions, "Still turning giddie, till they reele like drunkards" (I.v.24–32) and an allusion to Borachio's whirling votaries of fashion seems very likely (III.iii.110–112, 139–147). Cf. also *Much Ado,* II.i.97–100 with *Cynthia's Revels,* I.i.47–50; *M.A.,* V.ii.18–22 with *C.R.,* II.iii.41–43; *M.A.,* III.iv. 6–16 with *C.R.,* II.iv.1–8 and IV.i.22–24.

Interesting, in view of these other resemblances, and reading almost like a comment on Hero's experience, is Cynthia's statement: "Place, and occasion are two privie theeves; / And from poore innocent ladies often steale / The best of things an honourable name" (V.vi.63–65). Other more extensive likenesses, such as the use of Mercury and Cupid as invisible spectators of the strange show of the courtiers' follies (compare with the invisible spectators taking Cupid's role in the deception scene of Beatrice and Benedick) and the punishments of the courtiers and of Benedick and Beatrice for being "so odd and from all fashions," invite attention in passing.

Amorphus qualifies fully as the symbol of fashion for the play. His behaviors are not of "cheape or customarie garbe"; he is "alone in fashion" (I.iii.25, 31–32); he can mimic the "particular, and distinct face of every your most noted *species* of persons" (II.iii.16–17). Philautia acidly tells us that he looks "like a venetian trumpetter, i' the battaile of *Lepanto,* in the gallerie yonder; and speakes to the tune of a countrey ladie, that comes ever i' the rereward, or traine of a fashion" (IV.i. 48–51), and one is reminded how Borachio found the hot bloods fashioned "like Pharaoh's soldiers in the reechy painting." Though Amorphus, like other knaves, does not shift his clothes often (II.iii.97), his talk is all of fashion and courtly affectations, and he is recognized by the false courtiers as their "grand garbe-Master" (V.iv.540). As their leader he dominates the action of the greater part of the play, which centers around the follies of the courtiers, their eccentricities of dress, gossip, and frivolous entertainment, in which each betrays his special deformity.

In the final masque devised by Crites for Cynthia, the deformed courtiers all assume "the seeming face / Of neighbour-vertues, and their borrow'd names." For this "theft" of appearances Cynthia soundly rebukes them, banishes the offending Cupid, and gives to Arete and Crites the charge of punishing the presumption of the courtiers. Crites, after "citing" the female "follies" and "male deformities," sentences them to march, two by two, singing a palinode, by Niobe's stone and offer up two tears apiece upon it; then they are to pass to the well of knowledge, where, purged of their present ills, they are to become the goodness they have imitated. Then they are to return and offer their services to Cynthia (V.ix.104–113, 135–157). Claudio and Don Pedro have a somewhat like penance imposed on them. They, too, in formal procession ("*Enter* Don Pedro, Claudio, *and three or four others with tapers*"), march around Hero's supposed tomb and sing an "epitaph" (in content a palinode also; Jonson knew the correct term for the literary type specially involved here). Then, like the false courtiers, who return transformed to Cynthia, they go forward with chastened hearts to Leonato's house (V.i.281–298; V.iii).

The large intention of Jonson's play—the reformation of the manners and nature of the court to be achieved by grace of Cynthia's clear vision, aided by wise counselors (Crites, Arete, Mercury)—is summed up in his conclusion (V.xi.169–173):

> 'Princes that would their people should doe well,
> 'Must at themselves begin, as at the head;
> 'For men, by their example, patterne out
> 'Their imitations, and reguard of lawes:
> 'A vertuous *Court* a world to vertue drawes.'

Though Jonson has limited the scene of his action to the court, this final aim is not distant from the meaning of Shakespeare's play. Shakespeare's mood, however, is much more intricate and unobtrusive. Jonson is sharply, even savagely satiric. Shakespeare is the observer, urbane and mellow, reshaping life to an ideal pattern, but with gentleness and tolerance: Hero is innocent, but so are Claudio and Don Pedro who are only guilty of mistaking (V.i.283–284, iv.1–3). Benedick will devise brave punishments for Don John—but that will be tomorrow, outside the comedy. What Professor Barber has shown to be true of Shakespeare's gay plays preceding *Hamlet* and the problem plays, namely that they present the relation of man to his nature rather than the relations between social classes or social types, patently fits the nature of *Much Ado*.[30]

III

Iago, the "Complete Knave" and Demi-Devil[31]

The first act of *Othello*, a knave prologue to the main action, opens in the darkness of conspiracy. As Iago continues his conversation with Roderigo, the Jacobean audience first

30. C. L. Barber, "The Saturnalian Pattern in Shakespeare's Comedy," *Sewanee Review*, LIX (1951), 593–611.

31. For this study of Iago I am making use of my article, "The 'Arts Inhibited'

saw the very human ensign, disappointed because he had not been promoted to lieutenant. Then they saw, as in the phenomenon of reversible perspective, the shadow behind him, the familiar and subtle knave of appearance, with part ancestry, as Stoll has demonstrated, in the Devil and Vice of the early plays.[32] It is also clear that they would regard him as a machiavel, to be associated with Don John and Borachio and his thief Deformed and the other knaves of fashion and dissimulation of our study.[33] So much has been said about these matters in the past that only a short summary of Iago's knavery need be attempted here for the sake of our roster of knaves of appearance: the one "complete knave" must not be omitted.

At the very outset Iago reveals his knavish outlook on the world. He divides humanity into two classes: honest knaves, duteous and knee-crooking for nothing but provender (I.i.44–47), and knaves of his own sort,

> Who, trimm'd in forms and visages of duty,
> Keep yet their hearts attending on themselves;
> And, throwing but shows of service on their lordes,
> Do well thrive by them, and when they have lin'd their coats,
> Do themselves homage. These fellows have some soul;
> And such a one do I profess myself.

This philosophy is seen often in the play, as in the wit contest with Desdemona, in which Iago belittles all women (II.i.118–

and the Meaning of *Othello*," *Boston Univ. Stud. in English,* I (1955), 129–147.

32. Of E. E. Stoll's several studies of Iago, that in *Shakespeare and Other Masters* (Cambridge, Mass., 1940), pp. 230–280, offers the most complete view in this light. See also his helpful "Sources and Motive in *Macbeth* and *Othello*," *RES,* XIX (1943), 25–32.

33. See my article (note 31) for the relationship of Iago to the *maleficus* or *veneficus,* practicer of the arts of black magic and witchcraft. See also Professor R. B. Heilman's study of the relation between Iago and the false doctor (a common knave remarked in Copland and other rogue literature), "Dr. Iago and his Potions," *Va. Quart. Rev.,* XXVIII (1952), 568–584. Professor Bernard Spivack also studies at length the demonic character of Iago's villainy and finds a kinship between Aaron, Richard III, Don John, and Iago (*Shakespeare and the Allegory of Evil,* New York, 1958, pp. 28–59, 415–453).

161): the virtuous and good woman, if such a one exists, is only fit "to suckle fools and chronicle small beer." Naturally when he estimates the character of Cassio it is in terms of knavery, and the portrait he draws of him is almost his own image and would serve as an idealized sketch of a knave of fashion (II.i.242–253): "A knave very voluble: no further conscionable than in putting on the mere form of civil and humane seeming for the better compassing of his salt and most hidden loose affection? . . . A slipper and subtle knave, a finder-out of occasions; that has an eye can stamp and counterfeit advantages, though true advantage never present itself; a devilish knave! . . . A pestilent complete knave!"

The relation of Iago as master knave and cozener to his gull Roderigo is established in the first three lines of the play through the apposite image of the purse. This image is never far from Iago's thoughts; the first act ends with his soliloquy beginning, "Thus do I ever make my fool my purse; / For I mine own gain'd knowledge should profane / If I would time expend with such a snipe / But for my sport and profit." Later on, in the Temptation scene, with greater sport in view, he uses the metaphor to establish his honest-seeming unwillingness to taint Cassio with suspicion, and the expression is a masterpiece of seeming piety couched in imagery of theft suited to the knavish speaker (III.iii.155–161):

> Good name in man and woman, dear my lord,
> Is the immediate jewel of their souls.
> Who steals my purse steals trash; 'tis something, nothing;
> 'Twas mine, 'tis his, and has been slave to thousands;
> But he who filches from me my good name
> Robs me of that which not enriches him
> And leaves me poor indeed.

As Iago arouses Brabantio in the night with the shocking cry, "Thieves, thieves!," the audience must have felt the irony of the subterfuge. Brabantio recognizes that Iago and Roderigo are disturbing his quiet for "malicious knavery," but he does not begin to surmise the sinister depth of Iago's mischief. Most striking are the demonic features of this knave both as revealed by his own remarks and those of others, features that relate him to the devil-knaves of Lodge and Nashe. Both knave and demon are suggested as he assures Roderigo that he will be able to seduce Desdemona (I.iii.362–366): "If sanctimony and a frail vow betwixt an erring barbarian and a super-subtle Venetian be not too hard for my wits and all the tribe of hell, thou shalt enjoy her. Therefore make money." As he conceives his scheme for cozening Othello, he muses how to plume up his will in double knavery (a knavery more than natural); and as the scheme takes shape in his mind, he exclaims (I.iii.409–410): "I have't! It is engend'red! Hell and night / Must bring this monstrous birth to the world's light." And with Machiavellian cynicism he justifies his practices of pleasant seeming in terms of the demonic knave (II.iii.354–359):

> How am I then a villain
> To counsel Cassio to this parallel course,
> Directly to his good? Divinity of hell!
> When devils will the blackest sins put on,
> They do suggest at first with heavenly shows,
> As I do now.

Iago's great victim, Othello, is far from being a simple gull, one who can be easily led by the nose as asses are (here again we have the effect of double perspective: Othello is not naive, and it will require fiendish cunning to ensnare him: but honest Iago can delude any one). After years of discussion of this character in the world of scholarship, it must be clear that Shakespeare meant Othello to be considered as a man wise in the ways of the world, well acquainted with the hesitations and stammerings used for effect by clever rascals ("such things in a false disloyal knave / Are tricks of custom," III.iii.121–122), and who is shrewd and astute (Venice has no other of his fathom in ways of war, and these are scarcely less subtle than ways of peace, despite all casuistry to the contrary). Iago's consummate skill as a knave of seeming can have no credit (nor does he claim it) for the gulling of Roderigo; indeed his skill cannot even be perceived unless it is exercised in the deception of as wise a man as the times could offer, the Renaissance Complete Man, as John Holloway describes Othello.[34] The large meaning of Iago as a knave of appearance lies in the fact that he is able to deceive even the wisest person if that person trusts circumstantial evidence and his own eyes and ears rather than his inner vision of truth, his heart. "If she be false, why then heaven mocks itself." When Othello trusts to his human senses and loses this vision and renounces love (III.iii.445–460), he is lost. In this slippery world we cannot even trust the evidence of our own eyes and ears. If, as Chaucer's yeoman with his black-fringed hat says, even a lousy juggler can deceive us, how much easier it is for "honest, honest Iago"!

Moreover, as Professor Paul A. Jorgensen has demonstrated, it is through his pose of honesty that Iago has a very special connection with the Elizabethan world of knaves.[35] The painful stress on the terms "honest" and "honesty" throughout the play and Iago's posing as the blunt honest friend of Othello, reluctantly discovering to him the slippery knavery of Cassio and Desdemona, would doubtless recall to Shakespeare's audience not only such knaves of dissimulation as those already noted, but also invite association with the blunt, forthright character of Honesty in the popular morality-comedy, *A Knack to Know A Knave* (1594).[36] In that play,

34. *The Story of the Night, Studies in Shakespeare's Major Tragedies* (Univ. of Nebraska Press, 1961), p. 47.

35. *"Honesty in Othello," S.P.*, XLVII (1950), 557–567. Jorgensen calls attention also to the Vice Dissimulation in Robert Wilson's *The Three Ladies of London* (1584) who poses as an honest man and swears by his honesty.

36. *A most pleasant and / merie new Comedie, / Intituled, / A Knack to knowe a Knave. / Newlie set foorth, as it hath sundrie / tymes bene played by Ed. Allen / and his Companie. / With Kemps applauded Merriementes / of the men of Goteham, in receiving / the King into Goteham. /* [Printer's device] / *Imprinted at London by Richard Iones, dwelling / at the signe of the Rose and Crowne, nere / Holborne bridge. 1594.* This work, often edited, has been reprinted recently by the Malone Society (ed. G. R. Proudfoot, 1963).

Honesty, a "plaine man of the country," who has a knack to know knaves, engages to expose to virtuous King Edgar the caterpillars corrupting his state (A4). In the course of the action Honesty unveils the deceptions of the four vicious sons of a vicious bailiff, namely Perin the Courtier, a Priest, a Conycatcher, and a Farmer.

In *Othello,* Iago is accepted by everyone as an embodiment of the virtue of honesty. Professor Jorgensen emphasizes the irony of his posture in relation to the knave hunter, Honesty:

> What complicates his rôle in the drama is not simply, as has been supposed, that he is a villain posing as an honest man. The irony goes one fold deeper. Iago is a knave posing as Honesty, a hunter of knaves. Hence the effect of Emilia's words, uttered though they are in ignorance of her husband's guilt:
>
> The Moor's abus'd by some most villanous knave,
> Some base notorious knave, some scurvy fellow.
> O heaven, that such companions thou'dst unfold,
> And put in every honest hand a whip
> To lash the rascals naked through the world
> Even from the East to th' West!
> (*Othello,* IV.ii.139–144)
>
> Iago, present during this speech, is startled, for he finds himself in it in a double capacity: as the "most villanous knave," the "base notorious knave," and as the "honest hand" bearing a whip in the service of Othello.

In the end, however, with his "honesty" unmasked, the strongest impression left with us about the cozening Iago is the aura of the demonic when Othello queries his identity as a devil and Iago's answer seemingly confirms it (V.ii.285–289).

These several occurrences of the theme and of creatures illustrating the devices of the knaves of fashion are only indicative, not exhaustive of the literature of the time bearing on the subject.[37] Borachio himself reappears (distinctly a

37. It was but a step from the concept of the knave of fashion and the thief in society to the idea that everyone and everything in the world are thieves,

knave of seeming) in Tourneur's *The Atheist's Tragedy,* and Face and Subtle, Volpone and Mosca, belong in the category. Such knaves accenting fashion and pious seeming are not uncommon in later drama, one obvious example close to the coloring of the "thief Deformed" being Joseph "Surface" with his agent Snake.

---

and Timon of Athens takes this step in his unmitigated disillusionment as he talks with the bandits (*Timon of Athens,* IV.iii.425–451).

VII

King Lear: Unthrift-Fool of Fortune and Bedlam

IN THE LIGHT of the literature that we have been examining, two features in Shakespeare's portrait of King Lear stand out with fair clarity, namely that in the course of his experience he becomes an unthrift-fool and, for a brief period, a madman, and hence he belongs in the great procession of the destitute and lost on the highway. In this tragedy, which is perhaps most validly explained as arising from a Hegelian conflict between two great rights, Lear's right to respect and love and Cordelia's devotion to truth, rights both just and good in themselves but needing adjustment in their relation to each other, two good people on the height of happiness are separated, fall into misery, and end wretchedly because of a momentary and, one may believe, uncharacteristic lack of sympathy with each other's needs.

In Renaissance thought, a moment's folly can make any one a lifetime's fool, and all are victims of folly to a greater or lesser degree:[1] all are actors, Lear reminds us, on the great

1. It seems certain that Shakespeare knew Copland, and this source would be perhaps enough to help him to his many reflections on folly without recourse to any other; but it would be strange if he had not also read Barclay. It would appear unlikely that he had in mind Erasmus's *Encomium Moriae,* since the special tone of that work is not evident in *Lear,* except for the passage remarked by Empson, who believes that the theme of folly may trace to this source (see *The Structure of Complex Words,* London, 1951, p. 130). Folly in *Lear* is more serious, less mocking than in Erasmus, and though it would be

stage of fools.[2] (It was the most natural thing in the world for Shakespeare to substitute this metaphor for that of the ship of fools, and the effect, as will be seen, is comparable.) There is one consolation for this predicament: folly may lead to wisdom through repentance, as Barclay observes in his Prologue (fol. xi):

> And certaynly I thynke that no creature
> Lyvynge in this lyfe mortall in transytory
> Can hym self kepe and stedfastly endure
> Without all spot / as worthy eternall glory
> But if he call to his mynde and memory
> Fully the dedys both of his youthe and age
> He wyll graunt in this shyp to kepe some stage
>
> But who so ever wyll knowledge his owne foly
> And it repent / lyvynge after in sympylnesse
> Shall have no place nor rowme more in our navy
> But become felawe to pallas the goddesse
> But he that syred is in suche a blyndnesse
> That thoughe he be nought he thynketh al is well
> Such shall in this Barge bere a babyll and a bell

We are apt to become victims of folly even when we are proceeding with admirable caution and sanity. As is demonstrated in the fortunes of Othello, even the wisest and best of us may be deceived by appearances if we rely on them rather than on our instinct in determining good and evil. Lear seems to surmise this truth when he strikes his head and exclaims, "O Lear, Lear, Lear! / Beat at this gate that let thy folly in, / And thy dear judgment out!" (I.iv.292–294). This great theme of

---

hard to select specific passages in Barclay that may have been directly suggestive to Shakespeare, the lines from fol. xi, quoted below certainly fit the general sense of *Lear*.

2. R. B. Heilman (*This Great Stage*, Louisiana State Univ. Press, 1948, pp. 182–192) and Empson (pp. 125–157) have so extensively discussed the theme of universal folly in Lear that it is unnecessary to recapitulate its many elements here. See also Enid Welsford, *The Fool / His Social and Literary History* (London, 1935), for an enlightening discussion of the Fool in *Lear*.

folly, together with the concomitant theme of madness, is first given expression by Kent (I.i.147–150):

> Be Kent unmannerly
> When Lear is mad. What wouldst thou do, old man?
> Thinkest thou that duty shall have dread to speak
> When power to flattery bows? To plainness, honour's bound
> When majesty falls to folly.

Like Cordelia, Lear has made a great mistake, but it may be argued that the mistake was not characteristic of him. Kent does not take this occasion to remind Lear of any mistakes in the past when he has served as cleansing priest (a function which Leontes even in his obsession credits to Camillo), but this fearless and outspoken man here speaks as if this were the first occasion that he has ever crossed Lear's will. And indeed, save for this one tragic error, Shakespeare fundamentally pictures the King as a man of clear judgment, sound understanding, and, judged by the accepted view of kingly conduct, eminently proper behavior. If, after the first scene, any opposite impression is given at any time, Shakespeare appears always to correct it somehow in Lear's favor.[3] Unless Albany is badly mistaken, this "gracious aged man, / Whose reverence even the head-lugg'd bear would lick" (IV.ii.41–42), in general conduct seems to have been a man full of grace and fair regard.[4] Even in the terrible first scene Shakespeare begins

3. The interpretations of Kittredge, Stoll, and C. B. Watson that demonstrate Lear's behavior as usually proper and considerate of others seem more consistent with the total impression of Lear's character than those of such critics as Bradley and Granville-Barker who consider him lacking in self-government. The grandeur which Bradley, as well as Schücking, attributes to Lear is simply not consonant with the assumption that his character is habitually "foolish and self-willed." Bradley's assumption that Lear's curse of Goneril is a manifestation of hubris seems strained in view of his admission that the situation calls for passionate indignation on Lear's part. Even till the beginning of the present century the fear of a father's curse was an effective force in family life, a dread that an erring child had to fear. The Jacobean audience would almost certainly have regarded the curse as justified.

4. It is interesting to compare Albany's image of the head-lugged bear licking Lear in reverence with the picture in Barclay's *Ship of Fools,* fol. XLVIII, of

drawing in the lines that establish Lear as a good king who illustrates that the best of mortals may be a victim of folly unless he trusts to his inward vision.

At the very start it is clear that Lear attempts to plan wisely (though we cannot pry into the mystery of things, it is our lot to try). He sanely (not senilely) realizes that he is old, and surmising to some degree the natures of Goneril and Regan (who can know all in advance?), he hopes to prevent future strife in the kingdom by settling the problem of inheritance before his death, as a wise man should. The assumption that Lear should not have divided the kingdom is not made by Shakespeare, and does not seem a concern with him (at the end of the drama even the newly wise Albany proposes a split government of the realm, if not a division, to Edgar and Kent).[5] No better solution of the problem could have been devised. For Lear to have retained the kingship till his death could not conceivably have prevented strife and division, save, dubiously, for his own lifetime,[6] and the one hope of satisfying the conflicting interests of his daughters lay in the plan conceived by Lear. The one hope failed, not because the plan was ill-advised—it might have worked—but because the plan itself was abrogated by the unforeseen and unpredictable tragic error.

---

the fool counting his wealth while dogs lick the feet of a reverend beggar outside his window (see Plate 19). This woodcut illustrates the canto "Of riches unprofitable," which concludes with Barclay's envoy, "Ye great estatis and men of dignyte / To whome god in this lyfe hath sent ryches / Have ye compassion on paynfull povertye / And them confort in theyr carefull wretchedness"—lines which carry the same message as Lear's great plea for houseless wretched folk.

5. The assumption that the audience would have at once considered that Lear was unwise in dividing England (they knew that England had been variously divided in early history) is a view neatly tailored to fit one reading of the play, but it is not based on any expressed or implied opinion in the play itself. The same objection applies to Tillyard's suggestion that the audience would have regarded Lear's abdication in favor of his children as unnatural because such an abdication in *Gorboduc* was called so. Shakespeare does not give any support for these views.

6. Goneril and Regan appear to have been trying to get him to yield the kingdom earlier; the partition in Scene i is his "last surrender" (I.i.311).

Quid tamen hoc ꝓdest? quod deuorat oia auarus
Semper habens; nihil & ieiuno sufficit ori?
Nec modus aut requies: non hũc cumulauit aceruũ
Is sibi. sed lites subitas post funera linquet.
Vtilis est nũmus multis: inglorius illi
Qui nescit seruare modum: legemq̃ modestam
Qui nil pauperibus doni elargitur amicis:
Hunc deus omnipotens extremo fine relinquet:
Nec capiet vultu placido sua vota precesq̃.

Eccle.iiij.
Psal.xxxviij.
Amos.ij.
Prouer.xi.
Math.xix.
Marci.x.
Luce.xij.
Thobie.iiij.

Of ryches vnprofytable.

Yet fynde I folys of another sorte
Whiche gather and kepe excessyfe ryches
With it denyeng their neyghboures to conforte
Whiche for nede lyueth in payne and wretchydnes
Suche one by fortune may fall into distres
And in lyke wyse after come to mysery
And begge of other/whiche shall to hym deny

Qui obturat aurẽ suam ad clamorem pauperis ipse clamabit et ñ exaudietur Prouer.xxi.

It is great foly/and a desyre in vayne
To loue and worshyp ryches to feruently
And so great laboure to take in care and payne

h.iij.

Diuitiarũ solicitudo.
Noli anxius ee in diuitiis iniustis non eni ꝓderũt tibi in die obductionis & vindicte Nil proderũt thesauri impietatis: Iusticia vero liberabit a morte: ve vobis diuitibus: quia hẽtis hic cõsolacionem vestrã. Diues & paup obuiauerũt sibi vtriusq̃ opator est dominus.

Eccle.v.
ꝓuer.x.z.xi.
Luce.xvi.

PLATE 19. "Of Riches Unprofitable." *Ship of Fools,* Fol. XLVIII. British Museum, G.11593.

Though with instinctive good judgment (and Shakespeare seems to wish us to consider Lear as naturally endowed with this; if he were to be regarded as erratic and but slenderly knowing himself, his character would be more easily fathomed and the tragedy much less moving), Lear affects Albany more than Cornwall, he is impartial in allotting shares to Regan and Goneril and possibly (Bradley agrees) even to Cordelia. The actual giving of the predetermined shares is only a ritual—a necessary ritual as any such great action would have to be in an ordered society, and one that should, in the relation of a loved monarch-father and his daughters, include marks of gratitude and filial affection. As the ritual proceeds, Lear does not wait to evaluate comparatively what Goneril and Regan say; indeed, so far from having his vanity fed, we may assume that Lear hardly heard them except to note that they were behaving with proper decorum: kings are accustomed to flattery, and all his daughters' extravagance does not cause him to have any doubts about whether he has misjudged them in preferring Cordelia, to whom he now turns, smiling and secure in his feeling that she loves him as truly as he loves her. But the ritual is broken by Cordelia's "Nothing." Unlike the audience, Lear does not have the benefit of Cordelia's asides (as Kittredge pointed out, the audience would have found her response intolerable without them), and the tragedy begins. The shock to Lear of Cordelia's seeming lack of any deep affection for him, her affront to his dignity as a father and a king, neither his nature nor his place can bear.

One hardly needs to stress the attitude involved here, the reverence for the laws regarding the respect due a king and a father, and Cordelia's violation of a sacred principle of decorum. Even Goneril and Regan remind us of the accepted code when they accuse Cordelia of scanting obedience. Unlike us, the first audience of this play was deeply conversant with the respect due a king, an obligation that was a foundation stone of their society, as exemplified in the following passage from

A Perfite Looking Glasse for all Estates by Isocrates, translated in 1580 by Thomas Forrest (Cii):

> Have in admiration the nature and princelie maiestie of the King thy governour, conforming thy selfe in all thinges to his will and pleasure, studying most earnestly to immitate, the sincereness and integritie of his life so shall the people the better like of thy dealinges, and the King himselfe have greater cause to be well affectioned towardes thee, and that so muche the more if thou showe thy selfe a faithfull obeyer of his lawes and commaundementes, as also an earnest maintainer of the same, not seeking to conseale or to keep counsayle with any other which by worde or deede shall goe about to doe contrarie to the Kinges pleasure, or to impaire the royal estate of his Crowne and dignitie . . .[7]

The Jacobean audience would understand all these views much better than we, and would apply them to the situation and not in Lear's disfavor, as Schücking has well argued:

> The predominant impression is . . . that of the monstrous irreverence shown to three of the most venerable human qualities here united in one person: fatherhood, old age, and kingship. Stress is laid, above all, on the unspeakable insult offered the pride of a king who yet retains his dignity in his association with beggars as well as in his madness. The trait has been given a special prominence. It agrees with the thought that we constantly find in Shakespeare, that the true king is best shown by the way in which he preserves his dignity. (Katharine, the wife of Henry VIII, is a model of humility and Christian charity; yet even she, though on the point of death, dismisses from her service a messenger [IV.ii] merely because in his hurry he had entered without kneeling, and without the address 'Your Grace' instead of 'Your Highness'.)[8]

And Curtis Brown Watson has also recently demonstrated that the modern views of such critics as Stopford

7. Huntington, 59300 (STC 14275): *A Perfite Loo- / king Glasse for all / Estates: Most excellently and eloquently set forth by / the famous and learned Oratour Isocrates . . . / Imprinted at London by / Thomas Purfoote, dwelling in Newgate / Market, within the new Rents, / at the Signe of the / Lucrece / 1580.*

8. Levin L. Schücking, *Character Problems in Shakespeare's Plays* (New York, 1922), p. 183; see also p. 34.

Brooke, Granville-Barker, and others essentially representing Lear as a tyrannical fool in his dotage[9] would have been completely incredible to the Jacobeans who first saw the play and who would have understood Lear's dilemma. It is doubtful if they would have been willing to accept even the kinder and more tentative evaluations of Bradley and R. W. Chambers. Stoll, as is well known, regards the first scene as contrived against all likelihood to produce the tragedy, and he remarks the inconsistency of those who suppose Lear a foolish tyrant and yet worthy of the admiring devotion and love of Kent, Cordelia, and Albany.[10] As Shakespeare has elsewhere observed, " 'Tis mad idolatry / To make the service greater than the god."

In this scene Lear makes the tragic mistake of interpreting Cordelia's seeming lack of love (no one wishes to be loved simply because of an obligation) as the actual truth of her feeling; he could not foresee that she would one day demonstrate that she loved him more than eyesight, space, liberty, and life itself (all the extravagances of the sisters, except for their professed willingness to sacrifice grace and honor, become fulfilled in Cordelia's devotion to Lear). But now, as Lear ironically remarks, she prefers "truth." Rapp in a telling

9. Curtis Brown Watson, *Shakespeare and the Renaissance Concept of Honor* (Princeton Univ. Press, 1960). See pp. 186–190, order and degree; 194–197, kingly authority; 228–234, pride and humility; 371–374, respect for father; 374–376, respect for elders.

10. E. E. Stoll, *Shakespeare Studies* (N.Y., 1927), p. 112: "So Lear, Cordelia, and Kent, though devoted to each other, in the first scene fairly conspire to contrive their tragedy. Who could be more uncompromising than Cordelia or more provocative than Kent, though they know the nature of the King's other daughters into whose clutches they are throwing him? Characters so fine and devoted as they, and the King too, later show themselves to be could not have acted so in real life; but so they act, to bring about the complication—grief at the ingratitude of the favored daughters mingled with remorseful thoughts for the one he loved best, and death at the end from heartbreak for the loss of the child he has recklessly sent away. In the contrast, in the irony, lies the tragedy." See also Stoll's *Art and Artifice in Shakespeare* (Cambridge, 1934), p. 138.

way sums up the conflict (though like all attempts at generalizing, his statement needs qualification):

> [Cordelia] is proud of being in the right, in contrast with her vulgar sisters, and this feeling she opposes to her sisters and to her old father. The weak old father has a right to a few flattering expressions from a loving child, because he needs them. She offers him, on the contrary, what he cannot bear, the truth. A woman, whose nature is love, and who is straightlaced for truth, is a doubly perverted creature. Truth and love are completely antipodal; what else is love for an individual but the taking of a finite object for an infinite, and worshipping it as such? Thus love is essentially a lie, not a truth, and Cordelia misbehaves like her sisters, only in a different way, by egoism and lovelessness. One for whom she cannot tell a little lie, she does not love as she should. On this fine ground, which the poet has laid very close to us, now rests the whole piece.[11]

This view is perceptive and true in the main; but it must be qualified by the well-known doctrine that this love is symbolic of higher love, and that in concentrating on the iniquity of her sisters, Cordelia is for the moment blind to the needs of Lear and thus loses sight of the higher love. Similarly, Lear, stunned by the shock to his self-esteem and to the sanctity of order and degree, is blind for the moment to the fact that he is honoring flatterers rather than the worthy, a fault that Isocrates admonishes the ruler to avoid:

> And above all things be most carefull to shew thy selfe able to discerne, and to know those which artificially and craftily shall seeme to fawne and flatter thee, from them whiche with a true harte, and zelous affection reverence and obey thee: least that being fedde and reduced by their glosing and dissembling, thou shouldst rashly advaunce the wicked and evill to greater honour, than thou dost the godly and well disposed: or else to suffer the lewd person to receive more profite by thee, than they that bee honest and virtuous.[12]

And so the King banishes those who love him most. But this devotion of Cordelia and Kent is a most important point

11. *Variorum* ed., p. 17.
12. *A Perfite Looking Glasse,* Fiii^{v}.

in itself, as Coleridge indirectly suggests. Kent's approval of Lear, apparently a complete approval except for this moment of error, is a tremendous argument for Lear's goodness as king and father: "Kent is the nearest to perfect goodness of all Shakespeare's characters, and yet the most *individualized.* His passionate affection for and fidelity to Lear act on our feelings in Lear's own favor; virtue seems in company with him."[13] Briefly it would appear that this king who had planned to set his rest with Cordelia, who had perceived the superiority of Albany to Cornwall, who had the complete devotion and approval (with the exception before excepted) of blunt, critical Kent, and who had the real though tardy love of Cordelia, was not a man who characteristically lacked vision. It would appear also that his retention of the name and dignities of a king was an argument for his normality and soundness (who expects a king of eighty years who has governed well to change his way of life?),[14] and that the audience would accept his reservation of such dignities as natural and laudable; and it is inconceivable that had he been able to live with Cordelia any unhappiness would have ensued on this score. As Lear avers (Kent never suggests otherwise and Edgar's consorting with them supports Lear's statement), his men know all the particulars of duty "And in the most exact regard support / The worships of their name."

At the end of Scene I, the wicked sisters reveal themselves rather than their father. As Kittredge pointed out, this contradiction of accepted values ("The best and soundest of his time hath been but rash"), together with evidence pro-

13. *Coleridge's Writings on Shakespeare,* ed. Terence Hawkes (New York, 1959), p. 183. Bradley's criticism of Kent and the Fool as lacking tact in dealing with Goneril and Regan does not weigh the necessity for their acting as they did. Their choice was to acquiesce or to protest.

14. Empson (p. 125 ff.) seems half converted by the argument of George Orwell ("Lear, Tolstoy, and the Fool," *Polemic,* 1947, p. 10 ff.) to the effect that the subject of Lear is renunciation, but admits some of the objections to such an interpretation. It seems strikingly clear that Lear has no intention of renouncing his dignities.

vided in the rest of the play, demonstrates that what they say about their father, save for their facile criticism of his fault in rejecting Cordelia, is false. And Watson observes convincingly that after this revelation, with its obvious inversion of the relations of parent and child, the audience would have regarded the sisters as monstrous and would not have credited then or thereafter any statements they made against Lear.[15]

But whatever our virtues, we pay dearly for our mistakes, and the wheel of Fortune turns down for Lear, or better, Lear becomes, in his fallen estate, more perceptibly the fool of Fortune (see Plate No. 20). It is interesting that just at this point when Fortune has deserted Lear that the Fool appears. The audience hardly needed to be shown a picture of the turning wheel to remind them that the Fool could be taken almost to objectify Lear in his new fortunes, as has been observed in separate studies by Enid Welsford and Norman Maclean.[16] The Fool makes the identification often enough; even in his first appearance he mocks Lear's hiring of Kent and offers both Kent and Lear his coxcomb. Lear is, the Fool implies, a sweet fool who has given away his land and is now by an inversion of roles, a bitter fool (I.iv.154–161):

> The lord that counsell'd thee
> To give away thy land,
> Come place him here by me—
> Do thou for him stand.
> The sweet and bitter fool
> Will presently appear;
> The one in motley here,
> The other found out there.

Constantly the Fool, like Lear's own inner meditation (Empson says his conscience), drives home the theme of Lear's improvidence which has brought him to "play bopeep and go

15. Watson, pp. 186–189.
16. Enid Welsford, *The Fool His Social and Literary History* (London, 1935), p. 264; Norman Maclean, "Episode, Scene, Speech, and Word: The Madness of Lear," *Critics and Criticism,* ed. R. S. Crane (Univ. of Chicago Press, 1957), p. 104. Maclean also sees Poor Tom as an objectification of Lear's madness.

Atq; rates pariter turritas meruit in vndis:
Et Nabuchodonoſor ſceptro Babilona gubernans
Fortunę nimium dum fidit: tentat honores
Diuinos pręſtari ſibi: ſed ſũma poteſtas
In ſpeciem bruti regem mutauit inanem.
Magnus Alexander cui vix ſufficerat orbis
Immenſus: graiis primus dominator in oris:
Non ſecum ad ſtygiam ſua vexit regna paludem.
Quid Cyrum refero? lambens in morte cruorem
Sanguinis ipſe ſui: ſic tranſit gloria mundi.
Crœſus quandoquidem regniſq;/opibus vel opimis:
Non contentus erat: tamen hunc fortuna fefellit:
Euertitq; ſuum regnum: atq; potentia ſceptra.
Omnia regna cadunt: ruit & mundana poteſtas:
Exemplum dat Roma potens: Carthago: Mycene:
Et Solymę. atq; Tyros: & Grecia tota: ſubibit
Mox latium. pereunt quia nam mortalia cuncta
Quę facimus: cunctis exitus vnus erit.

Nabuchodo-noſor. dañ. iij.
Alexãder. m.
Iuuenalis
Cyrus Hero-dotus & Iuſti nus li. i.
Creſus Hero-dotus li. i.
Eccleſi. x.
Eccleſi. xlix.
Iob. iij.
Apoca. xviij.
Sapien. vij.

¶ Of the ende of worldly honour and power and of Folys that truſt therin.

Potẽtatus ſe-culi finis.

Cunctis die-bus ſuis impi us ſuperbit: & numerus ãno rũ incertus eſt tirãnidis eius. Multi tiranni ſederũt i thro no: & iſuſpica bilis portauit diadema Mul ti potẽtes op-preſſi ſunt va-lide: & glorio-ſi traditi ſũt in manus altoꝝ.

v. ii.

PLATE 20. Fortune's Wheel. *Ship of Fools,* Fol. CXI. British Museum, G.11593.

the fools among."[17] Even a snail has a house to put his head in, not to give it to his daughters (I.v.30–34), and though the imagery of Shakespeare is derived from many sources, the homely wisdom here is the constant subject matter of Brant, as reflected in Barclay and Copland. Lear should not have become old until he was wise (I.v.47). Unthrifts like Lear, says the Fool, should accept the vicissitudes of Fortune, acknowledge themselves as Fortune's fool (III.ii.74–77):

> He that has and a tiny little wit—
> With hey, ho, the wind and the rain—
> Must make content with his fortunes fit,
> For the rain it raineth every day.

Lear will presently see this, but he is too great to be passive. Like Job he may yield ultimately to power, but he will not yield while he can protest, and Lear is never "regenerated" as Bradley and others wish him to be.[18] He is never regenerated, one may add, for the very good reason that except for his initial error (which he repents almost at once) he does not need regeneration; as will presently be shown, the regeneration of a character is not the central meaning of this play. Shakespeare went longer to school to the philosophy of Barclay and Copland than he did to Aristotle. Yet suffering should deepen the perception of a good person, as the completely good Hermione suggests: "The action I now go on / Is for my better grace."

When Lear, fleeing Goneril, comes to Regan at Gloucester's castle, he finds his messenger stocked, subject to a punishment "such as basest and contemn'dest wretches / For pilf'rings and most common trespasses / Are punish'd with" (II.ii.150–152), and presently he himself, with the dismissal

17. Kittredge (*Sixteen Plays,* p. 1170) remarks the Fool's "perfect pun" on Lear's folly: "Take the fool with thee."
18. G. W. Knight observes that the last scene makes the idea of regeneration irrelevant: "In the face of the last scene any detailed comment of purgatorial expiation, of spiritual purification, is but a limp and tinkling irrelevance" (*The Wheel of Fire,* London, 1930, p. 223).

of his followers, and with nothing left of his own, is reduced to the ranks of the rogues and vagabonds, and it is at this point that the theme of madness, foreshadowed at the end of Act I, begins to take shape. And immediately, as with the introduction of the theme of folly, a fitting symbol anticipating that madness is projected for us in Edgar's description of the guise that he is going to assume,[19] much the best description of a Bedlam beggar that literature affords (II.iii.5–21):

> Whiles I may scape,
> I will preserve myself; and am bethought
> To take the basest and most poorest shape
> That ever penury, in contempt of man,
> Brought near to beast. My face I'll grime with filth,
> Blanket my loins, elf all my hair in knots,
> And with presented nakedness outface
> The winds and persecutions of the sky.
> The country gives me precedent and proof
> Of Bedlam beggars, who, with roaring voices,
> Strike in their numb'd and mortified bare arms
> Pins, wooden pricks, nails, sprigs of rosemary;
> And with this horrible object, from low farms,
> Poor pelting villages, sheepcotes, and mills,
> Sometime with lunatic bans, sometime with prayers,
> Enforce their charity. "Poor Turlygod! poor Tom!"
> That's something yet! Edgar I nothing am.

This portrait of the Bedlam beggar appears largely original with Shakespeare, presumably based on his own observation of these creatures.[20] In his turn, Dekker seems to have found

19. As Norman Maclean has shown, p. 104 ff.

20. Shakespeare most likely knew both Awdeley (who seems to be the first to list the name "poore Tom" in his description of the Abraham man) and Harman, but I have not found any description to account for the particular details set down by Shakespeare. Kittredge notes that Edgar's expression "Turley-god" is used nowhere else. In addition to past unsatisfactory attempts to explain the word, the following may be added: "Turley" may have some connections with a whirling or jig type of dance possibly practiced by Bedlams: see *Terley-ginckt, thurlerie, Turlery ginke* in *Nashe,* ed. McKerrow, III, 178 (19); III, 320 (4); I, 296 (14). Interesting also is the association of "poor Tom" with the Bessy ballad (*Lear,* III.vi.27–30). Malone (*Variorum* ed., 208) notes that Bessy and Tom are represented as travelling together in *The Court of Conscience or Dick Whipper's Sessions,* 1607.

this sketch suggestive, using it along with Harman's description of the Abraham man to describe his own Tom of Bedlam.[21]

To complete his portrait, as several commentators have remarked, Shakespeare appears to have drawn presumably upon the actual street cries of the Bedlam beggars. Edward H. Fellowes calls attention to one version of these cries, "The London Cry," set to music by Orlando Gibbons, which has been preserved in three differing manuscript part-books in the British Museum.[22] The "Cry" (Plate 21), which reminds one of the pleas of the Bedlams in *O per se O,* and which is echoed importantly in Edgar's various cries, runs as follows:

> Poor naked Bedlam, Tom's a-cold,
> a small piece cut of thy bacon
> or a piece of thy sow's side, good Bess,
> God Almighty bless thy wits.[23]

The stock phrase "Poor Tom," employed either as a cry or as a commiserative self-label from the time of Awdeley, beats insistently through Edgar's simulated ravings, which are also punctuated here and there by the cries, "Tom's acold" and "Bless thy five wits."[24] At one moment on the heath the opening of the "London Cry" is almost evoked, when Gloucester says, "Sirrah, naked fellow–" and Edgar responds, "Poor Tom's acold" (IV.i.51–52). Moreover, as Charles Garton has shown,[25] when Lear offers his great prayer for houseless,

21. See *The Belman of London,* D2.

22. *Orlando Gibbons and his Family* (Oxford Univ. Press, 1951), pp. 85 86. Fellowes cites B.M., Add. MSS. 17792–6; 29372–6; 37402–6. For this reference I am indebted to F. W. Sternfeld ("Poor Tom in *King Lear," TLS,* Jan. 5, 1962, p. 9), who remarks other discussions of the subject by Sir Frederick Bridge ("Musical Cries of London," *Proc. of the Musical Assoc.,* XLVI, 1919–20, 13–20) and Professor F. P. Wilson ("Illustrations of Social Life III: Street-Cries," *Shakespeare Survey 13,* 1960, 106–110).

23. This is the complete "Cry" as given in B.M., Add. MS. 17792, f.110.

24. For "Tom's a-cold" or "Poor Tom's acold," see III.ix.59, III.iv.85, III.iv. 152, IV.i.52; for "Bless thy five wits," see III.iv.58, III.vi.60.

25. "Poor Tom in *King Lear," TLS,* Dec. 15, 1961, p. 904. Garton studies in interesting detail the ways in which Shakespeare weaves phrases of the "Cry" into Edgar's various speeches.

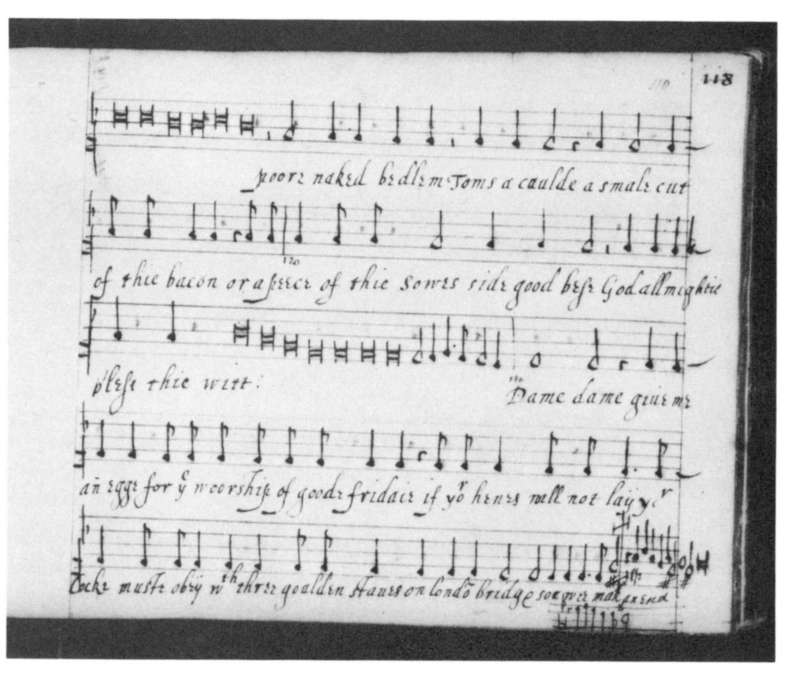

PLATE 21. "The London Cry" by Orlando Gibbons, British Museum Add. MS. 17792, f.110.

unfed wanderers, which is dramatically terminated by the cries of Poor Tom (III.iv.37), his opening words, "Poor naked wretches," may possibly have been inspired by the beginning of the "Cry," "Poor naked Bedlam."

Edgar's choice of this disguise is a particularly happy one for the meaning of this play. Shakespeare might have made him a counterfeit crank or a common swigman (peddler), but the artistic need here is for a symbol of madness. Thus Edgar, for his safety in a world of disorder, has been outfacing the winds and persecutions of the sky when Lear, the unthrift-fool, "attended with a desperate train" (the image summons up visions of the wandering bands of masterless men) rushes out into the hostile night. And in the storm (at once a symbol of a world of disorder and of the storm within his being), Lear's mind gives way, and the unthrift-fool, reduced to basest penury, undergoes a new metamorphosis into a Bedlam, stripping off his lendings, and becoming unsophisticated man. In this world of storm, in which all values seem repudiated (the humanity of Gloucester is only a feeble torch in the darkness and even Kent cannot help Lear), the only true philosopher is the Bedlam beggar and Lear must keep with him, both of them victims of an unfeeling world.

In the trial scene the new theme of madness mounts high with the Fool and two Bedlams conducting the trial. ("Prithee, nuncle, tell me whether a madman be a gentleman or a yeoman. *Lear.* A king, a king!") The King Madman appoints his court and arraigns the prisoners. The robed justices in this mad world are the blanketed Bedlam beggar and his yoke-fellow of equity, the Fool. Kent, who has qualified earlier as fool, sits too. Mad justice and foolish justice!—no wonder that in this symbolic court the criminals escape, as they do (for a time) in the really mad world now apparently controlled by Goneril, Regan, and Cornwall (Albany is still bemused by appearances).[26]

26. See Professor Heilman's thorough study of this theme as applied to Goneril, Regan, and Edmund (*This Great Stage,* pp. 225–253).

The Fool goes to bed at noon: the theme of Lear as foolish unthrift is completed, and when Lear next appears it is in the new guise of madness, that of a Bedlam, "mad as the vexd sea, singing aloud, / Crown'd with rank fumiter and furrow weeds" (IV.iii.2–3). In this mad world in which authority is vested in the hands of the corrupt, Lear's madness finds sham in all pretensions to justice—and the indictment that follows does not concern simply himself and his daughters but rather the whole world. Since justice itself is corrupt, who can judge? The author of *A Defence* of *Cony-catching* had essayed this theme; now it reaches its supreme expression:

> Change places and, handy dandy, which is the justice, which is the thief? Thou hast seen a farmer's dog bark at a beggar?
> *Glou.* Ay, sir.
> *Lear.* And the creature run from the cur? There thou mightst behold the great image of authority: a dog's obey'd in office.
> Thou rascal beadle, hold thy bloody hand!
> Why dost thou lash that whore? Strip thine own back.
> Thou hotly lusts to use her in that kind
> For which thou whip'st her. The usurer hangs the cozener.
> Through tatter'd clothes small vices do appear.
> Robes and furr'd gowns hide all. Plate sin with gold,
> And the strong lance of justice hurtless breaks;
> Arm it in rags, a pygmy's straw does pierce it.
> None does offend, none—I say none! I'll able 'em.
>
> (IV.vi.155–172)

If this social bedlam represents all of life, then indeed our values are all illusions and all are fools in the darkest sense.

But Lear has one daughter "Who redeems nature from the general curse / That twain have brought her to"; and at the moment when Lear in madness thus indicts mankind as evil, the forces of love are mustering in his behalf and humanity is redeemed in part. With the coming of love, the fever of madness departs. Love strips off the Bedlam and arrays Lear in fresh garments, and Lear is the King again. In the great reconciliation scene that follows, as Lear awakens he fancies himself in purgatory, expiating his sin against Cordelia, a soul in bliss. As he comes to himself, Cordelia asks the renewed benediction of his love, and he kneels to her for forgiveness. But her love is not tardy now, and to Lear's statement that she has cause for not loving him, she cries, "No cause, no cause."

Lear and Cordelia, having acknowledged their initial mistakes, are reunited in their love. That this love is heightened as a result of their suffering would appear manifest. That a very proper pride and love for truth set in motion the events that produced this suffering cannot be doubted. That Lear's momentary failure of insight and the initial lack of sympathy of Cordelia were characteristic faults simply would not be accepted by the audience that first saw the play. Nor need we assume that suffering arises only out of confirmed individual faults. In this world of fools in which even the wisest may mistake the shadow for reality and in which from a Christian point of view only grace finally can save, suffering is essential for the ripening of the soul. "Men must endure / Their going hence even as their coming hither; / Ripeness is all" (V.ii.9–11).

This philosophy of the value of suffering in attaining wisdom may have come to Shakespeare from his own observation and from several literary sources. One source that very probably influenced him, as Kenneth Muir has shown,[27] is found in the speech of Plangus following the story of the Paphlagonian king in the *Arcadia,* a speech in which Plangus, like Lear, cries his woes to the skies, in a world whose inhabitants are like players, fools on a filthy stage:

> Alas how long this pilgrimage doth last?
> What greater ills have now the heavens in store,

27. *King Lear,* ed. Kenneth Muir (London, 1952). p. xl. Muir says: "The general tenor of the debate between Plangus and Basilius about the rights and wrongs of suicide, on the justice of the gods, and on the slaughter of the innocent, may have caught Shakespeare's eye before he wrote of the attempted suicide of Gloucester and of the death of Cordelia." Since as Muir shows, the following story of Plangus is also used by Shakespeare in composing his

To couple comming harms with sorrows past:
Long since my voice is hoarse, and throat is sore,
With cries to skies, and curses to the ground,
But more I plaine, I feele my woes the more.
Ah where was first that cruel cunning found,
To frame of Earth a vessell of the minde,
Where it should be to selfe-destruction bound?

. . .

Balles to the starres, and thralles to Fortunes raigne;
Turnd from themselves, infected with their cage,
Where death is feard, and life is held with paine:
Like Players pla'st to fill a filthy stage,
Where chaunge of thoughts one foole to other shewes
And all but iests, save onely sorrowes rage.
The child feels that; the man that feeling knowes,
Which cries first borne, the presage of his life,
Where wit but serves, to have true tast of woes.

. . .

Griefe onely makes his wretched state to see
(Even like a toppe which nought but whipping moves),
This man, this talking beast, this walking tree,
Griefe is the stone which finest iudgement proves:
For who grieves not hath but a blockish braine,
Since cause of griefe no cause from life removes.[28]

In sum, it would appear that the Jacobean audience saw Lear at least partly in terms of familiar lore, that of the foolish unthrift who has put his trust in gratitude and has been disillusioned and transformed into a madman. Love alone can restore him, and it does, but even love cannot save him from the vicissitudes of blind fortune; as Kent says of Lear, "If Fortune brag of two she loved and hated, / One of them we behold."

Gloucester subplot, this supposition is most likely. Muir compares with Sidney's lines the following lines of *Lear:* IV.i.36–37; V.iii.184–186; IV.vi.192–193; IV.vi.180–185; V.iii.257.

28. B.M., C.30.d.22 (STC 22539a): *The / Countesse / of Pembrokes / Arcadia, / Written by Sir Philippe / Sidnei. /* [Heraldic insignia] */ London / Printed for William Ponsonbie. / Anno Domini,* 1590, fol. 156–158ᵛ (Lib. 2, Ch. 12).

VIII

Autolycus the Shape-Shifter and Jonson's Nightingale

JUST WHEN HE IS NEEDED in *The Winter's Tale,* Autolycus emerges, rogue and unthrift extraordinary and prince of shape-shifters, with all the characteristics that these words connoted to the audience. Shakespeare found no suggestion of him in his main source, but it was natural that with his knowledge of *The Triumphs of Pandosto* and his awareness of Greene's penchant for rogue-gallants, he should perceive the aptness of using a rogue here who might serve with symbolic effect in the great scenes to come; and the conception of Autolycus solved one of his dramaturgical problems.

When Shakespeare set about composing the play, he was faced with the problem of inventing some figure to fill the part of the Fool, the usual choragus of many of his dominant themes. He did not wish to recreate Feste or Touchstone. There was no place in Leontes's absolute rage for the self-questioning that marks Lear and makes him aware of his own moment of folly, and makes the Fool seem an objectification of the processes of his thought. The Fool for *The Winter's Tale* could come into the drama only after Leontes had become self-critical, if he was to appear at all. Moreover, the conversion of Leontes from his crimes (very different from the tragic mistakes of Lear and Cordelia) is so complete that he has become enlightened and hence needs no stronger spur of conscience than that supplied by the tutelary Paulina. If a fool or clown were to be used, he might well fulfill instead a role relating to the remaining problems of the play, the recovery of Perdita and the values lost with her, and the equally symbolic restoration of Hermione. In a richly suggestive way Autolycus appears to fulfill this role.

Never has there been a more completely representative ideal rogue than Autolycus; that is why his name springs unbidden to our lips when we think of the type. In his nature all the ingredients of roguery and vagabondage are blended except violence and malice. He is an amiable outlaw. In this respect, as well as others, he reminds us of his mythic ancestor, who was, like him, "littered under Mercury" and a "snapper-up of unconsidered trifles."[1] The classical Autolycus, the son of Hermes (Mercury), was endowed with the gift of stealthiness, and as the son of Hermes presumably shared Hermes's outstanding characteristics.[2] His known career in theft parallels that of Hermes (Hermes stole the cattle of Apollo; Autolycus stole the cattle of Sisyphus). It seems evident that, like his father, he was a trickster, not merely a thief. It would take little imagination to assume that he might have shared his father's gifts in song and heraldry,[3] or, better, for

1. S. L. Bethell calls attention to the fact that Autolycus's description of himself reads like a Theophrastan character of a rogue (*The Winter's Tale,* London, 1947, p. 51). An actual example of such a character may be found in John Webster's *Characters,* "A Canting Rogue," *The Complete Works of John Webster,* ed. F. L. Lucas (London, 1947), IV, 40.

2. For the relationship of Hermes to Autolycus, and their shared characteristics, see Norman O. Brown, *Hermes the Thief* (Univ. of Wisconsin Press, 1947), pp. 6, 8, 10, 13, 18, 53. The source of Shakespeare's knowledge of the nature of Autolycus is uncertain. Perhaps he found it in one of the editions of Natale Conti's *Mythologia;* see his *Mythologiae sive Explicationum Fabularum Libri Decem* (Venice, 1568), fol. 135, sec. 20; 188, sec. 33. Professor Douglas Bush notes the wide influence of this book in the Renaissance (*Mythology and the Renaissance Tradition in English Poetry,* New York, 1957, p. 31). Shakespeare's knowledge of Hermes (Mercury) could have come from the same source and from his familiar Ovid.

3. Brown, p. 25.

Shakespeare to see a Hermes in him. For it is this mythic pattern that our Bohemian rogue appears to represent in the fabric of the play.

Like so many other vagabonds, Autolycus was formerly a serving-man: he wore three-ply in the service of Prince Florizel, but now he is a wanderer. His ragged state is his profit from dice and drabs, and his revenue is the "silly cheat" (IV. iii.13–28).[4] But he is circumspect in his knavery, though he does not worry about religion: "Beating and hanging are terrors to me. For the life to come, I sleep out the thought of it." In these features he is a cousin of the conycatcher with whom Greene quaffed a cup of wine on Turnmill Street:

> Tut, sir, quoth he, calling me by my name, as my religion is smal, so my devotion is lesse, I leave God to be disputed on by divines, the two ends I aime at, are gain and ease, but by what honest gaines I may get, never comes within ye compasse of my thoughts . . . my resolution is to beat my wits, and spare not to busy my braines to save and help me, by what meanes soever I care not, so I may avoide the danger of the lawe . . . (C3^v^).[5]

As Autolycus summarizes his philosophy, he spies the clown and exclaims, "A prize! a prize!" A silly "cheat" (by synecdoche) has arrived, and Autolycus practices his art of conycatching, though it is interesting to note that Shakespeare avoids conycatching terminology here (perhaps he was aware that Rowlands, Dekker, and others were critical of these terms). Autolycus grovels on the ground, crying "O, that ever I was born!" and implores the astonished clown to pluck off his rags. He tells how he has been beaten with a million stripes and robbed of his purse and apparel by a footman who has dressed him in his own rags. The kindly clown helps him to rise, and Autolycus feigns acute pain. But watch the smooth rogue at his mystery:

> *Aut.* O, good sir, softly, good sir! I fear, sir, my shoulder blade is out.

4. Shakespeare might have derived his information about the "silly cheat" from *A manifest detection* or *Mihil Mumchance.*
5. *A Notable Discovery,* ed. Harrison, pp. 35–36.

Clown. How now? Canst stand?

Aut. Softly, dear sir! good sir, softly! [*Picks his pocket.*] You ha' done me a charitable office.

Clown. Dost lack any money? I have a little money for thee.

Aut. No, good sweet sir; no, I beseech you, sir. I have a kinsman not past three quarters of a mile hence, unto whom I was going. I shall there have money or anything I want. Offer me no money, I pray you; that kills my heart.

Clown. What manner of fellow was he that robb'd you?

Aut. A fellow, sire, that I have known to go about with troll-my-dames. I knew him once a servant of the Prince. I cannot tell, good sir, for which of his virtues it was, but he was certainly whipp'd out of the court.

Clown. His vices you would say. There's no virtue whipp'd out of the court. They cherish it to make it stay there; and yet it will no more but abide.

Aut. Vices I would say, sir. I know this man well. He hath been since an ape-bearer; then a process-server, a bailiff; then he compass'd a motion of the Prodigal Son, and married a tinker's wife within a mile where my land and living lies; and having flown over many knavish professions, he settled only in rogue. Some call him Autolycus.

Clown. Out upon him! prig, for my life, prig! He haunts wakes, fairs, and bearbaitings.

Aut. Very true, sir; he, sir, he. That's the rogue that put me into this apparel.

For this episode, as Professor Harrison points out, not only does Shakespeare parody the parable of the Good Samaritan, but at the same time he probably had recourse to Greene's narrative in *The Second part of Conny-catching,* "A kinde conceit of a Foist performed in Paules":[6]

> Ther walked in the middle walke a plaine country farmar a man of good wealth, & that had a well lined purse, oncly barely thrust uppe in a round slop which a crue of Foists having perceived, ther

6. G. B. Harrison (*Shakespeare, The Complete Works,* New York, 1952, p. 1430) seems to have been the first to note this probable relationship. For Greene's text (1592), see Chap. III, Note 18. In Harrison's edition, see pp. 40–41.

harts were set on fire to have it, and every one had a fling at him, but all in vaine, for he kept his hand close in his pocket, and his purse fast in his fist like a subtil churle, that either had been fore-warnd of Paules, or else had afore time smoakte some of that faculty, well, how so ever, it was unpossible to doe any good with him he was so wary . . . At last one of the crue, that for his skill might have bene Doctorat in his mistery, amongst them all chose out a good Foist, one of a nimble hand & great agility, and said to the rest thus: Masters it shall not be said such a base peasaunt shall slip away from such a crue of Gentlemen Foists as wee are, and not have his purse drawen, and therfore this time Ile play the staule my selfe, and if I hitte him not home, count me for a bungler for ever, and so he left them and went to the farmar and walkt directly before him & next him three or foure turnes, at last standing still he cryed alas honest man, helpe me, I am not well, and with that suncke downe suddenly in a sowne, the poor Farmer seeing a proper yong Gentleman (as he thought) fall dead afore him, stept to him, helde him in his armes, rubd him, and chafte him: at this there gathered a great multitude of people about him, and the whilst the Foiste drewe the Farmers pursse and awaye: by that the other thought the feate was done, he began to come somthing to himselfe again, and so halfe staggering, stumbled out of Poules, and went after the crue where they had apointed to meet, and there boasted of his wit and experience (D4^{v}).

But Autolycus is not only a conycatcher; he tries his hand, as we have seen, at several of the mysteries of his profession as knave and vagabond, thereby illustrating the view advanced earlier that the various "orders" represent the several devices practiced by most rogues as they found them advantageous.[7] As he himself says, he has flown over many knavish professions and at last settled only in rogue.

It is as pure ballad singer, however, that Autolycus excels, and he is right in describing it as his occupation (IV.iv. 301–302). As he enters he is singing a ballad that is the ver-

7. See p. 28 of this study. Christopher Sly, it will be remembered, was also a rogue of several trades: "Am not I Christopher Sly, old Sly's son of Burton Heath; by birth a pedlar, by education a cordmaker, by transmutation a bearherd, and now by profession a tinker?" (*The Taming of the Shrew,* Induction, Scene ii, 16–21).

itable apotheosis of vagabondage, an idealization of the life of the unrestrained wanderer (IV.iii.1–12), and there is something of eternal spring in the lines:

When daffodils begin to peer,
  With heigh! the doxy over the dale—
Why, then comes in the sweet o' the year,
  For the red blood reigns in the winter's pale.

The white sheet bleaching on the hedge—
  With heigh! the sweet birds, O how they sing!
Doth set my pugging[8] tooth on edge,
  For a quart of ale is a dish for a king.

The lark, that tirra-lyra chants,—
  With heigh! with heigh! the thrush and the jay—
Are summer songs for me and my aunts,
  While we lie tumbling in the hay.

Meditating on his loss of service makes him less joyous, but not melancholy:

But shall I go mourn for that, my dear?
  The pale moon shines by night;
And when I wander here and there,
  I then do most go right.

If tinkers may have leave to live
  And bear the sow-skin budget,
Then my account I well may give,
  And in the stocks avouch it.

Autolycus, like Hermes,[9] has magical qualities as a musician; his songs penetrate to the "bright mystery at the heart of things"; "He hath songs for man or woman, of all sizes. No milliner can so fit his customers with gloves" (IV.iv.191–193), and the goods of his peddler's pack share the magic: "Why, he sings 'em over as they were gods or goddesses. You would think a smock were a she-angel, he so chants to the

8. *Pugging:* very likely a misprint for *prigging,* sentiment and various conjectures (see *Variorum* ed., pp. 164–165, and *OED*) notwithstanding.
9. Brown, pp. 29–30, 66–70.

sleeve-hand and the work about the square on't" (IV.iv.209–212). Surely so gifted an entertainer may have some special meaning to the play, as the clown intimates: "You have of these pedlars that have more in them than you'ld think, sister" (IV.iv.216–217) and Perdita reinforces the idea: "Ay, good brother, or go about to think." Statements like these are a convention in Shakespeare and usually suggest a hidden meaning; this particular one may be interpreted as an index pointing to the deeper significance of Autolycus, warning the audience not to miss it.

The ballads of Autolycus, to say no more of the pure poetry of the songs, are marvels in themselves—records of fantastic events (though hardly more fanciful than many of the ballads of the age) also stressing shape-changing—the usurer's wife who bore money-bags and the metamorphosis of a woman to a cold fish; "he utters them as he had eaten ballads and all men's ears grow to his tunes" (IV.iv.184–186), and later exults in his success:

> Ha, ha! what a fool Honesty is! and Trust, his sworn brother, a very simple gentleman! I have sold all my trumpery. Not a counterfeit stone, not a ribbon, glass, pomander, brooch, table book, ballad, knife, tape, glove, shoe-tie, bracelet, horn ring, to keep my pack from fasting! They throng who shall buy first, as if my trinkets had been hallowed and brought a benediction to the buyer; by which means I saw whose purse was best in picture; and what I saw, to my good use I rememb'red. My clown (who wants but something to be a reasonable man) grew so in love with the wenches' song that he would not stir his pettitoes till he had both tune and words, which so drew the rest of the herd to me that all their other senses stuck in ears. You might have pinch'd a placket, it was senseless; 'twas nothing to geld a codpiece of a purse; I would have fil'd keys off that hung in chains. No hearing, no feeling, but my sir's song, and admiring the nothing of it! So that, in this time of lethargy, I pick'd and cut most of their festival purses; and had not the old man come in with a whoobub against his daughter and the King's son and scar'd my choughs from the chaff, I had not left a purse alive in the whole army. (IV.iv.606–631)

It seems certain that Shakespeare drew some of his inspiration here from Greene's story in *The Thirde and last Part of Conny-catching* of the ballad-singing rogues which, as has been remarked,[10] was to prove useful, together with Shakespeare's version, to Jonson also.

Greene's story is worth attention, then, not only as a page in the history of Autolycus but also for the light it throws on the responses of Shakespeare and Jonson to the same material:

> a roging mate, & such another with him, were there got upõ a stal singing of balets which belik was som prety toy, for very many gathered about to heare it, & divers buying, as their affections served, drew to their purses & paid the singers for thẽ. The slye mate and his fellowes, who were dispersed among them that stoode to heare the songs: well noted where everie man that bought, put up his purse againe, and to such as would not buy, counterfeit warning was sundrie times given by the rogue and his associate, to beware of the cut pursse, and looke to their pursses,

10. See p. 125. A possibly earlier example of a cutpurse incident of this sort is to be found in Sir John Davies's *Epigrammes and Elegies* (c.1590), Epigram No. 38. In this epigram Philo, a "thief in society," practicer of many professions, also practices "Physicke," and his reputation increases

> As doth the Ballad-singer's auditory,
> Which hath at Temple-barre his standing chose,
> And to the vulgar sings an Ale-house story:
> First stands a Porter; then an Oyster-wife
> Doth stint her cry, and stays her steps to heare him;
> Then comes a Cut-purse ready with a knife,
> And then a Countrey clyent passeth neere him;
> There stands the Constable, there stands the whore,
> And listening to the song, heed not each other;
> There by the Serjeant stands the debitor,
> And doth no more distrust him then his brother;
> Thus Orpheus to such hearers giveth musick,
> And Philo to such patients giveth physick.

Grosart (*Works of Sir John Davies,* I.23–26) calls attention to Wordsworth's imitation of this poem (omitting of course the Cutpurse) in his "Power of Music."

Yet another example of the influence of Greene's story, through the usages by Shakespeare and Jonson, may be seen in Fletcher's *Night-Walker,* III (*Enter Lurcher and Boy*).

> which made them often feel where their pursses were, either in sleeve, hose, or at girdle, to know whether they were safe or no. Thus the craftie copesmates were acquainted with what they most desired, and as they were scattered, by shouldring, thrusting, feigning to let fall something, and other wilie tricks fit for their purpose: heere one lost his purse, there another had his pocket pickt, and to say all in briefe, at one instant, upon the complaint of one or two that saw their pursses were gone, eight more in the same companie, found themselves in like predicament. Some angrie, others sorrowfull, and all greatly discontented, looking about them, knewe not who to suspect or challenge, in that the villaines themselves that had thus beguiled them, made shewe that they had sustained like losse. But one angrie fellow, more impacient then al the rest, he falles upon the ballade singer, and beating him with his fists well favouredly, sayes, if he had not listened to his singing, he had not lost his purse, and therefore would not be other wise perswaded, but that they two and the cutpurses were compacted together. The rest that had lost their purses likewise, and saw that so may [many] complaine togither: they iumpe in opinion with the other fellow, & begin to tug & hale the ballad singers, when one after one, the false knaves begin to shrinke awaie with yᵉ pursses. By means of some officer then being there presēt, the two roges were had before a Iustice, and upon his discreete examination made, it was found, that they and the Cutpurses were compacted together, and that by this unsuspected villanie, they had deceived many. (C3ᵛ–C4)

Autolycus is manifestly a much more clever knave than Greene's ballad singers: he is able to entrance his listeners and cut their purses at the same time. Shakespeare is aware of this straining of reality (it could not have been acted convincingly) as is shown by his apparent division of the faculties involved, when he makes Autolycus speak of his song as if it were being sung by another ("my sir's song") while he was picking the purses (IV.iv.623–628). The situation obviously calls for a rogue copesmate, as in Greene's version, but Autolycus is a magician in cunning (his ancestor had the gift of performing his thefts invisibly). Greene's ballad singers warn their auditors of the danger from cutpurses and observe them as they reach for their purses to make sure of them.

Autolycus warns the Clown of the danger of cutpurses (IV.iv. 256–261) and also studies the purses of those buying his trinkets. Greene's knaves are apprehended, but Autolycus gets away with his rascality, though he has a bad moment when he fears that Camillo and Florizel have overheard him (IV.iv.640–660).

Jonson's use in *Bartholomew Fair* is much more complete, freely combining both Greene and Shakespeare. Greene's story reads almost like a rough synopsis of Jonson's use of the material, which practically employs all Greene's details. Jonson has the two "roging mates," Nightingale and Edgeworth. Nightingale does better than merely warn his auditors of cutpurses: he sings a clever ballad on the theme. Greene's ballad singer is beaten by an angry fellow. Jonson gives us an interesting double play possibly based on this incident: first, the Justice in his disguise as a mad fool preaches to the crowd and thus innocently serves Nightingale's function of distracting his hearers while their pockets are picked by Edgeworth; subsequently the Justice is beaten by Wasp (Jonson's angry man), who suspects him as the patrico of the cutpurses (II.vi.137–150). Later, as will be seen presently, Nightingale plays his own role, singing his song of warning while Edgeworth acts as his hands in taking purses. Greene's rogues are haled before a Justice; Jonson's rogues are ultimately exposed before Justice Overdo, and the story so expands in Jonson that it becomes a large part of the plot (the exposure of enormities).

Jonson's use of Shakespeare here is more tenuous, but it appears to be none the less a genuine debt of inspiration. Nightingale is, to be sure, not a peddler of knickknacks and trifles. Jonson has several such peddlers crying their wares in the Fair (Trash, Leatherhead,[11] and others); instead Night-

11. Lantern Leatherhead, the hobby-horse seller, is also the puppeteer of the play. It will be recalled that Autolycus was also a puppeteer (IV.iii.98), though Shakespeare ignores the possibilities that this skill might offer in the development of his plot.

ingale's sole ware is ballads, but his second song, through the imagery of its ballad titles reminds us curiously of the usual peddler's wares:

> Ballads, Ballads! fine new ballads:
> *Heare for your love, and buy for your money.*
> *A delicate ballad o' the* Ferret *and the* Coney.
> A preservative again' the Punques evill.
> *Another of* Goose-green-starch *and the* Devill.
> *A dozen of divine points, and the* Godly *garters.*
> The Fairing of good councell, *of an ell and three quarters.*
> What is't you buy? . . .
>
> (II.iv.10–17)[12]

Later in the main pickpocket scene (III.v) Jonson very happily seizes on the theme of the warning against cutpurses and converts it through Nightingale into one of his best dramatic songs, entitled *A caveat against cutpurses,* a "gentle admonition" to purse-cutter and purse-bearer. As Nightingale sings the song, Bartholomew Cokes, a splendid example of the cony, serves in somewhat the same function as Shakespeare's Clown in his relation to Autolycus, though the Clown "wants but something to be a reasonable man," whereas Cokes must be writ down an ass. The ballad concludes, to general applause, with the following stanza:

> But O, you vile nation of cutpurses all,
> Relent and repent, and amend and be sound,
> And know that you ought not, by honest mens fall,
> Advance your own fortunes, to die above ground,
> And though you goe gay,
> In silkes as you may,
> It is not the highway to heaven, (as they say)
> Repent then, repent you, for better, for worse:
> And kisse not the Gallowes for cutting a purse.
> Youth, youth, thou hadst better bin sterv'd by thy Nurse,
> Then live to be hanged for cutting a purse.
>
> (III.v.146–156)

12. *Ben Jonson,* ed. C. H. Herford, Percy and Evelyn Simpson (Oxford, 1938), VI, 47–48.

And at once Edgeworth, acting as conycatcher, asks to be permitted to buy the first ballad. Cokes, however, asserts his prior right and buys them all. In this action he seems to be imitating the Clown who asks Autolycus for first choice and even also asks him to bring his pack after him as if he were planning to buy the lot.

Yet one other resemblance is worth noting. As Edgeworth is about to leave the scene of his triumph in serving as Nightingale's hands ("Where hadst thou hands, I pray thee?" III.v.188),[13] Quarlous and Winwife, who have been observing his cunning, intercept him and oblige him (now much concerned for his safety) to perform a theft of a license for them to make possible the marriage of Quarlous and Dame Purecraft. The situation is roughly parallel to that faced by Autolycus, who, after recounting his triumph over the purses of the festival crowd, fears that he has been overheard by Camillo and Florizel, and is made their instrument to help in the flight of Florizel and Perdita.

Nightingale has no apparent symbolic function in *Bartholomew Fair,* nor do we expect him to have one; but Autolycus is a larger figure and we expect more of him, and there are at least some hints of more, in addition to those already observed, as the drama continues to unfold.

At this point, Autolycus undergoes another transformation, together with Prince Florizel: Florizel turns peddler and Autolycus turns courtier. Surely, as Autolycus says, "the gods do this year connive at us, and we may do anything extempore." Florizel goes about his own brand of cozening, his special "piece of iniquity—stealing away from his father with his clog at his heels." Autolycus will not betray him, because he finds it more knavish to hide the fact than reveal it to the King.

13. It is tempting to read this line as a subtle thrust at Shakespeare's Autolycus, who (except as a magician) could not have been a foist and a ballad singer at the same time.

Autolycus is not very convincing as a courtier even to the elder shepherd ("His garments are rich, but he wears them not handsomely" IV.iv.776), but the younger is taken in: "He seems to be the more noble in being fantastical. A great man, I'll warrant; I know by the picking on's teeth." Far from bearing malice because of his dismissal from court, Autolycus hopes to do his Prince a service; instead of taking the shepherd and his son to the King, he will take them to Florizel. Thus Shakespeare achieves his purpose of having the revelation of Perdita's recovery revealed in Sicily at the precise moment when Polixenes arrives at Leontes' court.

It is possibly meaningful that our new rogue-courtier serves as the herald (one of the functions of Hermes) of the revelation. He puts only two questions, but they invite the narration, and he also concludes the scene. Our shape-shifter says, "I would most gladly know the issue of it," and the First Gentleman replies, describing people almost transfixed with wonder: "They seem'd almost, with staring on one another, to tear the cases of their eyes. There was speech in their dumbness, language in their very gesture. They look'd as if they had heard of a world ransom'd, or one destroyed" (V.ii.13–17). We have already met this imagery of transformation before in connection with Autolycus; his auditors at the ballad-singing, we recall, were senseless save for the music, with "no hearing, no feeling, but my sir's song." This time, though Autolycus has only unwittingly helped to achieve the discovery (he has a neat way of appearing at the right moment), he seems by his inviting questions to preside over its communication to the audience.

The Second and Third Gentlemen bring confirmation and more news: "The oracle is fulfill'd; the King's daughter is found. Such a deal of wonder is broken out within this hour that ballad-makers cannot be able to express it." And so the wondrous tale is told, as the ballad-maker listens. And the grief at the story of the Queen's death as related to Perdita causes like transfiguration: "Who was most marble there changed colour; some swounded, all sorrowed. If all the world could have seen't, the woe had been universal." All were transformed. And we might well be ready for the final shape-shifting, the story of the statue of Hermione.

Already Perdita and the rest of the Court have set forth to see the marvellous work of Julio Romano, the perfect ape of nature, who has so recreated Hermione that "one would speak to her and stand in hope of answer." All except unthrifts will go along (V.ii.118–121). Autolycus pauses a moment to explain why even now he cannot thrive (V.i.122–133):

> Now, had I not the dash of my former life in me, would preferment drop on my head. I brought the old man and his son aboard the Prince; told him I heard them talk of a farthel and I know not what; but he at that time overfond of the shepherd's daughter (so he then took her to be), who began to be much sea-sick, and himself little better, extremity of weather continuing, this mystery remained undiscover'd. But 'tis all one to me; for had I been the finder-out of this secret, it would not have relish'd among my other discredits.

But those whom he has benefited thus by accident promise to give him a good report, provided he amends his life. He promises to do so, and he will also prove a tall fellow of his hands—"by any means," as the Clown says (does he already have the Clown's new purse?). And he goes along with his new patrons to see the "Queen's picture," and the last transformation (the best of the old tales) is wrought.

The audience has had every reason to suppose Hermione dead, but the coming of Autolycus with his dual nature, in one aspect a mere rogue ballad-singer, in the other a figure of mystery invested with magic, perhaps was meant as a clue to suggest that something phenomenal was going to happen. Hermione's resurrection in this life, with all its symbolic force, is the significant ending of the tale of winter and of a man who dwelt by a churchyard.[14]

14. These lines (II.i.29–30) read like the preparation in a modern motion-picture for a fade-out: all that follows somehow seems like the story Mamilius is presumed to tell. In any event, it is clear that Leontes was a man who lived for fifteen years with remorse for his dead. See G. W. Knight, *The Crown of Life,* pp. 76–128, for a full study of the resurrection motif in *The Winter's Tale.*

IX

The Moon-Men: The Gypsies of Tudor and Jacobean England

SEPARATE AND ALIEN, but sharing the characteristics of our other knaves and vagabonds—rogue, cozener, tinker, horse-courser, and the rest of the devious crew—are the fabulous Gypsies (Plate 22). Their origins lost in mystery, variously described as descendants of Cain or of other people of Palestine,[1] Bohemians,[2] and Egyptians, speaking a

1. See A. H. Sayce, "Travelling Tinkers in Ancient Palestine," *Academy,* Nov. 26, 1886. Sayce finds that the Gypsies have traditions tracing them to the Kenites, a nomadic tribe of tinkers whose ancestry was thought to derive from Cain. This article is reprinted and accepted as plausible by David MacRitchie in "The Race of Cain and the Modern Gypsies," *The Journal of Gypsy Lore Society,* II (1890–1891), 62–63, though he prefers a Hamite origin.

MacRitchie (*JGLS,* I [1889], 143–145) notes that the well known Gypsy tribal name of Faws was related by the Gypsies to Melchior, one of the three wise kings. In "Notes of the Three Magi," *JGLS,* I (1889), 246–247, Charles Leland conjectures (with MacRitchie's approval) that the three Magi were Chaldeans or "Egyptians" and that their gifts of gold, frankincense, and myrrh relate to Gypsy charms.

But, as Dr. John Sampson observes ("On the Origin and Early Migrations of the Gypsies," *JGLS,* Third Ser., II (1923), 156–169), the evidence of the language itself is the best source for knowledge of the history of the race. After rejecting conjectures tracing the origins to the Jats of India and speculating on the possible origins in the Doms (still existing as low caste wandering tribes in Behar and the West and Northwest Provinces of India), Sampson examines the linguistic problem and says that we are (p. 161) "justified in regarding Romani as the oldest example of the neo-Aryan languages, saved by its isolation from the decay which has affected the others." See also Brian Vesey-Fitzgerald, *Gypsies of Britain* (London, 1944), pp. 1–11, 175–179.

2. This was the most common French term for the Gypsies. According to

PLATE 22. Jacques Callot, *L'avant-garde*. Meaume Collection, British Museum.

language tracing in its basic elements to a north Indian dialect,[3] these archwanderers and fortune-tellers of the world first came to England in groups early in the sixteenth century.[4] On their arrival in Western Europe in the first quarter of the preceding century,[5] they had told stories about how their ancestors dwelling in Lower Egypt had earlier given up their Christian faith for paganism, and on their return to the faith, were assigned the penance of wandering the earth for as long as their ancestors had lived in error.[6] The story

---

OED, bohème, bohémien were applied to the Gypsies because the French thought they came from Bohemia or through it on their arrival in Western Europe. The first recorded English use is the example in *Measure for Measure,* alluding to Barnardine (IV.ii.134).

3. Holger Pedersen, *Linguistic Science in the Nineteenth Century,* tr. J. W. Spargo (Cambridge, Mass., 1931), pp. 16–17.

4. Various attempts have been made to show that the Gypsies may have come into the British Isles quite early. Jusserand (*Wayfaring Life in the Middle Ages*) lists travelling jugglers, mountebanks, and fiddlers as common in medieval England, but accepts the view that the "Bohemians or Gypsies remained entirely unknown in England till the fifteenth century" (p. 182). MacRitchie ("Scottish Gypsies under the Stewarts," *JGLS,* II [1890–1891], 177–179) traces tinkers or tinklers back to the beginning of the thirteenth century in Scotland, but acknowledges that it has not been proved that these (and later or earlier medieval tinkers) were definitely Gypsies. See also H. T. Crofton, "King John of England and the Tinkers," *JGLS,* I (1889), 244. Paul Bataillard (*De l'apparition et de la dispersion des Bohémiens en Europe,* Paris, 1844, p. 53) believes that the Gypsies could not have come to England earlier than 1440.

5. Bataillard finds that the Gypsies came into Western Europe from or by Southeastern Europe in two waves of immigration, one from 1417 to 1438 and the other from 1438 to the seventeenth century. ("Beginning of the Immigration of the Gypsies into Western Europe in the Fifteenth Century," *JGLS,* I [1889], 187 ff; II, 27–53.)

6. Robert Pitcairn (*Ancient Criminal Trials in Scotland; compiled from the Original Records and MSS.,* Edinburgh, 1833, III, Part Second, p. 591) says, "in the fifteenth century, the *Egyptians* gave themselves out to be *Christian Pilgrims*—and their leaders assumed the titles of *Kings, Dukes, Counts,* or *Lords of Little Egypt;* from which country they always pretended they had been expelled by the *Saracens,* on account of their *Religion.* Certain it is, that at present they appear to profess *no religious belief* whatever . . . With their characteristic cunning, it is likely that this assumption of the appearance of *Pilgrims* was only in accordance with the superstitious and prevailing customs of the times: under this character they had the address to impose upon almost

of their supposed Egyptian origin was generally accepted at first, as is implicit in Andrew Borde's description of them in his *First boke of the Introduction of Knowledge* in 1542: "The people of the coũtry be swarte and doth go disgisyd in theyr apparel, contrary to other nacions they be lyght fyngerd and use pyking they have little maner, and evyl loggyng & yet they be pleasunt dauncers. Therbe few or none of the Egipciõs y^t doth dwel in egipt for Egipt is repleted now wth infydele alyons."[7]

The Gypsies seem to have come first to Scotland. The earliest official record of their existence in the British isles appears to be the legal notation of a payment by King James IV of seven pounds to an unidentified group in 1505: "Apr. 22, 1505, Item, to the Egyptianis, be the Kingis command, vii lib."[8] Perhaps this was the group under the leadership of a professed lord of Little Egypt, Anthony Gagino [Gawin],

---

all the Sovereigns of Europe, and obtained passports and privileges from them . . ." See also Bataillard, *JGLS,* I (1889), 198–200. In an interesting variant (Bataillard, *JGLS,* I (1889), 339), one group claimed origin from Egyptians who had refused hospitality to Joseph and Mary with the infant Jesus, and had been condemned to a life of wretched wandering.

7. C.71.b.29 (STC 3383): *The fyrst boke of the / Introduction of knowledge. / The whych dothe teache a man to speake parte of / all maner of / languages, and to know the usage and fashion of / all manner of countreys . . . Made by Andrew Borde, of Phy- / sycke Doctor. Dedicated to / the right honorable & gra- / cious lady Mary doughter of our soverayne / Lorde king Henry the eyght.* [Woodcut of gallants conversing.] The dedicatory address is dated May 3, 1542.

Though the belief in their Egyptian origin was widely accepted in the Renaissance, many express doubt about it, chief among these being Sir Thomas Browne, who thoroughly discredits the supposition in his *Pseudodoxia Epidemica,* ch. 7.

8. Pitcairn, III, p. 592. Pitcairn also lists several earlier items which indicate that the Gypsies were probably in Scotland before 1505. Thus payments were made by the Lord High Treasurer on May 2, 1501, and February 24, 1503, to "Peter the Moryene" (Moor); on May 10, 1502, to the "Erle of Grece," and on June 28, 1502, to a "Knight of Grece"; and on Dec. 11, 1504, a gift of nine shillings to "put in the caudill" at the christening of the "More Lass." Regarding the "Erle" and "Knight" of Greece, it must be remembered that Greece was, as Pedersen tells us (p. 17), "the common home of the European Gypsies for a considerable period."

whom the Scottish king commended to the King of Denmark in July 1505 as being on a pilgrimage through the Christian world, which had been enjoined on them by the Apostolic See.[9] In any event, it would appear that the Gypsies entering Britain were still employing somewhat the same stories in explaining their wanderings that they had used on the Continent.

The few references to Gypsies which occur early in the century in chronicles, works of literature, and other sources suggest that they had not yet invaded England in numbers and that they were at first regarded as creatures of novelty. In 1514, perhaps the earliest specific reference to a Gypsy in England is found in *A dyaloge of syr Thomas More knyghte.* More is giving an account of an inquiry into the pathetic death of Richard Hunne in the Lollards Tower and tells of the questioning of a man who had professed to know someone who could reveal Hunne's supposed murderer (fol. xci):

> By my fayth my lords [quod] he, & she were w^t you she wold have tolde you wõders. For by god I have wyst her tell many marvylouse thyngs ere now. Why quod ye lordis what have you herd her tolde? For soth my lords quod he yf a thynge had bene stolen / she wold have tolde who had yt and therfor I thĩke she could as well tell who kild Hunne as who stole an horse. Surely sayd the lordys so thynke all we to I trow. But how could she tell yt by the devyll? Nay by my trouth quod he / For I could never se her use eny worse waye than lokyng in onys hande. Therwyth the lordys laughed and asked what is she. Forsoth my lord quod he an egypcyan / and she was lodged even here at Lambeth but she ys gone over see nowe. How be it I trow she be not ĩ her own countre / yet for they saye yet ys a grate waye hence / and she wente over lytell more than a moneth ago.[10]

9. Bataillard, *JGLS,* II, 235; Pitcairn, III, 592 (Pitcairn lists the letter as of 1506).

10. B.M., C.37.h.10 (STC 18084): "*A dyaloge of syr Thomas More knyghte:* . . . [*N.D.*]; Colophon: "Johannes Rastell / Enprynted at London at the / synge of the meremayd at Pow- / lys gate next to chepe syde, in the / moneth of June the yere of our lord.Md.Cxxix," Book III, ch. xv. Henry T. Crofton cites this and many of the following references in his summary of the known facts about the Gypsies in Renaissance England, "Early Annals of the Gypsies in England,"

Three years later, Edward Hall describes two ladies attending a court mumming as having their heads "rouled in pleasauntes [gauze] and typpets lyke the Egipcians, embroudered with golde" and their faces, necks, arms, and hands covered with black "pleasance" so that they appeared to be "nygrost or black Mores" (BBvi); and under the date of 1520 he notes the appearance of eight ladies at a state banquet dressed also like Egyptians.[11] In the same period (1515), Skelton described Elinor Rumming as having a characteristic Gypsy headdress (qualified with a memory of the Wife of Bath):

> Her kirtell Bristowe red,
> With clothes upon her heade,
> That they way a sowe of leade,
> Wrythen in wonder wyse
> After the Sarasins gyse,
> With a whym-wham
> Knit with a trym-tram
> Upon her brayne panne,
> Like an Egypcyan

JGLS, I, p. 7. See also Crofton's supplement to this study, "Supplementary Annals of the Gypsies in England before 1700," *JGLS,* New Ser., I (1907–1908), 31–34; and Eric O. Winstedt, "Early British Gypsies," *JGLS,* N.S., VII (1913), pp. 5–37.

11. B.M., C.122.h.4 (STC 12721): *The Uni- / on of the two noble and illu- / strate famelies of Lancastre & Yorke . . . 1548, BBvi, MMiv.* The second of these occasions (MMiv) in which eight lords were also masked in attire like that of the ladies may have been suggestive to Jonson for his *Metamorphosed Gypsies.*

In a note summing up the history of the influence of the Gypsies on the English masque (*JGLS,* Third Ser., XXXIII, 1954, 74), F. G. Blair calls attention to a document in the Loseley Manuscripts dating 1 Edward VI (1547) listing masking garments for men, which includes the following specifications: "2 frocks or und' garments for Egipcyans of tawny tilsent [tinsel] with sleves; two shorte mantells for Egipcyans of crymson gold baudkyn fringed wth colen [Cologne] sylver; two hed peces of the same of sondry color lawne; two children to the same, redy trym'd, having coyffs of Venys gold; 8 coyffs of golde and sylver lawne, sondry colors; 13 p^r of fore sleves, new, of sundry color lawne; 8 ptlettes of sylver lawne, 2 trymd wth Venys golde; 4 stonderds . . ." (*The Loseley Manuscripts . . . From the Reigns of Henry VIII to James I,* ed. Alfred J. Kempe, London, 1835, p. 77).

Lapped about
When she goeth oute.[12]

Sometime between 1513 and 1523 we learn also that Thomas, Earl of Surrey, entertained some "Gypsions" at Tending Hall in Suffolk.[13] And yet another curious allusion is cited by F. G. Blair, a record of July 20, 1535, concerning a vision experienced by Dan George Lasingby, a monk in Jervaulx Abbey in Yorkshire. In the vision "women lyke Egyepetces appered to hym, among whome one greeter then the eoder, the whych appered with one of hyr papkes rede, and the wyssage of houre lady eponne hyr breste; the whych wyssage comforted hym myche; the whyche he toke for Sanct Anne, for a grett ymmage of Sanct Anne doht stande in the closyd there as he sayd masse . . ."[14]

It seems, then, from these early allusions to the Gypsies and to those masquerading or otherwise appearing as Gypsies, that at first the English welcomed them and found them novel and entertaining, as did the peoples of other countries on their arrival in various places. But also like other established people, the English speedily found them costly amusement; and hence as early as 1530 (Crofton tells us they had been expelled from France a quarter of a century earlier)[15]

12. STC 22598: *Here after / folweth certayne bokes / cōpyled / by mayster Skelton / Poet Laureat / whose names here after shall appere / . . . Printed at London by Richard / Lant for Henry Tab dwelling in Pauls churche yarde at / the sygne of Judith* [1545].

13. *The Works of Henry Howard, Earl of Surrey,* ed. Nott (London, 1815), I, Appendix, p. 5; Crofton, p. 7. Crofton (p. 8) cites several other early allusions as follows: in October, 1521, William Cholmeley gave some "Egyptains" forty shillings (Brewer, *Letters and Papers, Foreign and Domestic, Henry VIII,* vol. III, pt. 1, 499(4); in 1522, some "Egypcions" hired the use of a church house in Stratton, Cornwall, for thirty pence (*Archaeologia,* XLVI); in 1526 Skelton in *The Garland of Laurel,* line 1455, abbreviates *Sancta Maria Aegyptica* as Mary Gipcy, apparently the earliest literary use of the nickname for these people (*OED*).

14. F. G. Blair, "The Monk's Vision," *JGLS,* Third Ser., XXXIV (Jan.–Apr. 1955), 78–80.

15. Paul Bataillard (*Nouvelles Recherchés . . . des Bohémiens,* Paris, 1849, p. 38) observes that this act was proclaimed on July 27, 1504; see Crofton, p. 7.

an act providing for their banishment (22 Henry VIII, cap. 10) was passed:

> For as mouch as afore this tyme dyv'se and many outlandysshe People callynge themselfes Egyptians, usying no crafte nor faicte of merchaundyse have cõmen into this Realme, and gone from Shire to Shire and Place to Place in greate company and used greate subtyll and crafty meanes to deceyve the people, beryng them in hande that they by Palmestre could telle menne and womens fortunes, and so many tymes by crafte and subtyltie have deceyved the people of theyr money and also hath cõmytted many and haynous felonyes and robberies to the greate hurte and deceyte of the people that they have comyn amonge: Be it therefore, by the Kynge our Sov'eign Lorde the Lordes Spirituall and Temporall and by the Cõmons in thys p'sente parliament assembled, and by the auctorytie of the same, ordeyned establysshed and enacted that from hensforth no such psones be suffred to come within this the Kynges Realme, And yf they do [then] they and ev'y one of them so doynge shall forfayte to the Kynge our Sov'eign Lorde all theyr goodes and catalls and then to be cõmaunded to avoyde the Realme wythin xv days next after the cõmaundement upon payne of imprisonament . . .

Juries trying such persons for crimes were to be composed entirely of Englishmen instead of half English and half foreign members as provided earlier under 8 Henry VI.c.27,29. Goods claimed as stolen were to be restored, after adequate proof, to their owners. Otherwise, justices of the peace and other officers who seized the goods were to retain half of them for their own and account for the rest to the Court of Exchequer.[16]

Enforcing this law, however, was not easy. Various attempts seem to have been made to round up the bands and deport them, but the law-enforcing agencies were not well enough organized for any concerted action against so quicksilver a crew. On December 5, 1537, Thomas Cromwell, Lord Privy Seal, wrote to the Bishop of Chester, president of the Council of the Marches of Wales, urging him to spy out all

16. *Statutes of the Realm . . . From Original Records and Authentic Manuscripts* (1817), III, 327; Crofton, p. 9.

such "egipcyans" and "compell them to repair to the nexte porte of the See to the place where they shalbe taken and eyther wythout delaye uppon the first wynde that may conveye them into any parte of beyond the Sees to take shipping or if they shall in any wise breke that commaundement without any tract to see them executed according to the kinges hieghnes sayd letteres patentes . . ."[17]

Some records exist of actual deportations under the act of 1530. Thus in the summer of 1544 a large group of Gypsies possessing seventeen horses was arrested by Robert ap Rice, the Sheriff of Huntingdon, and sent to Calais, a part of the fees due the Sheriff being defrayed by the sale of the horses;[18] in the Christmas season of the same year, a group was shipped from Boston in Lincolnshire to Norway; and on January 21, 1545, Phillip Lazer, a Gypsy governor, was given a passport for his company to sail from London.[19]

But the measures taken to enforce the law proved (as always) inadequate, and on December 10, 1554, a new, yet more stringent law (1 and 2 Philip and Mary, cap. 4) was passed, making the immigration of Gypsies a felony, and requiring, among other provisions, all Gypsies in England and Wales to depart within twenty days or forfeit their goods. Those remaining forty days after the proclamation were to be subject to the same penalties applied to the newly imported Gypsies. Exceptions were made for anyone willing to quit the "noughty idle and ungodly lyef and company, and be

17. Roger B. Merriman, *Life and Letters of Thomas Cromwell* (Oxford: Clarendon Press, 1902), II, 106; Crofton, p. 10.

18. John Hoyland, *A Historical Survey of the Customs, Habits & Present State of the Gypsies* (York, 1816), pp. 81–82. Robert ap Rice received £17.17s.7d. and the fees from the sale of the horses, £4.5s.; Thomas Warner, Sergeant of the Admiralty, was paid 58s. for victuals, and £6.15s. to hire shipping from John Bowles. Will Wever received £5 for conducting the party to Calais. See Crofton, p. 11.

19. For the deportation of Lazer, see *Archaeologica, or Miscellaneous Tracts Relating to Antiquity,* Society of Antiquaries, London, XVIII (1817), 127, quoted from *Proceedings of the Privy Council,* fol. 129b; Crofton, p. 11.

placed in the service of some honest and able Inhabitante . . . or honestlye exercise himself in some lawful worck or occupac̃on."[20] Even this hard law did not immediately achieve satisfactory results, as Samuel Rid remarks in his *Art of Juggling:* "But what a number were executed presently upon this Statute, you would wonder: yet notwithstanding all would not prevaile: but still they wandred, as before up and downe, and meeting once in a yeare at a place appointed: sometimes at the Devils arse in peak in Darbishire & otherwhiles at Ketbroke by Blackheath, or elsewhere, as they agreed stil at their meeting" (B2).

One of the various reasons for the failure of the law to achieve its purpose was that the authorities were too humane to administer it literally. Thus when a large group of Gypsies was arrested in Dorsetshire and brought to trial at the Assizes in September, 1559, the judge finally acquitted them of the charge of felony on the ground that they had imported themselves not from overseas but by land from Scotland the previous year. They were accordingly dispatched as in the law for ordinary vagabonds, to the places where they were born or had last dwelt.[21] But the authorities were not always so lenient in bending the laws to mercy. In the same year apparently some of this same band were arrested and whipped naked at the cart-tail through Gloucester: "1559–60—Also payed by the tyme of thys accompte for byrche to make roddes to beat the Egypcyans naked abowte the citie, *ob.* also payed to Thomas Whelar for his carte where at the seyde Egyptyans were tyed and so brought aboute the citie and scourged, viii[d]."[22]

20. Crofton, p. 13. Commons' *Journal,* I Philip and Mary, Vol. I, p. 38; Lords' *Journal,* I, p. 474; *The Statutes of the Realm* (1819), IV, 242–243.
21. Crofton, pp. 15–16, citing *State Papers—Domestic—Elizabethan,* VI, nos. 31, 39, 50, pp. 137, 138, 139. Crofton remarks that this same band seems to have been rearrested at Langhope in Gloucestershire.
22. Crofton (*JGLS,* III, 59) cites *Records of the Corp. of Gloucester,* Hist. MSS. Commission, 12th Report, Appendix, Part ix, p. 468.

Meanwhile, the Gypsies were having their influence on the native unthrifts and vagabonds and even, perhaps, some English folk of higher station, as is witnessed by the nature of yet another "Act for further Punishment of Vagabonds calling themselves Egyptians" (5 Elizabeth, cap. 26) passed in March, 1562.[23] This act provided that any person who for a month or more consorted with Gypsies "and imitated their Apparel, Speech, or other Behavior, should, as a felon, suffer death and loss of lands and goods," a law to be executed without the benefits of a mixed jury or sanctuary or clergy. From this time on there is more and more confusion between the native English rogues and the Gypsies, partly because the Gypsies found it necessary to feign that they were English rogues, and partly because the English rogues found it profitable to practice such Gypsy occupations as juggling, palmistry and other mysteries of fortune-telling, horse-stealing, and the ancient Gypsy craft of the tinker. And consequently, in the periodic searches to seize vagabonds, punish them, and send them to their supposed home regions, the orders specify "sturdy beggars commonly called rogues or Egyptians."

Five years later, in 1567, Thomas Harman was optimistic that the laws for banishing the Gypsies were working effectively. In his *Caveat* he hopes that the general fraternity of vagabonds will be dealt with as speedily:

> I hope their synne [that of the vagabonds] is now at ye highest, and that as short and as spedy a redres wyl be for these, as hath bene of late yeres for the wretched, wily wanderinge vagabondes, calling and naming them selves Egiptians, depely dissemblinge and longe hydinge and covering their deepe decetfull practises, fedinge the rude common people wholy addicted and geven to novelties, toyes, and newe inventions, delytinge them with the strangeness of the attyre of their heades, and practisinge paumistrie to suche as woulde knowe their fortunes. And to be short all theves and hores, as I may well wyt, as some have had true experience, a nomber can well wytnes, and a great sort hath well felt it.

23. Commons' *Journal,* I; Lords' *Journal,* I. 596, 597, 598, 599; cited by Crofton, *JGLS,* I, 16.

> And now (thankes bee to god) throughe wholsome lawes and the due execution thereof, all be dispersed, vanished, & the memory of them cleane extynguyshed, that when they bee once named hereafter, our Chyldren wyll muche marvell what kynde of people they were: and so I trust shal happen of these (Aiii^{v}–Aiiii).

But Harman's hope for the elimination of the English rogues was, as we have seen earlier, to prove as false as his belief that the Gypsies had been effectively banished. Perhaps this belief had been occasioned by the temporary success of the laws in ridding Kent of the Gypsies; or perhaps (and this is more likely) the Gypsies who came into his region found it expedient to claim English birth and, when in danger, to dissociate themselves from their bands and appear as common vagabonds. At all events they continued to wander the land, and often, it would appear, attracted others to imitate their behavior and join company with them. For example, on April 18, 1577, Rowland Gabriel, Katherine Deago, and six others were convicted of felony for keeping company with Egyptians and counterfeiting their appearance and language, and hanged;[24] but in 1594 William Standley, Francis Brereton, and John Weeks, yeomen of London, who were sentenced to hanging on a similar charge, were pardoned.[25]

The magnitude of the problems faced by the magistrates in executing the provision of the law against the Gypsies and their response to these problems may be illustrated by the official report of the proceedings at the Yorkshire Quarter Sessions on May 8, 1596, involving the examination of 196 persons of whom 106 were tried and condemned to death.

24. Crofton, p. 18; *The Annals of England* (Oxford, 1856), II, 287–288. A full investigation of the documents of this episode was made by T. W. Thompson in "Consorting with and Counterfeiting Egyptians," *JGLS,* Third Ser., II (1923), 81–87. (Thompson appends a valuable summary of anti-Gypsy legislation to his article, pp. 87–93.) The statute of Elizabeth (1563) against consorting with "Egyptians" was not repealed until 1783 (see *JGLS,* Third Ser., II, 47).

25. Crofton, p. 21, citing *Middlesex County Records,* vol. I; *Athenaeum* (Sept. 11, 1886), p. 330.

The document is so informative and poignant as to deserve extensive quotation:[26]

> To all Christian people to whom these our l'res [letters] testimoniall shall come, we, S'r Will'm Mallorye, Knight, one of the Queenes Ma'ty Counsalls established in the North Marches; John Dawney and William Bellasis, Knights; Philip Constable and John Holdham, Esquires, 5 of the Queens Majesties justices of the peace in the said Countie of Yorke, to all mayors, sheriffs, bailiffs, constables, headboroughs, and tithingmen and all other her Ma'ty officers, ministers, and loyal subjects whatsoever; Greetinge in our Lord God Everlastinge. Forasmuch as a great number of idle persons, the Queens natural born subjects, and some of them descended of good parentage, as we be credibly informed by some of their friends that heartily wish the amendment of their lives, the whole number of which company being one hundred, fourscore, and sixteen persons of men, women, and children, having wandered in diverse parts of this relme in this county of Yorke, some of them feigning themselves to have knowledge in palmistry, physiognomy, and other abused sciences, using certain disguised apparell and forged speeche, contrary to divers statutes and lawes of this realme, and especially the statute made in the Vth year of the Queenes Ma'ty most gracious reaigne that now is, whom the Lord longe preserve over us.
>
> We therefore, the said Justices willing to keep this lewde company to conform them according to lawe in that case provided, did therefore cause the whole number of them to be apprehended and committed to her Highness gaols in the said countie of Yorke; whereof so many of them of full age, one hundred and six persons, were arraigned the Tuesday being the viii day of May last, at a Quarter Sessions holden at Yorke aforesaid, at which Sessions the [ ] of those offenders were by lawful inquest, though not *per medietatem linguae* condemned. Whereupon judgement being given that the said offenders should receive pains of death,

26. R. O. Jones, "The Mode of Disposing of Gypsies and Vagrants in the Reign of Elizabeth," *Archaeologia Cambrensis,* Fourth Ser., XII (1882), pp. 226–231; reprinted by John Sampson, in "English Gypsies in 1596," *JGLS,* N.S., II (1908–1909), 334–338. Sampson speaks of this document as "the only existing record of an actual attempt to carry out the provisions of the statute of 5 Elizabeth, cap. 20, by returning every member of the band each to his own parish." Sampson suggests that Portyngton was a member of a well-known Yorkshire family.

> according to the provisions of the said Statute; whereupon issued execution, and nine of the most valiant persons having least charge of children, and found by the said inquest to be strangers, aliens born in foreign parts beyond the seas, and none of the Queen Majesty natural born subjects, suffered accordingly. The terror whereof so much appalled the residue of the condemned persons and their children which stood to behold the miserable end of their parents, did then cry out so piteously as had been seldom seen or heard, to the great sorrow and grief of all the beholders: lamentably beseeching reprieves for their parents, then ready to suffer death, alledging that they being sixty infants and young children, which could not help themselves, should perish through the loss of their parents; wherefore being moved with compassion upon so doleful cry of such infants, we, the aforesaid justices, reprieved the residue of their condemned parents, and sent them back to the gaols from whence they came, where they continued till the vii of July last, during which time the Right Honorable Lords, Henry Lord Darsye and Ralph Lord Yevers, pitying the said miserable persons had obtained her Graces free pardon for the said offenders, which was published the vii day of July, together with her Highness Warrant in the nature of a commission procured by the said Lords, directed to us the aforesaid justices, that we should give order and direction to the said offenders to reform their lives, and to be placed where they were born, and last dwelled by the space of three years; there to demean themselves in some honest faculty, according to the limitation of one Statute made in the 26th year of our late Soverign Lord of famous memory, King Henry the VIII, now revived by the late Parliament holden anno xxxv Elizabeth Reign.

And so in July 1596, the company, now comprised of 187 persons, set out for their respective places of origin or latest dwelling for three years, under the leadership of William Portyngton, who was allowed eight months to conduct them to their various places. The Queen's pardon was to be withheld until Portyngton should return a "true calendar" of the placing of the company. Any one who rejected Portyngton's authority was to be treated as a felon. All officers and subjects of the Queen were to permit the company to pass through their shires, towns, and villages without harm, helping them to lodging and "victuals competent for their money." They were not to stay in any place beyond a day and two nights save for urgent causes. Did Portyngton succeed in his desperate assignment?[27] We shall probably never know; but her Majesty's judges at York had solved their problem in the conventional way by passing it on to others.

The measures committing the Gypsies to deportation or obliging them otherwise to change the habits of their lives may well have led many of them to seek employment when they could find it, and occasional evidence of at least temporary conversion to normal citizenship may be seen in the scattered records of the baptism of some.[28] But as late as 1596 Edward Hext complains of the failure of the officials to execute the laws, a failure which had resulted in something like a resurgence of the Gypsies: "Experience teacheth that thexecution of that godlye law upon that wycked secte of Roages the Egipsions had clene cutt them of, but they seynge the libertye of others do begynne to sprynge up agayne and ther are in this Cuntry of them." Even so, he says, they are not so menacing as the native rogues: "But uppon perill of my lief I avowe yt, they weare never so daungerous as the wandrying Souldiers and other stout Roages of England, for they went visibly in on company and weare not above xxx or xl of them

27. Judges (p. xli) notes that Portyngton is suspected of being a Gypsy himself (but see Sampson, Note 26 *supra*), and wryly observes that it is "unlikely that he kept the group together for many days." Various Gypsy leaders appear to have been given power by the State of life or death over their groups, very like that of Portyngton; for example, such power was given to John Faw, Earl and Lord of Little Egypt, in Scotland, May 26, 1540 (Pitcairn, III, 592).

28. Crofton (*English Gypsies under the Tudors,* Manchester, 1886, p. 16) cites the baptism of three as being representative of the tendency, namely that of Joan, at Lyme Regis, Dorsetshire, Feb. 14, 1558; of William, at Lanchester, Durham, Feb. 19, 1564; and Margaret Bannister, at Loughborough, Leicestershire, April 2, 1581. Francis H. Groome (*In Gypsy Tents,* Edinburgh, 1880, p. 113n.) lists these and two others from the register of St. Paul's Church, Bedford: "1567 Robartt Ane Egyptic. bapt. same daie (viz. 'March xxxth daie')" and 1567 "April—John, Ane Egiptn bapt. xxvith daie."

in a shere, but of these sort of wandringe Idell people there are three or fower hundred in a shere . . ."[29]

Dekker, however, finds them as serious a menace to the nation as the more conventional rogues and beggars, and speaks of their numbers being swelled by the addition of native priggers, cheaters, morts, yeomen's daughters, and servants. He gives a fairly realistic picture of them and their behavior in *Lanthorne and Candle-Light,* designating them as "Moone-men" (an inspiration probably owed to Shakespeare),[30] "a strange wild people, very dangerous to townes and country villages." They are called moon-men because, like the moon, they continually vary in shape and station, he tells us, and goes on to describe them in picturesque detail (G2^v^ G4^v^):

> A man that sees them would sweare they had all the yellow Jawndis, or that they were Tawny Moores bastardes, for no Red-oaker man caries a face of more filthy complexion, yet are they not borne so, neither has the Sunne burnt them so, but they are painted so, yet they are not good painters neither; for they do not make faces, but marre faces. By a by name they are called Gipsies, they call themselves Egiptians, others in mockery call them *Moone-men.*
>
> If they be Egiptians, sure I am they never discended from the tribes of any of those people that came out of the Land of Eigpt: . . . Looke what difference there is betweene a civell cittizen of Dublin and a wild Irish Kerne, so much difference there is betweene one of these counterfeit Egiptians and a true English Begger. An English Roague is iust of the same livery.
>
> They are commonly an army aboute foure-score strong, yet they never march with all their bagges and baggages together, but (like boot-halers,) they forrage up and downe countries, 4. 5. or 6. in a company: as the Swizzer has his wench and his Cocke with him when he goes to warres, so these vagabonds have their harlots, with a number of little children following at their heeles, which young brood of Beggers, are some-times caried (like so many

29. Aydelotte, p. 172; British Museum MS. Lansdowne 81, Nos. 62 and 64 (reprinted in Strype, *Annals,* 1824, IV, 404–13, Nos. 212–214).
30. See p. 173.

greene geese alive to a market, in paiers of panieles, or in dossers like fresh-fish from Rye that comes on horsebacke, (if they be but infants.) But if they can stradle once, then as well the shee roagues as the hee roages are horst, seaven or eight upon one iade, strongly pineond, and strangely tyed together.

One Shire alone & no more is sure stil at one time, to have these Egiptian lice swarming within it, for like flockes of wild-geese, they evermore fly one after another: let them be scattred worse then the quarters of a traitor after hees hangd drawne and quartred, yet they have a tricke (like water cut with a swoord) to come together instantly and easily aganie [again], and this is their pollicy, which way soever the formost ranckes lead, they sticke up small bowes in severall places, to every village where the [they] passe; which serve as ensignes to waft on the rest.

Their apparell is odd, and phantasticke, tho it be never so full of rents: the men weare scarfes of callico, or any other base stuffe, *hanging* their bodies like Morris-dancers, with bels, and other toyes, to intice the countrey people to flock about them, and to wounder at their fooleries, or rather rancke knaveryes. The women as ridiculously attire them-selves, and (like one that plaies the Roague on a Stage) weare rags, and patched filthy mantles uppermost, when the under garments are handsome and in fashion . . .

. . . Upon daies of pastime & libertie, they Spred thẽ-selves in smal companies amongst the Villages: & when young maids and batchilers (yea sometimes olde doting fooles, that should be beaten to this world of villanies, & forewarn others) do flock about them: they then professe skil in Palmestry, & (forsooth) can tel fortunes: which for the most part are infallibly true, by reason that they worke upon rules, which are grounded upon certainty: for one of thẽ will tel you that you shal shortly have some evill luck fal upon you, and within halfe an houre after you shal find your pocket pick'd or youre purse cut. These are the *Egiptian Grashoppers* that eate up the fruits of the Earth, and destroy the poore corne-fieldes: to sweepe whose swarmes out of this kingdome, there are no other meanes but the sharpnes of the most infamous & basest kinds of punishment. For if the ugly body of this Monster be suffred to grow & fatten it selfe with mischiefs and disorder: it will have a neck so Sinewy & so brawny that the arme of ye law will have much ado to strike of ye Head; sithence every day the members of it increase, and it gathers new ioints & new forces by *Priggers, Anglers, Cheators, Morts,* Yeomens Daughters (that have taken some by blowes, and to avoid shame, fall into their Sinnes) and other Servants both men and maids that have beene pilferers, with al the rest of that Damned Regiment, marching together in the first Army of the *Bell-man,* who running away from theyr own Coulours (which are bad ynough) serve under these, being the worst.

On the other hand, in *The Art of Jugling* in 1612, Samuel Rid speaks of a decrease in their numbers and suggests that many Gypsies have deserted their companies to become peddlers, tinkers, and jugglers (B2ᵛ)—in other words, to join the larger but dispersed ranks of the ordinary rogues and vagabonds. One wonders if these varying impressions are not partly based on the periodic appearance and disappearance of the Gypsies; in their absence over a protracted time, people would regard the plague as diminished, only to become, with their reappearance, suddenly convinced anew of its enormity.

People such as these offer living models for any author in search of the unusual or bizarre, and at least a few Renaissance poets and dramatists, particularly Shakespeare, Jonson, Middleton,[31] Fletcher,[32] and Brome,[33] employed them in a variety of ways. Of these authors, Shakespeare and Jonson give us the most entertaining uses, particularly Shakespeare,

31. In *More Dissemblers Besides Women,* IV,i,61–310, Dondolo and Aurelia join the Gypsies, the former running away from his master, and the latter dissembling to win her love. But Middleton's Gypsies are what Dekker would call merely rogues and doxies, save that Middleton invents a jargon for them neither rogue nor Romani. This is characteristic of Middleton, who, though he likes rogue characters, never troubles to learn pedlar's French or Romani. Thus the members of the "Roaring School" in *A Fair Quarrel* employ a jargon invented for the occasion, like that in *More Dissemblers.* As remarked elsewhere, this fact indicates that Dekker, not Middleton, was responsible for the pedlar's French scenes in *The Roaring Girl.* As for Middleton's *The Spanish Gypsy,* only the plot (based on Cervantes) is Spanish, though Middleton knew that the Spanish Gypsies spoke *Germania* (II.i.13). The Gypsies of this play are all nobles in disguise, and have little resemblance to either Gypsies or rogues.

32. Fletcher's *Beggars Bush,* though primarily relating to English vagabond life, illustrates, like several other works, the tendency to mix Gypsy and rogue traditions; see pp. oo of this study.

33. Brome, like Fletcher, confuses rogue and Gypsy elements at times, but his *Jovial Crew* is predominantly a play in the Dekker rogue tradition; see p. 165 of this study.

whose apparent appreciation of their values helps him to achieve both strange and at times deeply spiritual effects in story and metaphor reflecting their impact on his mind. Some of these uses are slight in substance, almost illusory, but behind the shadows possibly lurks some reality. The uses are isolated, not thematically connected, and will be considered in their chronological order.

I

Amiens and the Gypsy Ideal

Though Dekker's sketch represents the bleak reality of Gypsy life seen in a dark light, the Gypsies are indeed "moon-men," and they glow at times with romantic illusion. Shakespeare grasps the idealistic aspect of their wanderlust in *As You Like it*. Gypsies are the perpetual seekers of the green world, and Amien's first song, and particularly the second stanza, phrases this ideal with a perfection unachieved elsewhere:

Who doth ambition shun
And loves to live i'th'sun,
Seeking the food he eats,
And pleas'd with what he gets,
Come hither, come hither, come hither!
Here shall he see
No enemy
But winter and rough weather.
(II.v.40–47)

And, as Charles Strachey argues,[34] Jaques's subsequent mockery of this ideal may even contain direct allusions to the Gypsies and their language:

34. "Shakespeare and the Romani: A Note on the Obscurities in *As You Like It*, Act ii, Sc. 5," *JGLS*, III, 96–97. Regarding the "Greek invocation," it should be remarked again (as Pedersen tells us, *Linguistic Science*, p. 17) that Greece was the home of the Gypsies for a long period; see Notes 3, 8, *supra*, and Note 35.

> If it do come to pass
> That any man turn ass,
> Leaving his wealth and ease
> A stubborn will to please,
> Ducdame, ducdame, ducdame!
> Here shall he see
> Gross fools as he,
> An if he will come to me.

Strachey suggests that the mysterious *ducdame* may be Shakespeare's version of Romany *dukdom me* ("I did harm") or *dukkerdom me* ("I tell fortunes, I cast spells"), and that Jaques's explanation of *ducdame* as "a Greek invocation to call fools into a circle" and his threat to "rail against all the first-born of Egypt" may be respectively allusions to the Gypsy jargon and the Gypsy leaders, self-styled lords of Egypt. It is interesting in this connection to note that a group of Greek-speaking Gypsies led by a handsome man on horseback had visited Utrecht in 1596, avowedly to collect a pension. Whether they returned to Egypt as they professed they were going to do, or continued their pilgrimage is not known.[35]

Curious also in this same play is the familiar picture Shakespeare evokes of Gypsy children on a horse when the second page agrees to sing "It was a lover and his lass" without a prologue of excuses: "I'faith, i'faith! and both in a tune, like two gypsies on a horse" (V.iii.15–16).

II
Barnardine

As has been observed, some Gypsies, for whatever cause, of heart or expediency, were willing to accept baptism, and without doubt the fathers of the church did their best to minister to the ghostly welfare of those who were imprisoned and in jeopardy of life. Those who did not respond to this spiritual comfort must have been a vexation to the priests

35. See Eric O. Winstedt, "Greek-Speaking Gypsies at Utrecht, 1596," *JGLS*, Third Ser., XIII (1934), 222–224.

who wished these strange creatures with their different view of life to see the light and to sanction with their own consent the measures taken against them. We have a lively picture of one such unregenerate in Barnardine in *Measure for Measure.* Introduced presumably, as has been remarked earlier, to add further reality to the prison scenes, which otherwise, even with Pompey Bum's catalogue of inmates (IV.iii.1–22), might seem merely taken from a house for the correction of lechery, Barnardine, born a Gypsy ("Bohemian") but, as Gypsies found it expedient to be in England, nursed and bred in the realm (IV.ii.135), appears to represent a subtle satiric sketch of the actual procedure in English law against such offenders.

Barnardine, whose name associates him with the rascally cozeners of the barnard's law, has been imprisoned for nine years on an unproved charge of murder. The evidence for his guilt was so substantial that he would have been executed had not his friends (presumably Gypsies) secured reprieves for him. Only now under the too zealous government of Lord Angelo has his guilt been established, and even not denied (though we are almost sure that it would not be confessed) by Barnardine himself. Barnardine does not seem a penitent character, capable of rehabilitation; he is "A man that apprehends death no more dreadfully but as a drunken sleep; careless, reckless, and fearless of what's past, present, or to come; insensible of mortality and desperately mortal" (IV.ii.149–153).[36] He has no use for spiritual counsel, and leads a life of revelry in the prison walls, with the liberty of the prison; drunk many times a day, he would not escape even if given the chance. To move him to repentance the jailer and his men have often awakened him with an apparent warrant for his execution, but he is completely hardened.

The Duke-Friar proposes to substitute the execution of

36. Barnardine's insouciance may be compared with that of Greene's knave and Autolycus (see p. 239 of this study). The characteristically English rogue usually acknowledged his sins and accepted his execution unrepiningly.

this lost wretch for that of Claudio, and arranges for the deed and goes himself to shrive him. But true to his pattern, Barnardine will not be confessed. He has been drinking all night and "will not die today for any man's persuasion." The Duke, though recognizing the evasion, shows the conscience that distressed the minds of all good magistrates when a prisoner did not accept his lot with pious resignation:

Prov. Now, sir, how did you find the prisoner?
Duke. A creature unprepared, unmeet for death,
And to transport him in the mind he is
Were damnable.

(IV.iii.70–73)

Most opportunely for Barnardine and the perplexed Duke, the Provost has a solution: the pirate Ragozine (another rogue) has just died of a cruel fever, and his head may be substituted for Claudio's, a clever bit of juggling that will not be detected by Angelo. In the end, after serving unaware as part of the Duke's and the Provost's device in the resurrection of Claudio, Barnardine is pardoned and left to the counselling of Friar Peter.

III
The Moor of Venice

More curious still are the elements of Gypsy lore in *Othello, The Moor of Venice.* Gypsies were also known as Moors,[37] and it has been suggested that the Morris or Moorish dancers were originally Gypsy dancers.[38] However that may

37. Brome in *A Jovial Crew,* speaking of Springlove with his Gypsy inclinations, says "I will no longer strive to wash [excuse and make white] this Moor" (*Dramatic Works,* 1873, III, 361), and in *The English Moor,* in a scene in which the jealous Quicksand paints his newly contracted wife black, Quicksand says, "Why thinkest thou, fearful Beauty, / Has heaven no part in Aegypt? Pray thee tell me, / Is not an Ethiope's face his workmanship / As well as the fair'st Ladies?" (*Dramatic Works,* II, 37–38). Many such references might be cited.
38. See David MacRitchie, "Gypsies and the Morris Dance," *JGLS,* III, 188–189; see also, *JGLS,* II, 232–233; and Wentworth Webster, "The Cascarrots of Ciboure," *JGLS,* I, 79–83.

be, Othello, the Moor of Venice, like the "Lords of Lower Egypt" who headed the Gypsy bands invading the West, is a romantic figure who derives from men of royal siege, and a lover of untrammeled freedom:

> But that I love the gentle Desdemona
> I would not my unhoused free condition
> Put into circumscription and confine
> For the sea's worth.
>
> (I.ii.25–28)

If, as Fernand Baldensperger conjectures,[39] Othello was an Ethiopian Moor, his connection with the Lords of Lower Egypt becomes still closer. Like them this "extravagant and wheeling stranger / Of here and everywhere" has been a wanderer, and he comes to Desdemona's house with stories of his "moving accidents by flood and field," of his redemption from slavery, into which he had been sold by the insolent foe, and of his conduct in the course of his travels (we are reminded that the Gypsies too were redeemed from bondage to error and hence their travels in expiation of their guilt). To Iago these tales are "fantastical lies," just as Dekker would regard the stories of the Gypsies.

The charges that Brabantio brings against Othello of being "a practicer / Of arts inhibited and out of warrant" are such as were brought against Gypsies practicing divination and witchcraft. In his eloquent self-defense Othello temporarily clears himself of the charge; but the Jacobean audience must have felt their doubts increase with the sinister evidence of the handkerchief. Othello himself clearly identifies this ob-

---

One of the prettiest passages of Sidney's *Arcadia* is based on this custom. In it, Selmane, Pamela, and Philoclea are confronted by six maids in scarlet petticoats with bells at their ankles and elbows who lure them into the woods where they are carried off to the castle of Cecropia (see *The / Countesse / of Pembrokes / Arcadia,* (1590), fol. 248, Book III, ch. 2. Ordinarily morris dancers are men; but poets bend custom to their will.

39. Fernand Baldensperger, "Was Othello an Ethiopian?" *Harvard Stud. in Phil. and Lit.,* XX (1938).

ject as a token of witchcraft—and of Gypsy witchcraft as well:[40]

> That handkerchief
> Did an Egyptian to my mother give.
> She was a charmer, and could almost read
> The thoughts of people. She told her, while she kept it,
> 'Twould make her amiable and subdue my father
> Entirely to her love; but if she lost it
> Or made a gift of it, my father's eye
> Should hold her loathly, and his spirits should hunt
> After new fancies. She, dying, gave it me,
> And bid me, when my fate would have me wive,
> To give it her. I did so; and take heed on't;
> Make it a darling like your precious eye.
> To lose't or give't away were such perdition
> As nothing else could match.
>
> (III.iv.55–68)

This token, so frightening and fatal to Desdemona and the Moor, has magic in its web. The very worms that produced the silk were hallowed, and a two-hundred-year old sibyl sewed the embroidery, which was "dy'd in mummy which the skilful / Conserv'd of maidens' hearts." Unless the audience looked upon this story as another of Othello's tall tales, they must have accepted the kerchief as a token of witchcraft;[41] and they knew that its use by Othello if it had been publicly revealed would have made him guilty before the law as a practicer of black arts and that according to the then current theology he would suffer damnation, as well as death, unless he repented his action.

40. I have studied this aspect of Othello's nature and its relation to the witchcraft elements of the play in "The 'Arts Inhibited' and the Meaning of *Othello*," *Boston Univ. Stud. in English,* I (1955), 129–147.

41. Kittredge points out that the Royal Acts of 1559 forbade, under penalty of death, the use of "charmes, sorcerye, enchantements, invocations, circles, witchecraftes, soothsayinge, or any lyke craftes or imaginations invented by the Devyll," and that the statute of 1604 (known as the statute of King James) has like restrictions (*Witchcraft in Old and New England,* Cambridge, Mass., 1929, pp. 104, 115, 282–284).

"Sure there's some wonder in this handkerchief." Why a handkerchief anyway? Though Shakespeare was presumably unaware of it, this token appears to relate in some fashion to the Gypsy *diclé*. According to John Sampson, the word *diclé* (*dikla, dilk*), meaning basically "cloth" or "kerchief," is defined by various authorities as an apron or girdle, and was regarded as a symbol of chastity.[42] Borrow's account of the object probably reflects a continuous tradition: "There is another word in the Gypsy language, *Diclé*; and this word is closely connected with Lacha [chastity]—indeed is inseparable from it, in unmarried females; for to lose their Diclé is tantamount to losing Lacha." A few pages later Borrow alludes to the custom in describing a Gypsy wedding: "First of all marched a villainous jockey-looking fellow, holding in his hands, uplifted, a long pole, at the top of which fluttered in the morning air—what? the mysterious diclé, and yet more mysterious handkerchief of cambric—the latter unspotted—for otherwise there would have been no bridal, and the betrothed girl would perhaps then have been a corse."[43]

The situation in *Othello* itself accounts sufficiently for the menace in Othello's words regarding the possible loss of the handkerchief; but how precisely that menace and the resulting death of Desdemona correspond with the Gypsy tradition!

Where did Shakespeare acquire this lore? Professor Lois Whitney has argued for the possible derivation of many significant features of Othello's life from John Pory's translation of *A Geographical History of Africa Written in Arabic*

42. "English Gypsy Dress," *JGLS,* III, 155–159; see also T. W. Thompson, "Gypsy Marriage in England," *JGLS,* Third Ser., VI (1927), 109. Thompson observes that perhaps the commonest gift in Gypsy lovemaking is that of a colored handkerchief by the young man, and the acceptance by the girl indicates that she is willing to marry him (p. 115). This tradition of the diclé traces back at least to the time of *Othello,* as is witnessed by its use in marriage ceremonies in John Porys' translation of Leo Africanus's *Geographical Historie* (1600), p. 143 (see Note 44).

43. George Borrow, *The Zincali* (1841), I, 333 (cited by Sampson, p. 159).

and Italian by Iohn Leo a More (London, 1600).[44] In many respects Leo Africanus, as he is commonly known, is very like Othello. His parentage, though not of royal siege, was not ignoble; his uncle and he were royal ambassadors. A great traveler (for the most part in caravans) who has left no region of Africa unvisited, Leo causes Pory to marvel how ever he should have escaped so many thousand of imminent dangers, and one is reminded of the dangers that Othello faced in his travels, his "hairbreadth scapes i'th' imminent deadly breach" (I.iii.134–136): "Moreover as touching his exceeding great *Travels,* had he not at the first been a More and a *Mahumetan* in religion, and most skilfull in the languages and customs of the *Arabians* and *Africans*, and for the most part travelled in *Carovans,* or under the anthoritie, safe conduct, and commendation of great princes: I marvell much however he should have escaped so manie thousands of imminent dangers." Also like Othello, he has traversed vast deserts: "For how many desolate cold mountaines, and huge drie, and barren deserts passed he?" And, as Miss Whitney adds, he describes vast caves in his book.[45] He was also often in hazard of being captured by the Arabians who sold their captives (I,25–26) (and one thinks of Othello's being sold into slavery and his redemption thence).

All these details relating to Leo's wandering life recall

44. "Did Shakespeare know Leo Africanus?" *PMLA,* XXXVII (1922), 470–483. It should be added that Miss Whitney does not relate this subject matter to Gypsy lore. My quotations from Pory's work are from B.M., C.4258 (STC 15481): *A Geographical / Historie of Africa, / Written in Arabicke and Italian / by Iohn Leo a More, borne / in Granada, and brought up / in Barbarie. / . . . Translated and collected by Iohn Pory, lately / of Gonevill and Caius College / in Cambridge.* / [Ornament] / *Londini, Impensis George Bishop. / 1600.* Most of the resemblances between Othello and Leo occur in the unpaged address "To the Reader" written by Pory.

45. III, 211–212; V, 242 (Miss Whitney cites the Hakluyt Soc. ed., II, 555–557, III, 710–711). Miss Whitney also finds noteworthy resemblances in traits of character between Othello and the Arabs and Moors of Leo (p. 40): "Most honest people they are, and destitute of all fraud and guile." They tend to be steadfast in friendship, credulous, highly jealous.

familiar Gypsy lore; but more arresting still are other parallels to known Gypsy history. Thus Pory tells us, Leo, along with his book of geography, was delivered by God's providence into the hands of certain Italian pirates who presented him to Pope Leo X, and we are reminded how the Gypsies on their first invasions into Western Europe are reported to have been cordially received by the Pope and the Emperor and given letters of safe conduct.[46] Leo X seems to have given Leo Africanus a yet more lavish welcome: "Being thus taken, the Pirates presented him and his Booke unto Pope Leo the tenth: who esteeming of him as of a most rich and invaluable prize, greatly rejoiced at his arrivall, and gave him most kinde entertainement, and liberall maintenance, till such time as he had woone him to be baptized in the name of *Christ,* and to be called Iohn Leo, after the Popes owne name."

One may conclude that both Pory and Shakespeare thought of their heroes as Moors, not as Gypsies, just as the Pope and various monarchs at first accepted the Lords of Little Egypt and the Earls of Greece at their face value, unaware of their actual nature as *mori capitani.* Through some alchemy these Gypsy leaders appear to have been translated into Leo Africanus and the Moor of Venice.

IV
Cleopatra

The most exciting Gypsy of them all is obviously Cleopatra, Queen of Egypt and an archetypal Gypsy Queen. Mercutio early associates the word *Gypsy* with her, not in a pejorative sense but mocking Romeo's supposed obsession: "Laura to his lady was a kitchen wench . . . Cleopatra a gypsy . . ." (II.iv.41–44); but the association is made, and we are not surprised when the first image of Cleopatra presented to us in *Antony and Cleopatra* is the contemptuous one of a

46. See Bataillard's study of these claims, *JGLS,* I (1889), 198, 261–283.

Gypsy wanton. The eyes of Antony, once like those of plated Mars,

> now turn
> The office and devotion of their view
> Upon a tawny front. His captain's heart,
> Which in the scuffles of great fights hath burst
> The buckles on his breast, reneges all temper
> And is become the bellows and the fan
> To cool a gypsy's lust.
>
> *Flourish,* Enter *Antony, Cleopatra,* her *Ladies,*
> the *Train,* with *Eunuchs* fanning her.
>
> Look where they come!
> Take but good note, and you shall see in him
> The triple pillar of the world transformed
> Into a strumpet's fool. Behold and see.

Philo's speech here has the force of an initial chorus, epitomizing the action to come.

That Shakespeare immediately distracts our attention from this theme by introducing the story of a supposedly unbounded love between Antony and Cleopatra does not really cancel the basic intention of the play; we do behold and see the triple pillar of the world metamorphosed by a creature as wayward and lawless as a Gypsy. A true Gypsy in her love of liberty, Cleopatra is ever her own mistress, and Antony ever her soldier, servant, slave. Even while she waits for news from him at Rome she reflects on her earlier conquests:

> Broad-fronted Caesar,
> When thou wast here above the ground, I was
> A morsel for a monarch; and great Pompey
> Would stand and make his eyes grow in my brow;
> There would he anchor his aspect, and die
> With looking on his life.
>
> (I.v.29–34)

Once having established the Gypsy metaphor, Shakespeare does not belabor it, perhaps in part because the image was so powerful and so familiar that it did not need frequent repetition. Instead he spends his effort on sustaining the image through his portrayal of the Egyptian Queen. Teasing, capricious, and "riggish," aware that she is "with Phoebus' amorous pinches black / And wrinkled deep in time," she exercises her charms (the metaphor is still new and peculiarly appropriate) on the self-indulgent Antony, enslaving his judgment and eroding his honor till nothing is left of the man; her tires and mantle grotesquely fit him, and in his erratic conduct he has become a Gypsy too. At moments he recognizes the truth:

> These strong Egyptian fetters I must break
> Or lose myself in dotage.
>
> (I.ii.120–121)

> I must from this enchanting queen break off.
> Ten thousand harms more than the ills I know
> My idleness doth hatch.
>
> (I.ii.132–134)

And this recognition reaches its high point with the fall of his fortunes:

> Betray'd I am.
> O this false soul of Egypt! this grave charm—
> Whose eye beck'd forth my wars and call'd them home,
> Whose bosom was my crownet, my chief end—
> Like a right gypsy hath at fast and loose
> Beguil'd me to the very heart of loss!
>
> (IV.xii.24–29)

Antony here perceives that he has been beguiled much as Gypsies trick their victims at the cheating game of "fast and loose,"[47] basically the familiar scarf trick in which an appar-

47. Reginald Scot in *Discoverie of Witch-craft* (1584) alludes to this game in Book XI, Chap. x: "The counterfeit *Aegyptians,* which were indeed coosening vagabonds, practising the art called *Sortilegium,* had no small credit with the multitude, howbeit their divinations were, as was their fast and loose"; in Book XIII, Ch. xxix, "Of fast and loose, how to knit a hard knot upon a handkercher, and to undo the same with words," Scot describes the trick. Crofton (*JGLS,* I, 19–20) notes that the game is described also in *Brand's Popular Antiquities,* ed. Hazlitt (London, 1870), II, 325.

ently secure knot is untied by sleight of hand (the term gradually came to signify a variety of such deceptions); and it is grimly ironic that at this crucial moment Cleopatra tricks the vengeful Antony with yet another variant of "fast and loose," which suggests that despite her protestations that all is naught and that her lamp is spent, she is ready to make provision for the future, a trick betrayed by Seleucus. Cleopatra's final trick, by which she cheats Caesar of his triumph, is nobler than her other deceptions, though still characteristic: she dies with courage (and beauty), exemplifying, as in her life, so in her death, an apotheosis of the Gypsy spirit.

V

A Masque of the Metamorphosed Gypsies[48]

Shakespeare credited Cleopatra with foreseeing that some squeaking Cleopatra boy would mock her greatness on the stage; and a touch of this mockery may be seen in the passing allusions to her as the "gypsies grandmatra" in Jonson's *A Masque of the Metamorphosed Gypsies* which was presented on three different occasions before King James I and his court in 1621. Though it is not one of his best masques, Jonson spent considerable effort on it, varying it to suit audiences at Burley in Rutland, Belvoir in Leicestershire, and Windsor. More interesting as spectacle than as literature, the masque was primarily designed as an extravagant means to compliment James and the lords and ladies of the court.

In developing his plot Jonson draws rather indiscriminately on the beggar lore of the pamphlets by Dekker and Rid. A fresh touch, perhaps suggested by Dekker, and not unlike a picture by Jacques Callot, opens the masque as a Gypsy leads in "a horse laden with five little children, bound in a trace of scarffes upon him: a second leading another

48. W. W. Greg, Jonson's *Masque of Gypsies in the Burley, Belvoir and Windsor Versions* (London, 1952). I am using the Burley version except for one passage indicated in the text.

horse, laden with stolne poultry, &c." Immediately Jonson reveals his reliance on Dekker by adopting for his Gypsies the professions of Dekker's vagabonds, particularly those of the Jackman and the Patrico (described as nonexistent types by Harman), and thereby exhibiting the general tendency of the Jacobeans of confounding the native English vagabonds with the Gypsies.

The Jackman introduces the five children as five Princes of Egypt, begotten upon several Cleopatras in several counties, one of whom is Justice Jugg's daughter in Flintshire. The Jackman's speech is interspersed with terms of pedlar's French which he refuses to interpret (a fact which may argue that Jonson knew that the terms were somewhat familiar to the audience, most of whom would doubtless have read the pamphlets). After several dances and songs describing the nature and behavior of the Gypsies, the Captain tells the fortune of the Gentry Cove with rather sickening adulation, only to find in his Jupiter's mount that he is the King in person. Hardly less saccharine are the following fortunes of the ladies and lords of the court; yet Jonson deserves some credit for his ingenuity in expressing the same ideas in many ways.

After all have been dully complimented, an antimasque of clowns enters, admiring the glitter of the earlier masquers: "Well said Tom Foole! why thou simple parish asse thou, didst thou never see any Gypsies? these are a covy of Gypsies, and the bravest new covy that ever constable flew at: goodly game Gypsies! they are Gypsies o'this yeare, o'this moone, in my conscience" (p. 154). These are indeed, as the rustics tell us, true Moon-men, very gentlemanlike Gypsies, not hedge-frequenters. They do not know how to cant and beg, for they are bachelors in the craft and have not had time to become lousy. After the ensuing country dance, the rustics have their mock-fortunes told while the various Gypsies take their purses, a device which Jonson had used successfully in *Bartholomew Fair* as we have seen. In this version, however, Gypsies cannot be thieves; hence the patrico presently restores all that was lost. The rustics query: what sort of Gypsies are these?

In response the Patrico briefly outlines his wanton biography and then sings the ribald ballad on Cocke Lorell feasting the devil at the celebrated meeting place of vagabonds, the Devil's Arse a-Peak in Derbyshire. When the rustics in envy wish they could become Gypsies like these, the Patrico tells them that it is not easy to become a son or brother of the moon; he describes in detail some of the fine arts in theft. As they continue to admire him (Cockrell would "give anything to see him play loose with his handes when his feet are fast" [Windsor Version]), the Patrico reveals the truth. In a trice the Gypsies are all transformed: all are lords and ladies. Even the clowns are knights and their lasses are pages. The Patrico then sings a song blessing the King and his five senses, to which the Clowns sing the burden. The masque concludes with five songs, each followed by a recitative, all glorifying King James.

That James liked this masque well enough to endure it three times indicates not only that he had a strong stomach for praise, but also suggests that like his ancestors he was personally not hostile to the Gypsies.[49] Jonson, seeking to please, and apparently succeeding in pleasing the King, probably would not have deliberately used subject matter repulsive to him. The masque ends with reformed Gypsies, to be sure; but the tradition of the Gypsy life is laid bare through the masque in a way which suggests that the presence of the Gypsy was an accepted fact of life in England as it had

49. David MacRitchie, "Scottish Gypsies under the Stewarts," *JGLS,* II (1890), 296: ". . . the Gypsies of the sixteenth century appear as the protégés of the Scottish monarchs, and not as men living under the ban of the law . . . from the time they are first mentioned in 1505 through three successive reigns." In the reign of James VI (James I of England), however, as MacRitchie observes (II, 343), the Scottish were more hostile: ". . . the last quarter of the sixteenth and the first quarter of the seventeenth century is a period more adverse to the Gypsies, by reason of its stern and continuous anti-Gypsy legislation, than any period before or since."

been for a century in Scotland, and that though there were laws and constables to keep these wanderers in check, their nature and behavior would continue to fascinate a tolerant, orderly people who saw in them the fulfillment of their own suppressed longings (see Plate 23).

* * *

We leave our Renaissance knaves and unthrifts with a cumulus of myth around them that invests the sad actuality of their lives spent usually in physical hunger and harried by fear. At the outset, as we have seen, they were commonly regarded as faceless outcasts, a swarm of idle caterpillars devouring the good of the realm. As knaves it was understood that, unless they repudiated their ways, they had forsaken God and committed themselves to the devil; they had chosen the primrose path leading to the sordid hospitals on Earth which prefigure in their sin and misery their final hospital in Hell. As unthrifts, they had chosen ways of folly and become passengers on the Ship of Fools, also to end in the hospitals side by side with the knaves and other misfits of all kinds.

The myth that these knaves and unthrifts had an established order, a myth which goes back at least as far as the *Warnung* of the Senate of Basel, was fostered by many writers such as Harman, Greene, Dekker, and Rid who variously make much of their initiations, quarterly meetings, and the "laws" supposed to direct their activities. The numerous shifts and subterfuges of individual rascals thus became codified as the set practices of an order that did not exist. Throughout the sixteenth century and well into the seventeenth, these authors more or less uniformly see these creatures as a horde of vicious wasters who should be exposed as a menace to the state—though it must be added that some of these writers took a curious delight in the tricks of the knaves they condemned.

But to counterbalance this harshness we find evidence of

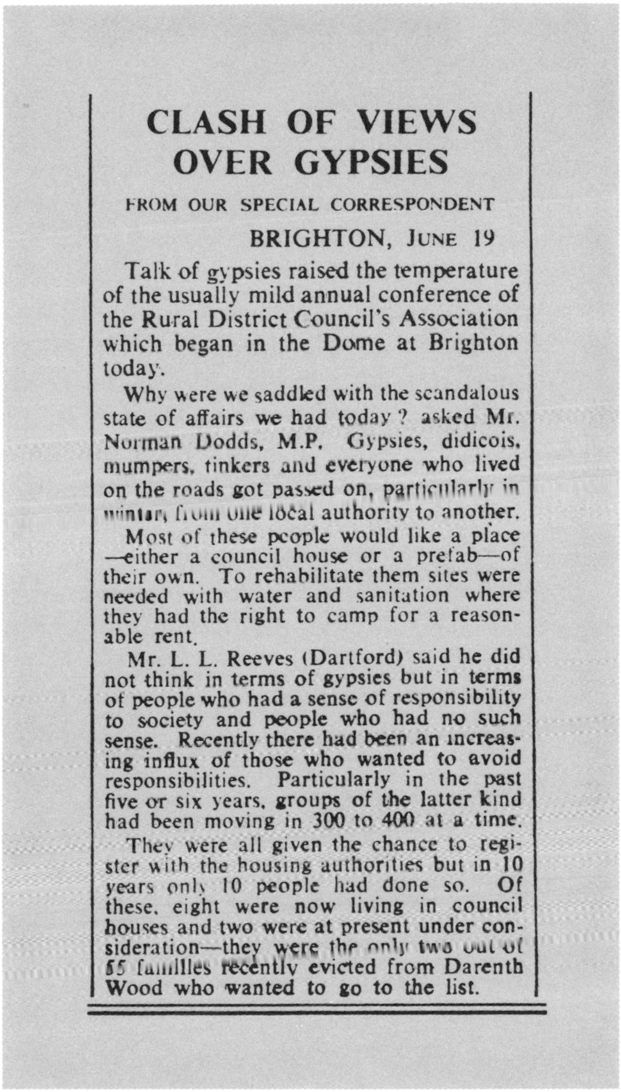

CLASH OF VIEWS OVER GYPSIES

FROM OUR SPECIAL CORRESPONDENT

BRIGHTON, JUNE 19

Talk of gypsies raised the temperature of the usually mild annual conference of the Rural District Council's Association which began in the Dome at Brighton today.

Why were we saddled with the scandalous state of affairs we had today? asked Mr. Norman Dodds, M.P. Gypsies, didicois, mumpers, tinkers and everyone who lived on the roads got passed on, particularly in winter, from one local authority to another.

Most of these people would like a place—either a council house or a prefab—of their own. To rehabilitate them sites were needed with water and sanitation where they had the right to camp for a reasonable rent.

Mr. L. L. Reeves (Dartford) said he did not think in terms of gypsies but in terms of people who had a sense of responsibility to society and people who had no such sense. Recently there had been an increasing influx of those who wanted to avoid responsibilities. Particularly in the past five or six years, groups of the latter kind had been moving in 300 to 400 at a time.

They were all given the chance to register with the housing authorities but in 10 years only 10 people had done so. Of these, eight were now living in council houses and two were at present under consideration—they were the only two out of 55 families recently evicted from Darenth Wood who wanted to go to the list.

PLATE 23. "Clash of Views over Gypsies." London *Times*, June 20, 1962, p. 7e.

a growth in sympathy for the hapless unthrifts and even for unregenerate knaves. As we have seen, Sir Thomas More, Francis Bacon, and others inveigh against the injustice of penalizing the dispossessed, the victims of the enclosures, and there is ample evidence that many magistrates were too humane to enforce the utmost penalties of the laws against knavish misdemeanors. Even the pamphleteers had moments of sympathy for the wretches they were attacking, and the author of *A Defence of Conny-catching* was among the first to point out the inequity of condemning petty knaves when greater ones, fox-furred gentlemen, committed their frauds unchallenged. The satirists and dramatists in their turn reflect these attitudes and emphasize and sharpen this growing social consciousness. The sympathy of such men as More and Bacon becomes transmuted into telling art in Jonson and Shakespeare. The Brueghel-like world of *Bartholomew Fair* and the large humanity of *Measure for Measure* and *King Lear* illustrate the Renaissance conscience at work on these social conditions. In these plays and many other works *knave* and *unthrift* become fruitful metaphors, as seen in the "honest" ensign crying thief in the night, and in the greatest of unthrifts with houseless head stumbling through the tempest. As the period closes, however, no effective solution to the complex problems presented by this multitude of the wayward and the lost was in sight. The doubtful Utopia of the welfare state was centuries ahead.

INDEX